AUTUMN VOICES

Scottish Writers over 70 talk about cre

AUTUMN VOICES

Scottish writers over 70

talk about creativity in later life

Robin Lloyd-Jones

Editor

Playspace Publications

Published in United Kingdom in May 2018 by
PlaySpace Publications
14 Garrioch Drive, Glasgow G20 8RS, Scotland
www.playspacepublications.com

ISBN: 978-0-957334-0-4-5

Edited by Robin Lloyd-Jones
Cover image © Petr Vaclavek/www.shutterstock.com
Typeset & designed by Gerry Cambridge
in Walbaum 10 and Walbaum 120
gerry.cambridge@btinternet.com

For the distribution of *Autumn Voices*, Playspace is an imprint
of Scotland Street Press (SS Press Ltd): scotlandstreetpress.com

Printed by ImprintDigital

To my wonderful wife, Sallie,
with whom I have shared the Spring, Summer
and now the Autumn of my life.

—RLJ

Contents

Acknowledgements

The *Autumn Voices* project would not have come into being, nor finally emerged as a published book without the help of a great many people. In particular my thanks are due to:

Creative Scotland for the generous funding which enabled the project to happen; the twenty writers who agreed to be interviewed and who gave me their precious time, their support, their valuable insights into matters not always easy to talk about and inspiring samples of their work; Larry Butler, editor of PlaySpace Publications, who believed in this project and helped and encouraged me at every stage — from conception to final book — and with whom it has been a pleasure to work; Luminate: Scotland's Festival of Creative Ageing for support, encouragement, advice, contacts and much else. I would like to thank its director, Anne Gallacher for her interest in everything connected to *Autumn Voices*.

I would like to thank all those who entered the *Autumn Voices* Over 60 Writing Competition; Marc Sherland, President of the Scottish Association of Writers, for hosting the competition and Janice Johnston, the competition secretary and the winner and runner-up, Jeanne Dron and Morelle Smith, for agreeing to have their entries published in this book.

I wish to thank the various authors from whose works I have briefly quoted (as acknowledged in the text); and Lizzie MacGregor and the Scottish Poetry Library for permission to use a longer quote from *Whatever the Sea*.

The *Autumn Voices* blog has been an important tool in gathering information for the book and promoting discussion. Thanks go to Jim Convey of Ladder IT Limited for his expertise and technical assistance in setting up and maintaining the blog; and to Simon Berry for making valuable suggestions about the blog's questionnaire; and to all those who completed it.

There are yet more people and organisations to whom I am indebted: the members of the Helensburgh Writers' Workshop for comments and suggestions at all stages of the project; the Scottish Poetry Library & the Scottish Book Trust, from whose websites come most of the introductory information about each writer; the many people and organisations who have spread the word about the *Autumn Voices* project, including Mary Irvine, Jean Rafferty, Pat Byrne (Pat's guide to Glasgow West End), Ruby McCann (Scottish Writers' Centre) and Lesley Traynor (Federation of Writers), Mary McCabe (Scottish PEN Newsletter) and many club secretaries.

In the later stages of production I was extremely thankful to have the thorough and painstaking services of Helen Boden as proof-reader. And I'm grateful for and delighted with the fine layout/ design of *Autumn Voices* by Gerry Cambridge.

I am most grateful to John Gillies for writing the Foreword and Valerie Gillies (no relation) for writing the Preface, both providing valuable insights and perceptive comments.

Finally a huge thank you to my wife, Sallie, for freeing up so much of my time to work on *Autumn Voices*.

PREFACE

One symbol of autumn is the cornucopia, that horn of plenty which signifies that the possessor will always have everything in abundance: grain and wine, flowers and fruit. This book is brimming with ripe autumn fruit. As we reach for one after another, we realise that we are reading the work of writers and artists who are resilient and who are ageing in an optimum way. What brings them to maturity? What can we learn from them that will help us stay connected to our regenerative sources?

It is clear that the wise elder writers who contribute their thoughts here will keep asking similar questions about the energies that renew us and the enlivening power of the arts. They continue to discover the full range and potential of their art forms, and to integrate the arts into their lives with growing wholeness.

They make good companions, too, choosing a path for us where every page is part of the harvest, and a hope for our future. Here's to life!

—*Valerie Gillies*

Note

Valerie Gillies is a former Edinburgh Makar and Royal Literary Fellow. She facilitates the Creative Writing and Journalling groups at Maggie's Centre, Edinburgh.

FOREWORD

In 1972, my mother's aunt, Flora Macaulay, reached the age of 100 years. She was a weaver of blankets and tweeds and spent most of her life in a thatched house in Baleshare, North Uist. To reach 100 then was quite uncommon. Among many letters from friends and family, she received a handsome message from the Queen, hand-written by a private secretary.

Now in 2018, it is not uncommon for people — still many more women than men — to make it to 100, and I would be surprised if the Palace issued handwritten messages now. This is true across the UK, and indeed all rich Northern countries, as life expectancy continues to grow. It is a big success story, due not just to some extraordinarily effective medical advances, but to less arduous oc-cupational practices, better food, reduced smoking, education, less overcrowding and warmer better housing. As a GP working for nearly 30 years in rural Scotland, it was heartening to see this happening at an individual and community level. Not only length but quality of life has got better, and many 80-year-olds are much fitter than their predecessors of a generation ago. We should not ignore, though, the fact that there are still gaps of up to 20 years in both life expectancy and *healthy* life expectancy between the most deprived and the most privileged Scots. In Glasgow this is obvious even in adjacent postcode areas; it diminishes our stand-ing as a society. This theme, of continuing and avoidable injustice and inequality, features strongly in several of the interviews.

Autumn Voices explores promoting reading and writing for well-being. Both the *Autumn Voices* website and the book ask the ques-tion: 'What gifts has ageing brought to you and how are these reflected in your writing?' At the heart of the project, therefore, is an assets-based approach to getting older. My experience as a GP is that this works for many. Those who engage with, explore and articulate what happens to them as they age often have later lives of better quality.

Autumn Voices explores creativity through interviews by Robin Lloyd-Jones with writers over the age of 70 who are living in Scotland. He was 80 when he began, 83 when he finished, and the successful completion of the project is testament to his own curiosity, creativity and stamina! Yeats's idea that creative energy stems from 'the quarrel with ourselves', quoted by the editor, emerges strongly through the book. The writers laugh, celebrate, mourn, curse, complain and create in their own unique and personal voices.

The Portuguese doctor-writer Miguel Torga called his fictionalized autobiography *The Creation of the World*. 'We all create the world to our measure. The enduring world of the long-lived and the short one of the ones who depart prematurely.' These interviews with some of the longer-lived show these different measures very clearly. Some are more passionate, some more scholarly and some are both passionate and intellectually provoking.

I was fascinated by the way that that Torga's different measures appear through the dialogues with the editor. Loss of friends and loved ones, illness, disability and the fear of dementia figure largely of course, but our human ability to survive, not undamaged but each creating the future in some of sort of complex emergent way, is both moving and encouraging. The joys of grandchildren, nearby or far away, are often mentioned. As George Mackay Brown, who never had any, said 'they sweeten our old age'.

It is hard to pick out individual contributions but I will. I found the creative energy of the 92-year-old David Donnison awe-inspiring. He plays in a ceilidh band, draws, paints and writes. His maxim 'If something is worth doing, it's worth doing badly' is a good minding for perfectionists. His 'Die-a-logue' group to reflect on death is a model of how to approach this 'distinguished thing'. The poet and children's writer Diana Hendry has 'an eight-year-old in her head', surely a wonderful way to retain and reflect her creativity. 'Kaddish', her poem to the Lord about her mother ends: 'May she be dumbfounded by love.' Amen to that for all of us. And as an Uibhisteach, I give thanks to the Yorkshire woman Pauline Prior-Pitt for her celebration of her later life in North Uist. 'Rinn thu gu math!'

This book is, as the cliché goes, for all ages. Read an author every night. You too may laugh, mourn, complain, celebrate, curse…and learn a lot.

—John Gillies
Selkirk
February 2018

Note

Dr. John Gillies is Deputy Director of the Scottish School of Primary Care, Senior Adviser Global Health Academy, Co-Director University of Edinburgh Compassion Institute, and former Director of the Royal College of General Practitioners. He was awarded an OBE in 2015 for services to general practice.

1. BY WAY OF INTRODUCTION

INTRODUCTION

Autumn Voices is based on interviews with Scottish writers who are over seventy years old and still actively writing. By over seventy I mean over seventy in 2017, i.e. born in 1947 or earlier. I, myself, was eighty when I began this project and eighty-three at the time of publication. I have no definition of 'old' or 'later life.' It varies from person to person and from generation to generation. Young adults tend to see it starting at sixty, the middle-aged are more likely to say seventy and for many seventy-year-olds it is still some-time in the future.

The three main areas of enquiry are: (i) the identification of role models of writers who are active in later life; (ii) an analysis of why they are still active; (iii) the changing nature of creativity in later life; (iv) a discussion of the problems and opportunities that arise for writers in their Third Age.

Obviously, most of the professional research into creativity has been done by people of pre-retirement age. The contribution of older artists themselves is a key factor in gaining insights into new meanings and ways of being for this age group. If we want to understand creativity in later life, elderly artists are the most ap-propriate people to define and interpret its characteristics.

Too often, because of the weight of negative expectations, so much potential that could be released on retirement and so many ambi-tions that could be fulfilled in later life come to nothing. By pro-viding positive role models and by furthering our understanding of the nature of creativity in later life, my aim and vision is to help future generations of septuagenarians and octogenarians to lead creative and fulfilled lives.

In studies of human development generally, most of the emphasis has been placed on the first half of life, especially on the early stages from infancy to adolescence. Where research has been done into ageing it has mostly been into its negative aspects such as physical decline and terminal illnesses, and on the quantity rather than the quality of life. In a society where those over 60 now outnumber those under 18 and where the UK population over 70 is projected to more than double in the next 30 years, the emphasis needs to shift.

Examining creativity in later life is an important strand in our society's need to acknowledge and understand that physical decline does not necessarily mean a decline in emotional, creative and personal growth; that creativity is linked to both mental and physical health; and that our economy will not survive unless we stop regarding our elderly citizens as a burden and start seeing them as potentially productive and useful people whose maturity, greater life experience and insights are valuable assets. The AgeUK survey (Sept. 2015) found that 76% of older people believe that the UK fails to make good use of their skills and talents.

A project which adds to the understanding of what contributes towards a healthy, productive old age is not only helping to improve quality of life, but also the productivity of an age group of growing economic importance. The Arts Council of England 2014 review, *The Value of Arts and Culture to Society*, states that the UK Arts and Culture industry generated an aggregate turnover of £12.4 billion in 2011. More and more this economic contribution from the arts will have to come from those in later life. A society that is better for older people is better for people of all ages. To address the problems and the opportunities of the elderly is to benefit the welfare of our society as a whole.

It would seem timely, therefore, to look at the relationship between creativity and ageing. There are a growing number of self-help books about how to stay younger longer and how to defy the ageing process. Basically, these are books which are against old age. I think we need more research that embraces ageing, that is about ageing well rather than doomed attempts at staying young, and which provides role models of happy, fulfilled lives in later life.

This enquiry is only one small corner of the vast and complex subject of creativity. The analysis of creativity in all its forms is beyond the competence of any one accepted discipline. The input of psychologists, neurologists, biologists, philosophers, computer scientists and artists of all kinds is required if anything like a complete picture is to be achieved. In writing about creative ageing I am all too aware that there is still a huge amount to be learned about the ageing process, a huge amount to be learned about the nature of creativity and even greater gaps in our knowledge about creativity in old age. If *Autumn Voices* has made some small contribution to filling these gaps, pointed the way to future projects and demonstrated that a creative old age is possible, it has served its purpose.

Perhaps it needs to be said that there are many other different expressions of creativity besides those found in what are accepted as the literary, visual and performing arts. For example, activities such as gardening, technology, dress-making, cooking, knitting, or creative play, making love, storytelling with one's grandchildren or conversation can be creative, as can one's whole approach to life.

Perhaps it needs to be said, too, that there are many other autumn voices in Scotland besides those in this book, writing wonderfully both in their later life and about later life. When I began looking for people to interview for *Autumn Voices* I found that there were far more active writers over seventy in Scotland than could be fitted into the project. My criteria for selection were somewhat arbitrary — a mixture of whom I knew personally, who was available; and an attempt to strike a rough balance between men and women, fiction and non-fiction, between prose, drama and poetry and to achieve a spread of ages so that those in their 70s, 80s and 90s were all represented.

All the twenty-one main interviewees in *Autumn Voices* (I include myself in this head-count) are successful, established writers, most of whom have been writing for quite a number of years. To redress the balance and at least take a sample of the huge number of part-time writers, those, for example, who belong to writing groups and are not often published; and those who did not take up writing until after retirement I organised the Autumn Voices Over 60s Writing Competition (see Section 6). The blog which I run in support of the *Autumn Voices* project (www.autumnvoices.co.uk) further extends the range of autumn voices discussing these issues through the monthly guest blogger, from visitors to the site and from the questionnaire for writers over 60 which I circulated.

The way the book groups the writers into different sections is also somewhat arbitrary. It could have been done in any number of different ways. I was trying for an element of common ground, but also variety. Some of the sections contain a unit at the end where the writers in that section ask each other questions. My intention in doing this was to introduce new angles and dimensions by having people other than myself ask questions.

Almost half of the interviewees originate from outside Scotland. There can be no doubt, though, that they count as Scottish writers. The cities and landscapes of Scotland, the strong sense of community that exists in the Scottish Arts world, the company and friendship of other writers, the Scottish literary scene and Scottish culture and society as a whole have seeped into them and become part of them.

Although the focus of each interview is on these men and women's lives, thoughts and creative output since passing seventy, quite a high proportion of each of their chapters is concerned with their lives before then. This is partly because I found their life stories so interesting that I felt compelled to include them, but mostly because the nature of a person's writing at seventy stands upon a platform of their previous writing history, their successes and failures and the skills honed when younger. Who they are now is largely determined by who they were in the decades leading up to this point and the development of character, personality, work habits and positive values that took place in these earlier years.

The age given for each interviewee is as at the time of interview. Between the first interview and the last there is more than a two-year gap, so direct comparisons in this respect cannot be made.

The interviews were either conducted in a public place previously agreed upon, or in the writer's home. Most interviews lasted between two and three hours. In most cases the questions were sent in advance, although some people opted to 'wing it.' About half of the questions were specific to each individual and their work. Other questions were common to everyone. However, not everyone chose to answer all the questions. Moreover, the questions evolved as the project progressed, so that those interviewed early in the project were not asked quite the same questions as those I met later on.

All profits from the sale of *Autumn Voices* (both the publisher's and the author's) will be donated to Age Scotland — a registered charity formed by the merger of Help the Aged in Scotland and Age Concern Scotland.

I would like to repeat my thanks to all those mentioned in the Acknowledgements who have contributed to this book and made it possible.

BLONDIN'S WHEELBARROW: *A General Discussion of Creativity*

Over the past thirty years I have led several workshops for writers' groups on the topic of Creativity. I asked these groups to jot down what they felt went into their own personal cocktail. Here is what, collectively, they came up with:

- recognising patterns
- making connections
- emotional intelligence, caring & empathy
- discipline & commitment
- determination & perseverance
- curiosity
- playfulness
- a sense of wonder
- spontaneity
- high intrinsic motivation
- willingness to let go & lose control
- self-honesty
- ability to access memory
- lateral thinking
- problem-solving
- thinking metaphorically
- being receptive to new experiences
- being in touch with your inner child
- challenging assumptions
- taking risks & taking advantage of chance
- seeing in new ways
- absolute focus and intensity and achieving flow

Many of the elements listed above connect with each other, overlap and intertwine.

As with cooking, a list of ingredients for creativity is not the same as the process itself. Finding and gathering the ingredients, the manner in which they are combined and applied, the transforming of the raw material into something else, the different phases and stages of the process, such as genesis, exploration, execution and revision; and the cyclical nature of much of it as one looks back as well as forward, the methods of work, the way the work develops an impetus of its own, achieving a state of flow — all these and more are part of the process and, in the following chapters, we catch a glimpse of these in action.

As the *Autumn Voices* in this book make clear, there is no formula for creativity, no list of ingredients that applies to everyone. The creative process is different for each person and, for that person, varies from one work to another. Creativity involves the translation of each individual's unique gifts and vision into an external reality that is new. We must keep in mind, too, that creative acts take place within a personal, physical, social and cultural context that is different for each of us. However, I think there is sufficient common ground for a dialogue to take place about the creative process, provided our approach is flexible and tolerant of diversity and individuality.

A fish doesn't need to know about oceanography or theories of salinity in order to thrive in the sea, so why should artists concern themselves with things which come instinctively to them? I can only answer for myself by saying that I want to know more about a very large and important part of my life. Rather than scaring away this shy and mysterious muse, I and others who appear in *Autumn Voices* have found that an examination of it brings understanding of how to nurture it and build on it.

As one would expect with so elusive and multi-faceted a talent as creativity, there are almost as many definitions of it as there are people writing about it.

Some definitions emphasise process:

Creativity is:

The joining of wonder, skill, intensity and discipline.

Adventurous thinking, getting away from the main track, breaking out of the mould, being open to experience and permitting one thing to lead to another.

Seeing the relationship between two items in such a way as to generate a third item; playing at the way things are interrelated.

The quality of mind which allows an individual to juggle scraps of knowledge until they fall into new and more useful patterns.

The search for truth — responding truthfully with one's whole being to what one sees and understands to be the truth.

Digging deeper.

Facing the fear of going inside yourself and coming out with what you find.

Other definitions focus on the end product:

Producing something that is different in some way from anything that has been produced before.

An act that produces effective surprise.

By 'surprise' Jerome Bruner, the originator of this definition, means the unexpected that strikes one with wonder and astonishment. Surprise need not be rare or bizarre. Often, once something has been pointed out, its effectiveness lies in the shock of recognition.

As we will see later in this book, yet more definitions arise from those interviewed for the *Autumn Voices* project.

One characteristic of creativity which these varying definitions all suggest is that it does not deal with the predictable and repeatable, but with the unique and unrepeatable. Despite this, most of the time at least ninety per cent of the material we use is not original. What matters is the way the material is transformed into something else by passing through a creative process unique to that artist. To quote Francois René de Chateaubriand: 'An original writer is not one who imitates nobody, but one whom nobody can imitate.'

Although this chapter is mainly a discussion of process, it does assume that this process has an outcome. How tangible such an outcome has to be is open to argument. If I compose a poem in my head but do not actually put words down on paper, have I created something or not? I think so.

Research into creativity has focused on four main areas: (i) the creative process itself, with focus on the mechanisms and phases involved as one performs a creative act; (ii) the criteria for and characteristics of creative products; (iii) the creative person and their personality traits; (iv) the creative situation — the creative environment and context. *Autumn Voices* touches upon all of these and certainly recognises that they all influence each other and cannot really be separated.

One of the questions put to a majority of the writers I interviewed was: Look at the list of some of the ingredients of creativity:

Which of them do you value most at the moment?

- Would your answer have been the same when you were younger?
- What would you add to this list?
- Have any of these qualities become stronger in later life?
- Have any of them diminished in later life?

Here are their responses:

Larry Butler:

I recognise everything on that list. The ones I feel less inclined to are: discipline & commitment; I think I am ADHD as well as dyslexic. It's one reason why I take on so many projects; and I have about 30 books by my bed which I dip into.

I would add to the list something to do with appreciation of beauty and being moved by aesthetic experiences. And throughout my life as a writer and an artist, collaboration has been an essential ingredient. Some of my best work has been done in partnership with other writers and artists.

I think self-honesty is getting stronger as I get older. I'm more open about my vulnerabilities. I can't be bothered hiding anything!

A.C.Clarke:

I found these questions difficult to answer probably because I am not used to thinking about my creativity in these terms. The abilities/qualities I value at the moment are: making connections, taking advantage of chance, discipline & commitment, determination & perseverance, accepting disorder, self-honesty. I suspect any difference in answers between then and now would be related less to my age when answering than to my mood at the time. I might have chosen the same set at 20 (but see below) and could choose a different set to highlight tomorrow!

In other words it's not easy to say if anything has changed since I was younger. I probably wouldn't have highlighted playfulness then but I think that's because when I began writing years ago creativity wasn't thought of in those terms or if it was I wasn't aware of it. Ability to access memory and to make *rapid* connections has certainly diminished with age but not the other things as far as I can judge. The most significant change ageing has brought is *time to explore* — in some ways my writing is more adventurous now, I think, though that may be a delusion.

This leads me to what I think is a significant omission from the list (leaving aside the perhaps best avoided, though to me interesting, question of the relation between sexual drive and creativity!) — some of the crucial changes in creativity as one ages have to do with the milieu in which one is creative having also changed significantly. What the list omits is interaction with other creative people and ideas. Creativity never takes place in a vacuum even with the most solitary writers and artists.

Robin Lloyd-Jones:

From that list, I would say that, in my own case, the one which has diminished with age is taking risks. This, I think, stems from a desire in later life, commented on by Cohen, to consolidate what you have already done; and to establish, for your own satisfaction and for posterity, something to be remembered by. I am tempted, at times, to think it is too late to branch out into something different. I ask myself how much time is left to pursue and develop something new. Also diminished is my ability to concentrate and focus for long periods at a time. I need more breaks.

On the other hand, the gains outweigh the losses. Fairly late in life I discovered the dérive, the unplanned creative wander, and that, I suppose, involves some kind of artistic risk, and involves taking advantage of chance (another item on the list), both of these serving as an antidote to the creeping caution I feel is waiting to claim me.

There are aspects of recognising patterns which have become stronger with the advancing years — well, at least as far as seeing some pattern to my own life is concerned. From the heights of later life, I see the landscape of my earlier years laid out below and recognise patterns which, before, were invisible to me. In another sense, my pattern recognition has been sharpened by contact with the natural environment and by slowing down and observing things more closely in a way that I never did before. I have acquired a greater appreciation for the natural rhythms and cycles of the environment and the similarity of design on all scales in obedience to natural laws. An outcome of this and of slowing down is a heightened sense of wonder.

As per list, I also feel more in touch with my inner child. Not that I'm saying I've reached my second childhood, but that, at least I acknowledge that I do have an inner child — something I would have regarded as a completely wet and unmacho concept in my callow youth. I have found paying attention to that child to be rewarding.

The list of traits, identified as often accompanying creativity, also includes an ability to access your own memory. Subsequent research has shown that memory is not some storehouse of past events that you can access, but a flexible, changeable, storytelling part of the brain. It fills in blanks, it erases uncomfortable episodes and reinvents itself according to your needs or shifting values and attitudes. Many writers, myself included, discover this for themselves when they attempt a memoir, or a biography which draws on the subject's unreliable memory. Becoming aware of the true nature of memory, which happened late in life for me, was an important and positive influence on my writing, and more important than an ability to access information from one's past, a great deal of which is probably fiction anyway.

Sheila Templeton:

I've got better at recognising patterns, particularly patterns in my own life.

I'm more laid back now and consequently less self-disciplined.

I would add — not minding looking ridiculous and also being willing to go with the flow and accept and act on opportunities as they occur.

Stewart Conn:

Making unexpected connections is happening less often. A lot of my poems have come about through converging and intersecting events. In my mind, they don't converge like they used to. They maintain their own separate, parallel trajectories. I think I value determination and perseverance more than I used to because these qualities are needed more than they used to be to reach the same result. A sense of wonder is still there and imbues the precious things in life and is a source of poetry. 'Be receptive to new experiences' is, I think, an instruction to oneself as an ageing person. Cartier Bresson talked about the decisive moment when taking a photograph. More and more I am aware of the decisive moment and, if I miss it, it's gone. Previously, I could revisit it. If I hadn't written down the words for my tide poem, I don't think I would have remembered them the next morning. I never used to be a jotter-down of things, but now I am.

I think there are two kinds of creativity. One is like rubbing two sticks together and creating fire; the other is the bolt from the blue and I don't know where it comes from. It remains something of a mystery. I quite like it remaining something of a mystery.

Jenni Calder:

I draw on most of these, but different things at different times. A lot of these qualities overlap, or cannot be separated. For example, making connections and emotional intelligence. I think an important part of my creativity is observation and an ability to step back slightly from what's going on and just watching. I've always done that. I really enjoy travelling on buses. I've overheard so many intriguing conversations! I may not use these in a direct way, but it's all fodder. Creativity manifests itself in so many different ways that to define it is almost impossible. Children find so many ways of being creative and it's tragic to see this being narrowed and confined.

Vicki Feaver:

I think creativity is a talent humans possess for making what already is known and exists into new forms. In the case of poetry, that is language. I like the idea that everyone is unique and different and therefore has the capacity to be creative. But it's difficult to be yourself because we are all brought up with these received ideas, and there are huge pressures to conform and be like everyone else.

I see everything on the list as being important. The one I need most at the moment is determination and perseverance to finish the collection I have been working on for so long. Accepting disorder to create a new order is one I identify with strongly. Some of my strongest poems have gone through a state of chaos in which it would have been easy to abandon them. Sometimes I have left them, then revisited them later to see — rather like solving a difficult jigsaw puzzle where the disordered pieces fit together. To the list I would add fearlessness, self-belief, shamelessness — the latter because I feel ashamed sometimes of writing almost totally from my own experience as a woman. I have to be brazen about it, because I can't write in any other way. There is still a feeling among a lot of male critics that to write as a woman is somehow on a lower level than if it was sexless. I think the male point of view is very interesting, but it is very different.

Douglas Dunn:

Everything on that list has validity for me, but they are not isolated ingredients. They are all working at the same time. To the list I would add patience. For me, creativity and confidence are related.

And, also, it's about being tuned into a place where things flow in a natural way or are cathartic.

Lee Gershuny:

Yes to all ingredients mentioned here. I am not disciplined, but I am committed. Doing whatever it takes to express what you want to express. I think, if you are working in theatre, you certainly have to be able to let go and allow others their input. Ability to access memory — not really, it's all in the now for me. What I would add to the list is being free and also caring for what you create. Also trust in yourself.

Diana Hendry:

I think creativity is tuning into yourself and the world around you. And it's a bit magical, too. Creativity comes in all sorts of ways, from gardening to painting.

John Purser:

I would say that a sense of wonder and of love, which is often exemplified in little children, is more precious than anything else. I would add to this list humour, also sexual energy — it is a prime motivator in human affairs. Music is very physical, and that includes sexual: so too can be poetry, though more by verbal association than physical inspiration.

Pauline Prior-Pitt:

The ingredients of creativity I value most at the moment are making connections; taking advantage of chance; willingness to let go and lose control and receptiveness to new experiences. When I was younger I would have wanted more control, discipline and commitment. To the list you provided I would add collaboration with other art forms and intuition. The qualities that have become stronger in later life are willingness to let go and lose control, receptiveness to new experiences, and intuition. The ones which have diminished in later life are determination and perseverance.

Sheena Blackhall:

Taking advantage of chance is important to me; and curiosity. If you're not curious, you're dead. You have got to have the motivation to write, nobody else is going to do it for you. Self-honesty is a very important one. I don't think I have ever lost the inner child.

The same question was put to other writers in their later life via a questionnaire which was accessed through the *Autumn Voices* blog.

Responses to the question, *What qualities have become stronger in later life?* included: an increased willingness to trample the fences round one's comfort zone, ability to listen to the opinion of someone else, however young; a wider perspective on life; a greater sense of optimism; admiration of the natural world; spontaneity; curiosity, especially since gaining access to internet; paying attention to dreams; consciousness of place; greater interest in other people and their motivations; listening to my other senses.

It seems to me that any discussion of creativity in later life should recognise that there are at least four important gifts old age can bring to writers (and other kinds of artists, too).

The first of these is confidence. Particularly destructive to a person's creative potential is the negative self-image and lack of confidence engendered by a repressive upbringing, sarcastic teachers who emphasised failure rather than success, and by the low expectations of peers and adults. By the time we are of advanced years, having weathered the storms of life, there's a good chance that we have gained in confidence and outgrown the low self-esteem of our younger years. Finding a publisher is a huge boost and something which, by the time a writer has reached seventy, is more likely to have happened than at (say) thirty. In later life we become more experienced and more comfortable in expressing our own opinions. We tend to care far less what other people think of us. This can be liberating and opens up opportunities to be honest in a way that evaded us when younger.

The second gift is that, by the time we are of advanced years, we have learned to trust our subconscious minds in the same way that we learn to trust a friend. Repeated evidence that it can be trusted and that its offerings are not to be ignored builds up confidence in it. So that, when something bubbles up from the subconscious, even if it seems inappropriate to what we are writing, we use it, knowing that it will eventually click into place.

Also, our ability to walk the tight-rope has improved. The French acrobat, Blondin, crossed Niagara Falls on a tightrope one thousand feet long, pushing a wheelbarrow. In the analogy between Blondin's daring feat and our creative processes, Blondin is the artist and the wheelbarrow is the work of art being pushed across the chasm which separates the idea and its realisation. The tension on the rope stands for the opposing forces which are an essential part of the creative process; and Blondin's skill at staying on the rope represents the delicate balance required to tread the narrow line between these opposites. For many writers it is one of the gifts of old age that we become more experienced and adept at this balancing act. We learn how to manage the loss of control, the disorder before a new order asserts itself; how to apply both discipline and freedom. We are better at walking the line between the humility to accept criticism and the arrogance required to believe we have something worth saying and to stick at it. By the time we reach later life we are more likely to have learned how to handle our co-existing contraries — believing two opposite things at once — that so often provides the 'quarrel with ourselves,' the creative tension. We have learned to accept ambiguity, knowing that paradox is often the only truth there is. We know how to reconcile the need to be both part of society and to step outside it as objective observers. When we are in our seventies and beyond, the tug between wanting to hide and needing to be found has become a recognisable part of creativity, rather than something confusing or frightening.

Finally, it is a part of growing old for most of us that we become more reflective. This, and seeing everything from a wider perspective, as if looking at life from a mountain-top, enriches our writing. Ageing can be a process of growth by which the mysteries of life are revealed to us.

I have mentioned some important gifts that ageing can bring. As the following chapters and interviews will show, there are many other gifts which make writing in the Autumn of our lives a rewarding and fulfilling experience.

DISCUSSION WITH ALISON PRINCE

Alison is a one-time Fellow in Creative Writing at Jordanhill College of Education. When I visited her in September 2017 to interview her for this book, I also showed her, in draft version, the section entitled 'Blondin's Wheelbarrow' which immediately precedes this. I was prompted to do this because, knowing her interest in matters related to the nature of creativity, I have corresponded with her on this topic, starting back in 1996. The following is a record of Alison's response to this draft version:

In my opinion, at some level, too much self-analysis can be damaging. I feel you should trust your subconscious and accept that it is part of who you are. For some people there is a danger of becoming self-obsessed, lost in self-interest and a bit over introspective. People vary enormously, of course. A giraffe has a very different view from that of a mouse. The giraffe, from its height, can see for miles, but it's never going to get down a mouse hole — and there are all sorts of fascinating things down there. The trick is to cultivate those things that enable you to come fully to fruition creatively and to discard those things which do not — and that includes the people who are a negative influence on you. This sounds rather ruthless, but you need to make full use of the gifts you are given.

There is no formula for creativity. The list of ingredients you provide is more to do with semantics, with trying to pin down elusive things with words. There is a huge difference between driving the car and being the mechanic.

Our system of education trains us to focus on the main task, but the sidetracks and peripheries we are encouraged to shed are often the most interesting bits. The system aims to produce citizens who are obedient, malleable and easy to control. The ones who don't toe the line are told to shut up — and that is counter to creativity. The proper meaning of education is from the Latin educare — to draw out, not to ram something in.

To be creative we need to be more like goats than sheep. In our formative years we are so often channelled by our social environment, education and training towards narrow modes of thinking. If I may quote a few extracts from my book, *The Necessary Goat & Other Essays* (Taranis Books, 1992):

'The connection between the goat and creativity is inescapable. The compliant, sheep-like child who is content to allow its cycle of experience to be filled with the approved names of things rather than with the things themselves will accumulate no bursting, inconvenient store of experienced phenomena which demand expression... Being disinclined to trust the evidence of direct experience, they seldom encounter any feedback which causes doubt about their own virtue or about the worth of what they are doing. They are narrow and forceful, as effective within a small target as arrows are... Goats, on the other hand, have an inbuilt suspicion of purpose. A multitude of alternatives are always present in the goat-mind, and total devotion to a single line of thought will always seem restrictive to them.'

If you are reaching for creativity, you are looking for some thought you haven't had before. I have to be in a state of readiness for such thoughts to visit me. I can't have an idea at will, any more than I can cause a plant to bloom by glaring at it and muttering, 'Come on, hurry up!' — but I can work towards that state of mind and body in which everything seems interesting and potentially funny. It's a sort of relaxed awareness, and it only comes when I'm feeling reasonably chirpy.

As I said before, we are all different.

2. FIRST AND LAST

Robin Lloyd-Jones
A.C.Clarke
Sally Evans

As I mentioned in the Introduction, the way the writers are grouped together is fairly arbitrary. I have put myself first because my account of my own experience of being an ageing writer was written well before any interviews took place. I used it to clarify in my own mind what I wanted Autumn Voices *to be about and what questions I wanted to ask other writers. As part of my funding application to Creative Scotland, I did a pilot interview with A.C.Clarke. This too, helped shape future interviews. By contrast, Sally Evans was the last writer I contacted, and by this time I knew more about the shape of the book and the kind of replies I was receiving, so my list of questions to Sally was honed and to the point, enabling her to answer directly to some of the emerging areas of discussion.*

ROBIN LLOYD-JONES (Age 80)

I have lived in Helensburgh for the last fifty years. I write novels (mainly historical), short stories, non-fiction (outdoor and environmental topics and biography); and I have, in the past, written radio drama. I spent nearly six years in pre-independence India as a child of the British Raj. On return to England at the end of the war I went, as a boarder, to Blundell's School in Devon. After that came Cambridge University and an MA Degree in Social Anthropology. I moved to Scotland in 1960, the main attraction being the mountains. In Scotland I attended Jordanhill College of Education, then taught social subjects, before becoming director of Dunbartonshire Curriculum Development Centre, then an Adviser in Social Subjects. I retired from education 1989 to become a full-time writer. I did six years as an evening class tutor in Creative Writing at Glasgow University. I was President of the Scottish Association of Writers 1993–96; and President of Scottish PEN International 1997–2000[1].

At the time of writing this I have been married fifty-five years to my wife, Sallie. We have three children. Our son, Glyn, is a former electronics engineer, now a translator of technical documents from Italian into English, father of our granddaughter, Cassandra (currently at Perugia University). Our elder daughter, Kally, is founder director of the award-winning dance theatre company, Company Chordelia, and she also often works freelance with Scottish Opera as their Movement Director and as Director. Our younger daughter, Leonie, is a Support Teacher in Grantown on Spey and is mother to our two other grandchildren, Chloe (now a nurse) and Andre (still at school, but soon to start studying computer gaming at Abertay University).

Being married to my wonderful wife, Sallie, has massively contributed to my physical, emotional and mental health. Second to that, but also hugely important, have been creativity and a sense of wonder. I am in no doubt that the feelings of fulfilment and joy and the sense of purpose and productivity that writing brings to me has had a positive impact on my health and general wellbeing — the first of several benign circles: good health has allowed me to live well beyond three score years and ten, and so to continue being creative; being creative has contributed to my good health, which...

Several inseparable strands have sustained my creative writing into later life. The first of these is that I do not subscribe to the myth and self-fulfilling prophecy that creativity declines with age. I was lucky enough to grow up with role models who clearly demonstrated that this was not the case. My father read widely and remained insatiably curious about everything until he died at the age of eighty-five. He explored the world through books and continued to expand his outlook on life until very near the end. My mother was still painting when she was ninety — not very well in my opinion, but that is beside the point. The creative urge was there, if not the technical skill; and my Uncle Lionel was living proof of Emerson's saying that we do not grow old, we become old when we stop growing. I never heard him say, 'in my day'. His day was always the here and now. I add my late brother David to this list. Two and a bit years older than me, he led the way for me into later life, his interest in the arts of all kinds never flagging despite being almost blind towards the end. Historical role models also bolstered my faith that creativity could be sustained into later life. For instance, I took heart from the fact that Verdi composed *Falstaff*, one of his greatest operas, in his eighties, and that the American poet, Robert Frost, was still writing poetry at eighty-seven.

Then there is my excellent support team — namely my wife who has freed up time for me to write by doing almost everything needed to keep the household running — shopping, cooking, paying the bills, changing the light bulbs, calling the plumber etc.

Strand number three is that I am a keen walker and sea kayaker. My walks are becoming shorter, slower and flatter as my body ages, and my kayak outings rather less challenging than they used to be. This is not a loss but a new opportunity. Slowing down has meant that I now notice and appreciate all sorts of things in the environment around me which, before, I hurried past. As the mountains become too steep for me, I am discovering, for the first time in my life, the delights of forests and rivers. As one door closes another opens. This is relevant to my writing not only because I often write about these things, but also because being close to nature refreshes my spirit and recharges my creative batteries. Walking and kayaking are steady, rhythmic activities in which the slowly changing scene stimulates the mind while leaving it free to roam.

Some of my best ideas have come to me this way.

I thought, when I retired from full-time employment with Strathclyde Education Department, that I would spend much more time writing. This has not happened. There are only so many hours a day that I can be creative. I might, on occasions, sit at my writing desk and my computer for more hours, but I can't honestly say that the amount of time when I am actually being creative has increased by much. The rest is playing at writing — shuffling papers, reorganising files, sharpening pencils and trying to fool myself into thinking I am being productive. It would be true to say, though, that not having to put in the writing hours on top of a day's work in the Education Department does mean I am more relaxed. It is not so much extra time, but blocks of uninterrupted time that are important to me as a writer, and finding these has been a great deal easier since retirement.

Becoming totally absorbed and lost in my writing now happens more regularly. That is to say, I reach a state of flow (sometimes called being 'in the zone'), when the words seem to flow effortlessly. This links with the thirty minutes of meditation I do every day. Research has shown that those who experience a state of flow are more likely to achieve greater depth when they meditate; and, conversely, that deeper states of meditation lead to increased incidences of flow.

At the same time, however, quite a number of the extra hours gained by no longer doing a nine to five job, are now being lost to the need to maintain my ageing body. I spend more and more time seeing my dentist, my doctor, my physiotherapist and various consultants. I seem to do everything slower than I used to. My stamina, both mental and physical, is not what it used to be, so that I need to take more frequent and longer breaks from any work I am doing.

These five strands — a positive attitude to ageing, a supportive, loving wife, being in the natural environment, flow state and meditation — reinforce and enhance each other, and they have grown stronger since I stopped working for a local education authority. Perhaps there is a sixth strand: self-belief. Some of the ingredients of this, in my particular case, are: an optimistic nature; having supportive friends and family; finding that most difficult tasks yield in the end to hard work and patience; and a fairly high degree of self-reliance acquired through kayak expeditions and days on the mountains. This self-belief carries into my Third Age, so that I see no valid reason for not remaining creative and productive for a good few years yet.

There are a host of other reasons why I think I have continued to be creative. Before I delve into these, let me say I do not necessarily equate creativity with the number of books published or awards won. Some of the work of which I am proudest has never been published (not yet, anyway).

I have used the word 'retirement', but I don't consider myself to have retired from work, rather to have exchanged employment by an Education Authority for self-employment. I did this at the age of fifty-five. This may have something to do with why I am still active creatively. I found officialdom crushing to the spirit. I felt at the time that, unless I got out early, something precious inside me would die. Creativity feeds off things like relinquishing control, embracing uncertainty and taking risks; but working in an office demanded qualities the very opposite to this. In the Education Department control was deemed essential, as was knowing the targets and outcomes before you began, with any deviation from them being regarded as failure. All this I chucked out of the window when I quit working for them. Now I was able to surrender to the creative spirit, following it wherever it might lead me. When writing a novel, if asked, 'Is everything going to plan?' I am happy to reply, 'No, thank goodness!' The term 'self-employed' is not quite accurate either. I don't regard writing as work. It is who I am, what defines me, creativity as re-creation. It is not something from which I would or can retire.

One theory of creativity is that creative energy stems from 'the quarrel with ourselves' (to quote Yeats), the inner tension, the grit in the oyster which produces the pearl. It would be a valid supposition, then, that the easing of stress, which I have described, and the tendency to be calmer and more tranquil in old age might have diminished my creativity. I don't think this is so, although the nature of it may have changed. There are different kinds of creativity and more than one reason for it. Besides, there is never any short-age of co-existing contraries in my life.

Not until I was seventy-three did I take up photography seriously, buying a decent camera and going on a landscape photography course. I am especially drawn to landscape and nature photog-raphy. Thinking about what would make a good shot and trying to record visually the beauty encountered has heightened my ap-preciation of the natural environment and also influenced how I record this in words. I have found that any kind of creative activ-ity stimulates, informs and illuminates my creativity in other ar-eas. My late arrival in photography links with the general slowing down I mentioned previously. I notice more because I go slower, which leads me to take more photographs and, in doing so, to focus more intently on the detail than before; taking photographs slows me down so that I notice more — another benign circle or upward spiral which has taught me the difference between seeing as compared to merely looking, and to finding the extraordinary in the ordinary.

Learning new things keeps the brain active, sharp and flexible. The kind of things I write — both non-fiction and fiction, books with a historical setting, biography — require a lot of research. Just about everything I have written has resulted in tottering piles of reference books filling my study — new learning, fresh view-points and perspectives on life. *The Sunlit Summit*, a biography of W.H. Murray, written in my late seventies, demanded a huge amount of research, as the bibliography at the end will testify.

I was confident that my creativity would not diminish as I aged, but was surprised by the unexpected release of new creative en-ergy. It wasn't so much that I was no longer permanently stressed and tired from work at the Education Offices, but other things which I was hardly aware of at the time. Only now, when I come to write this chapter do I begin to recognise them. The period when my grandchildren, Chloe and Andre, were of pre-school age coin-cided with my late sixties and early seventies. They came regularly to our house and I would play with them — games which invari-ably began 'Grandad, let's pretend...'; games in which the imagi-nation held sway and the boundaries between fantasy and reality were blurred. So much creativity stems from play, from allowing the mind to be playful. Playing with my grandchildren rejuvenated the playfulness in me.

From my mid-sixties onwards I have done a great deal of travelling abroad: as a representative of Scottish PEN at international conferences, as a speaker at literary gatherings, as a cruise lecturer, or on grants for research purposes, or simply going on holiday. Not only has this given me new material to write about, it has counteracted a growing fondness for the familiar and the routine which has been creeping over me. Travel gets me out of my comfort zone and stimulates and challenges my mind with new ideas, with different values and customs, and my senses with new sights, sounds, smells and tastes; and it enables me to meet and talk to a range of people outside my regular group of friends.

Learning to forgive has released huge amounts of creative energy that were imprisoned by anger and resentment. I used to think that forgiveness was some sort of magnanimous favour you bestowed on those who had wronged you. It needed the maturity that comes with age to see that, most of all, it is something you do for yourself, something liberating and healing. In 2007, when I was seventy-three, I attended a weekend course, run by psychotherapist Nick Duffel, entitled 'Boarding School Survivors'. It was for people like me who were still grappling with the damage caused by being sent to boarding school at age seven or eight, away from home, parents and pets, living in a loveless environment, and hiding behind a protective mask twenty-four hours of the day, seven days of the week. In such a confined society, hatreds and rivalries were intense. I found, aged seventy, that I was still having fantasies of revenge on various boys. Nick Duffel helped me get over this, to let go of it, to understand and forgive. It released so much new creative energy. That I left it so late before doing this is, I think, an age-related thing — the growing compulsion to tidy up loose ends and put one's house in order.

A fear of death and worrying about when it would happen and what it would be like was constantly in the back of my mind, surfacing whenever I heard or read of the death of someone close to my age or younger. The turning point came when my wife suggested that one way of coming to terms with my fear might be to look it in the face by planning my own funeral in detail. And it worked! Shortly after this I was diagnosed with prostate cancer. My PSA level was so high that the consultant could see no other outcome than death. At the best I had maybe a couple of years left, at the worst, only a few months. It didn't happen and I am now completely cured. Having planned my funeral and already accepted that one day I would die, none of this seemed so terrible at the time. It banished any lingering worries and fears and set a sizeable corner of my mind free to be creative.

Just as I was not the same person at twenty as I was at ten, or the same person at fifty as I was at thirty, so I am not the same now as I was in earlier phases. The things I wrote were different too. Cowboy and Indian stories for our gang comic; the John Buchan-type adventure novels I attempted in my twenties; the magical realism and surrealist fantasies of my forties and fifties and a growing liking for non-fiction as well. Different life experiences feed in at each stage, a widening of perspective, an increasing maturity. The decision to start on a new work is always an important moment — to invest so much of my time, emotional and creative energy in this piece of writing rather than another. I feel that there is a right moment for each book: any earlier in my life or any later it wouldn't have been the same book and, probably, would not have given me quite the same satisfaction. And *Autumn Voices* is clearly a book for the final phase of my life. I could not have undertaken it until now. I have become more patient with regard to my writing. In my earlier years I would be impatient to finish the book and rush the end because I was desperate to see it in print as soon as possible. I have learned that some novels are best left to mature and ripen in the mind, best left for several years, sometimes, before coming back to them; and also that there can be a moment when the time is right both to begin a book and to publish it — when you are really ready to write it, and when the reading public are ready to receive it.

In my work as a writer the motivations, the type of content and the style of execution have changed. Rather like a river, I have left the fast and furious torrents of youth and entered the calmer, slower, deeper stage before being united with the ocean. A changing hormone balance — less testosterone, more oestrogen — has something to do with it. It's not just that I can't physically do the challenging adventurous things any more, I actually don't want to do them. I want something else. Rather than conquest, I want connection. Conquest is about domination, putting a flag on the peak, naming a route, or earning bragging rights. Connection is about being part of the landscape, feeling a sense of unity and harmony with it. I became a devotee of the dérive. A dérive is an unplanned wander in which you respond creatively to whatever stimuli you encounter on the way. My enjoyment now lies in the journey rather than in reaching the destination. My choice of where I go is determined more by the desire to encounter natural beauty in all its forms than by the challenge it presents or the extent to which it tests my manhood. All this has been reflected in my writing.

As part of my treatment for prostate cancer I underwent a course of hormone treatment, designed to dampen down the level of life-threatening testosterone. This somewhat accelerated the natural process, to the extent that it made me impotent. Even this brought unexpected gifts. As Sophocles has been misquoted as saying, 'it was like being unchained from a lunatic' — yet more release of creative energy.

My earlier fiction was fast paced, quirky and sought to astonish and amaze on every page. I am beginning to discover that creativity is not necessarily linked to novelty. The older me would treat the same subject differently: less frenetic, more reflective and with slower passages contrasting with the fast ones, less striving after effect, less rushed. Much of the writing I did when younger now seems to me like a tightly packed suitcase, full of exotic and brightly coloured clothes. Octogenarian me would want to unpack that suitcase, take out each item, unfold it and hold it up to the light.

Dr. Gene Cohen in his excellent book, *The Creative Age: Awakening Human Potential in the Second Half of Life*, identifies various phases in our creative lives. One of these, which typically occurs in our seventies, is what he terms 'the summing up phase'. In this phase our creative expression is shaped by the desire to review and find a larger meaning in the story of our lives. I recognise this in myself, particularly in my non-fiction writing. I feel drawn to writing memoirs and autobiographical pieces. In this, I think I am more honest about myself than I would have been when younger. I am more accepting of who I am and I care less about what other people think. That censor, who used to sit on my shoulder and whisper, 'What will your friends think if they read this?' seems to have lost its perch. And the gatekeepers who guard my subconscious, refusing to let out painful or inconvenient thoughts and memories, seem to have gone off duty. I have become more accepting of who I am, more honest about my true feelings, and much readier to write freely about these things. There is a new vantage point and a broader perspective, making it possible to see patterns and themes in my life that I hadn't been aware of previously. I find that the writing seems less like hard work. As Dr. Cohen says, 'for many people, the optimal combination of knowledge, experience and emotional readiness comes more dramatically in later life.'

I have files stuffed with notes for future books, both fiction and non-fiction. I'm not sure whether these works-in-waiting are some kind of bucket list, or simply things I want to write about that are waiting their turn. The urge to create, to find an outlet for my imagination, the thrill of it, the self-fulfilment, the challenge of the craftsmanship involved and the satisfaction when I feel I've got it right (or nearly right, at least), the need to communicate my ideas to others, to share joy encountered, and to embark on the inner journeys that help me grow as a person — these have been constant throughout my writing life and are still there. There is a growing awareness, though, that I have now accumulated quite a body of work, not all of it published, and that there are new patterns, threads and themes within old material; and, of late, I have noticed a need to feel that at least some of my work will make a difference to society.

The thought that I might be counting the remaining years of my life in single figures does influence what I feel moved to write these days. Penelope Lively, in a perceptive article about ageing (*The Guardian*, 5/10/2013), refers to developing a new relationship with time in which the balance between time that lies behind and time that lies ahead has shifted. Yes, I recognise that, too. When I was in my thirties, two or three years spent on a novel that never found a publisher did not seem too much of a loss. Now, however, those two or three years might be as much as 50% of the time remaining to me. I want more certainty about the outcome of what I write before I start.

With old age has come a sense that everything is connected. This has made me much more aware of and open to metaphor, for seeing the dissimilar in the similar is about the connectedness of things. Poetry is particularly suited to making connections and drawing out new meanings. Since passing seventy I have felt moved to write much more poetry than previously.

Of all the things I have written since passing seventy what gives me the most pride and satisfaction? To that question I must add 'so far.' *The Sunlit Summit*, a biography of the Scottish mountaineer, writer and conservationist, W.H. Murray, gave me a lot of satisfaction because it took nearly six years to research, write and see through to publication in 2013. Several people were sceptical about whether, at my age, I could carry off a project of that length, particularly as I was undergoing radiotherapy for cancer at that time. About one third of *The Sunlit Summit* was written in trains on my daily journey to and from hospital or in the hospital waiting-room. Writing that book took my mind off the worries and discomforts of cancer. Another is *The Sweet Especial Scene* (2014): a collection of essays about natural beauty encountered. Nothing else I have written has so exactly expressed my feelings about things at the very core of me.

My advice to the youngsters who aspire to being productive into later life? Apart from 'read *Autumn Voices*,' it would be, 'don't even let it cross your mind that you can't or won't be productive in later life. Assume that you can and then you will be.'

Note

1. Scottish PEN, a branch of PEN International, champions freedom of expression and campaigns on behalf of persecuted writers. A. C. Clarke, the subject of the next chapter, has served on its Writers in Prison Committee (now Writers at Risk) and the Exiled Writers Committee.

I have mentioned *The Sweet Especial Scene* and my sample is taken from this. It is part of a chapter entitled 'A Sense of Place' which is a series of short sketches of places that have been special for me.

LOCH CORUISK: the one-eyed witch of the west.

On 'The Isle of Mists' I am not often granted a clear view of the Cuillin peaks. Frequently they are half shrouded, dark, austere and stern, and yet alluring, like a dusky maiden performing the Dance of the Seven Veils, revealing tantalising glimpses through vapour layers — hints of bare, bristling ridges, spires, crags, gullies, deeply gouged corries and long scree slopes. The Black Cuillin give the impression of being one enormous, solid, sculptured stone. Their coarse, crystalline gabbro provides so much friction that I can saunter, hands in pockets, up steep-angled rock. Even with sheets of water sliding down them, I have crossed sloping slabs, so pitted and abrasive that all fears of a slip are banished. Sunk deep in these hills is Loch Coruisk, a remote, wild place. Around it, in a horseshoe, swing the twenty peaks of the Black Cuillin. Intensified by the enclosing, near-perpendicular cliffs is the scent of bog myrtle and rain-sweet heather. At night, echoing mournfully across this dark bowl, is a fox's lonely cry. The Cuillin have been called 'the most beautiful witch of the western seas.' Beautiful undoubtedly, and witchlike too, with sharp talons piercing the sky, and unpredictable weather brewed in high rock cauldrons. Loch Coruisk is the witch's single eye, its all-seeing eye. On most days the loch lies still, unblinking, unruffled by winds that buffet the summits, reflecting the encircling mountains and their many moods, the changing sky, the moon, or the Northern Lights. Sometimes it brims with burnished silver, spilling liquid starlight; at other times it's black with unfathomable mystery. I return to the Cuillin and Loch Coruisk whenever I can, for the one-eyed witch has cast her spell on me, a spell that brings an undying hunger of the heart.

You may also wish to consult www.robinlloydjones.com

www.helensburghheroes.com/hall-of-fame

A.C.CLARKE (Age 75)

Anne Clarke, who writes as A. C. Clarke, is a poet and translator with a background in teaching and university administration. She has been widely published in magazines and anthologies but did not concentrate on her writing until retirement in 2002, when she also moved to Scotland. Her first full collection, *Breathing Each Other In*, was published by Blinking Eye Press in 2005. Anne has won a number of prizes, including Off the Stanza in 2011 and Second Light in 2012. Her second pamphlet, *A Natural Curiosity*, published by New Voices Press in 2011, was shortlisted for the Callum Macdonald award. From 2007–2008 she was Makar for the Federation of Writers. She is an active member of Scottish PEN, and has used her interest in translation to work with refugee poets.

Before moving to Scotland, Anne worked first as a lecturer in Medieval English, University of Southampton, then lecturer in General Studies Department, Marine and Technical College South Shields, Chichester College of Technology, then an administrator, Middlesex Polytechnic,[1] at the Senate House of London University and at University College, London.

For the interview, Anne and I meet in the Millennium Hotel, next to Glasgow's Queen Street Station. She begins by saying that she thinks there is a difference in the creative process between writing prose fiction and writing poetry. She tells me, she started writing poetry at the age of seven, but becoming a single mother in her mid-twenties and needing to hold down a full-time job kept her away from her poetry, from exploring 'that psychic wound that never heals,' as she puts it. I ask her to expand on this. She says, 'The "psychic wound" idea is so familiar to me and so often alluded to in discussions of poetry that I'm afraid I can't identify the source. The idea that it never heals is my own. I think the combined effects of my parents' unhappy marriage, a difficult relationship with my father, the disruption of the war and its aftermath and the rigours of a Catholic education all contributed to the "wound". The poetry comes out of a sense of being out of kilter with the world, familiar to many writers and especially to poets, and perhaps wanting to rebalance my relations with it. I have a natural empathy with those who similarly feel out of place and they too are subjects for my poetry.'

Hoping to make more time to write, she moved out of the academic world and into administration, but somehow these extra hours for her poetry evaded her. Those who know Anne will not find this surprising. She is an extremely conscientious person who always gives of her best to others and full value for money. She could have stayed on, but chose to retire at sixty, finally finding the time she needed for her poetry.

'The stage of my life that I began writing seriously and how long I've been doing it obviously influences the phase of development I've reached at the moment, and my creative pattern,' Anne says, and then adds, 'Some people expect wisdom to come with age. I don't know about that. A sense of perspective can look like wisdom, I suppose.'

In the nearly fourteen years since she retired, how has her poetry changed or developed?

'I think I have improved, in the sense that I have been writing steadily for a number of years now and therefore have more practice at it and I take more care over each poem.'

Having more time has enabled her to read the works of a wide variety of contemporary poets; to learn from and be stimulated by them (Anne has no TV in her house); to join poetry workshops and discussion groups; to attend and take part in poetry events — all of which have contributed towards her continuing development. Also, she points out, poetry is thriving in Scotland at the moment and the level of competition is high, which has forced standards up.

Are the themes running through her poetry the same as they used to be? When she was young, Anne says, she tended, like a lot of young writers, to write about herself and her own feelings and emotions. Later, though, she found it more interesting to write in the voice of other people, about lives forgotten and to get inside their heads and their viewpoints. This latter theme, only now finding expression, has its roots, she thinks, in the way her parents constantly quarrelled. As a child she was caught in the middle, trying to see both points of view. With the passing of the years has come a different perspective, understanding and forgiveness. And the kind of things she became involved with have influenced her themes. In her sixties and seventies these have been, first her work with the Campaign for Nuclear Disarmament, then her work with Scottish PEN and with refugees and asylum-seekers who have come to Glasgow. Themes change, too, with the changing perspectives of later life.

Anne was brought up as Roman Catholic and, for two years, went to a Catholic boarding school.

'I'm no longer a Catholic,' she says, 'But it stays with you. I couldn't have written about Jean Meslier or Margery Kempe[2] until recently. I would have been too close to it.'

Margery Kempe figures in Anne's most recent collection, *In the Margin* (Cinnamon Press, 2015), as do references to a passionate and traumatic love affair of more than thirty-five years ago — again something that needed the passing of time before she could write about it. Anne talks about how she was so totally absorbed in this affair that she hardly noticed the things that were making the news headlines at the time (IRA bombings, the Yorkshire Ripper, for example). In *In the Margin* she has experimented with framing intimate poems within extracts from the news.

Anne translates poetry from French and Latin into English. Has her approach to this aspect of her creativity changed over the years? 'I'd say I have become more careful at making sure that I'm not misinterpreting the original language when translating but I don't think my approach has changed otherwise. I have also tried translating into Scots — but that's to do with living in Scotland now rather than to do with becoming older.'

The discussion moves on to what kind of fears old age holds for her. Dementia, she answers and mentions Iris Murdoch who had Alzheimers in later life and whose thoughts and words in her later novels were said to have become simplified and rambling. 'Words, and a memory for words, are so important to a writer', Anne says. She thinks painters or visual artists in general might possibly continue to function under these circumstances, but not writers. An unpublished poem of hers, 'Losing it', refers to the dread moment when:

> Mirrors streaked with residue
> reflect a stranger whose eyes blank you.

And how 'One day you will open your mouth and utter disconnections.'

On the other hand, Anne points out, there are plenty of poets from the past who have written good poetry well into their seventies and eighties. Other artists, too, of course. She mentions Louise Bourgeois, a sculptor, who continued to do new work into her nineties.[3] In particular she cites W. B. Yeats, her all-time favourite poet, whose work, in her opinion, improved with the advancing years. She quotes a line from his poem 'A Coat' (1916): 'For there's more enterprise in walking naked,' and explains how Yeats, in his more mature work, stripped away the fripperies and adornments and went straight to the heart of things — something she herself tries to do, though she is also drawn to the opposite: the love of words for their own sake.

'It's a matter of finding a balance,' she says. 'Between what really matters and banality; between simplicity and lines lacking in imaginative energy.'

Returning to what she fears about old age, Anne says, 'I've been obsessed with death since I was seven.' At that age she witnessed her newly-born sister being rushed to hospital, only to die there. Aged ten, she was involved in a serious car crash which left her with a fractured skull and unconscious for two weeks. Then, on a school trip to the British Museum, she was terrified by the Egyptian Mummy room. Another fear is of becoming out-of-date — something that seems unlikely, considering her wide reading, and her interaction with poets of all ages through attending poetry events and belonging to groups such as St. Mungo's Mirrorball, Caledonian Poets and the Federation of Writers.

On the topic of motivation to write, Anne tells me it has become stronger as the years go by because of a sense of time running out, of wanting to do as much as possible before she has 'lost it.' But she does not feel under pressure, she says. 'I don't think about my creativity or analyse how it relates to ageing. I just do it. I'm rather opposed to too much analysis in case it frightens away that element of spontaneity, or I become too self-conscious about the whole process.' She doesn't think about herself as any particular age. 'I'm just me, although "me" has changed over the years.' It's an attitude of mind, she says. 'I don't think about the past, except in relation to the present. And I don't think of my life as a progression from youth to age, but rather where I am at as a poet.' She thinks the maturity of a poet, the stage or phase they have reached, is not necessarily related to their chronological age.

'Writing is what I always wanted to do. I write to survive — mentally, emotionally and as a way of understanding myself.' To make the most of her remaining time Anne has become more disciplined. 'But that's not a hardship not a difficult thing to do, because writing is such a pleasure.'

A driving motive behind Anne's work is the urge to keep developing and growing as a poet and to constantly challenge herself. To mark time, to stick to a successful formula, or repeat a theme already explored she regards as some kind of failure. As well as the reading and immersion in the Scottish poetry scene, a range of other stimuli fuel this growth. Some go back to childhood. Growing up in cosmopolitan London was, for her, a broadening influence. She was, from an early age, very aware of other cultures, other religions and lifestyles, visible both on the street and in the city's museums and galleries. 'And anything that opens you up to difference is a plus.'

Anne's parents, who ran a private boys' school, thought it best to send her away from home when she reached adolescence. So they sent her to a Catholic boarding school. There were many things she hated about it and she has now rejected Catholicism. 'But,' she says, 'The Catholic Church is rich in ritual. It's exotic, erotic, graphic, physical, tactile.' It took her years to overcome repressed feelings and the Church has given her a lifelong guilt complex. It has also fed her imagination and opened new pathways of poetry. In order to come to terms with that upbringing, she revisited much of it through her poetry and looked at it from a new perspective.

The 2014 Commonwealth Games, held in Scotland, presented her with another poetic challenge. Anne, who has no interest in sport, was one of the poets commissioned to write poems about one of the sports featured there. She chose the triathlon and found herself exploring themes which would not otherwise have occurred to her.

She says, 'I don't need to travel to get out of my comfort zone. The whole of life is beyond my comfort zone.'

This fear of ossifying as a poet and her need to grow and explore are major factors in maintaining the momentum of her writing into her seventies and will continue to drive her forward in the years ahead. Anne stresses how important mentoring has been to her in this process. Before retiring she had two sessions of being mentored by Martyn Crucefix.[4] Then, three years into retirement, The Royal Literary Fund granted her a mentorship with Mario Petrucci.[5] After moving up to Scotland in 2002, Anne was mentored by Donny O'Rourke.[6] 'He was particularly good at making me think about what I was trying to do, about ways of approaching it, and new avenues I might explore.' O'Rourke, she says, was instrumental in encouraging her to write her book on Margery Kempe and, before that, her poems about Fr. Meslier.

Anne is currently taking an online course with Poetry Kit, which, she says, challenges her in new ways, involving set tasks and analysis of other people's work. Anne speaks about Second Light Network which she has found helpful. It is a network of women poets who are published or beginning to get published and who are serious about developing their work.

Also contributing to her creative growth and the momentum of her work is the critiquing group she helps to run in Glasgow (by invitation only) and her work with Sheila Templeton and Maggie Rabatski in which they translate/respond to each other's work, writing their own versions of each other's poems in, respectively, English, Scots and Gaelic, exploring new themes, styles, moods and tones.

Anne, who has always enjoyed walking, began hill-walking in Scotland through holidays with her partner. Now that they have moved to Scotland permanently, they are on the hills regularly. 'Hill walking — and walking in general — is for me a key part of maintaining health, both in body and mind, and it is also a time for reflection and creativity. I have found subjects for poems on walks, revised poems in my head on walks, started new ones not to do with the walk.' Wordsworth, she says, found he could not compose poems unless he was walking.

From the work completed since retirement, Anne picks 'Fr. Meslier's Confession' (2012) as the one of which she is proudest. Jean Meslier (1664–1729), a French parish priest, was a closet atheist, who wrote in secret a Memoir or Testament in which he expressed his revolutionary zeal and his loathing of the monarchy, aristocracy and church hierarchies for their tyranny over the poor. I ask Anne to say more about the writing of these poems and she refers me to her introductory Author's Note to the collection, from which the following is an extract:

'For me the pull of the story is the dichotomy between Meslier's outward life as a parish priest and his inner life as expressed in the 'Testament' and the anguish this caused, to which he testifies himself. My version of Meslier embodies many of my own uncertainties, as a "cradle Catholic" turned agnostic. So powerful a pull did he exert that he seemed to walk onto the page almost unbidden and for three months entirely took over my writing, for good or ill. I would like the unprejudiced reader to be left not with a sense that the real Meslier was as I have depicted him but that the real Meslier *was*, and that the nature of his dilemma was real and pressing — and still is.'

She feels she got it right because it struck a chord with priests and staunch Catholics. A poem from it was read on the weekly BBC 4 radio programme *Something Understood*.

Anne expresses the thought that those who reach their seventies having already made a reputation for themselves in some particular genre of poetry or for their distinctive style might find it harder to live up to their past. It might not be so easy to better your past work. Those that depend on writing for their main source of income might also find it harder when they get older.

'I work slower than I used to,' Anne says. 'I produce less in a given time, and what I write is not always fashionable or marketable. But I'm not financially dependent on my writing, not many poets are.'

We touch upon the dwindling opportunities open to older writers: 'Especially older women,' Anne says. She mentions Grey Hen Press, run by Joy Howard in Yorkshire: a small independent press which publishes poetry by older women, concentrating in the first instance on producing themed anthologies. These showcase the particularity of women's voices, and give less well-known poets the opportunity of having their work published alongside that of established writers. It also runs a poetry competition open only to women over sixty. On the whole, Anne says, she prefers publishers, events and groups which are for all ages. 'Otherwise it's rather like going into sheltered housing where you only live alongside other old people.'

We discuss the shift that has come about in attitudes to modesty, self-confidence and self-promotion. Her generation, Anne says, was brought up to believe that modesty was a desirable quality and that to be self-effacing was considered an attractive trait in a person. 'If you thought well of yourself, your parents or your teachers soon squashed you,' she says. These days it's often regarded as a handicap to be self-effacing. She is not comfortable with the idea of promoting herself and her work through Facebook, blogs and other social media.

What advice would she give to younger writers who aspire to continue being productive into their Third Age? Anne's view is that the biggest obstacle to continuing one's writing is not being able to handle criticism. Women, in particular, she thinks, are more easily put off as they get older. She herself stopped writing for several weeks after an especially harsh critique which came at the wrong time for her. 'Learn not to take criticism to heart,' she advises. Her second piece of advice is: 'Do things that will stimulate your creativity.' In this, A.C.Clarke is certainly a role model for others.

Notes

1. Names of all institutions here are as they were when A.C.Clarke worked there. The names have since changed in some cases.

2. Margery Kempe (c. 1373–after 1438) was an English Christian mystic, known for dictating *The Book of Margery Kempe*, a work considered by some to be the first autobiography in the English language. Her book chronicles her domestic tribulations and her extensive pilgrimages to holy sites in Europe and the Holy Land, as well as her mystical conversations with God. She is now honoured in the Anglican Communion, but was never made a Roman Catholic saint.

3. Louise Joséphine Bourgeois (1911–2010) was a French-American artist. Best known for her large-scale sculpture and installation art, Bourgeois was also a prolific painter and printmaker. She explored a variety of themes over the course of her long career including domesticity and the family, sexuality and the body, as well as death and the unconscious. Although Bourgeois exhibited with the Abstract Expressionists and her work has much in common with Surrealism and Feminist art, she was not formally affiliated with a particular artistic movement.

4. Martyn Crucefix: (born 1956) is a British poet, translator and reviewer. His work ranges widely from vivid and tender lyrics to writing that pushes the boundaries of the extended narrative poem. His themes encompass questions of history and identity, particularly in the 1997 collection *A Madder Ghost* and — influenced by his translations of Rainer Maria Rilke — more recent work focuses on the transformations of imagination and momentary epiphanies.

5. Mario Petrucci: He moved into freelance writing after a stint in science teaching, a PhD in optoelectronics at UCL, organic farming / goat-herding in Ireland, and a further BA in Environmental Studies at Middlesex University. He was inaugural Royal Literary Fund Fellow at Oxford Brookes University and (later) the Fellow at Westminster and Brunel Universities. Most recently, he became RLF Fellow at the City and Guilds of London Art School. His

poetry performances attract international recognition. He is four times winner of the London Writers Competition and recipient of the 2002 *Arvon/Daily Telegraph* International Poetry Prize. Mario now works as an educator and creative writing tutor for all ages, and as a radio/tv broadcaster.

6. Donny O'Rourke: Poet, songwriter, film maker, critic, editor, teacher and translator, Donny O'Rourke was born, brought up and educated in Renfrewshire and has degrees from the University of Glasgow and from Cambridge. After several years (and very senior positions) in television and journalism, Donny went freelance. He still broadcasts regularly and is the author or editor of more than a dozen books, CDs and works for the theatre including translations, mostly from French. He edited the landmark anthology *Dream State: the New Scottish Poets*, published in 1994 and updated in 2001.

I wrote this poem last year [2016] and it does seem to me to relate to general themes of change, development and looking back.

Portrait of the author at ten

The girl in the gingham dress and pigtails
with her bucktooth grin leans into the picture
afraid of missing out, the only one
not facing the camera foursquare
with a ready-made smile.
Who is she? I don't remember.

Here is a family portrait
formal as a Gainsborough despite
Grandad's patched tweed, Grandma's florals.
A record? No, a testimonial.
Grandad smiling as ordered, Grandma
tucked in behind him, my cousin

seriously aware of her good girl pose.
Judgement is everywhere in the garden,
has crept into the Box Brownie
frowns through its lens. But the girl
in the gingham dress wants life to start
never mind the rules. I wish I knew her.

You may also wish to consult:

http://www.scottishbooktrust.com/profile-author/30627

http://www.overstepsbooks.com/poets/a-c-clarke

Photograph by Gerry Cambridge

SALLY EVANS (Age 76)

Sally Evans is a poet and editor, who lives above a bookshop in Callander. She moved to Edinburgh from the north of England in 1979. Soon after, she teamed up with Ian W. King, Scots poet and fiddle player, and they started bookselling together. Sally is editor of *Poetry Scotland*[1] and Poetry Editor, Scots Language Centre Website. Her publications include shorter poems, book-length poems, a memoir, translations of Gaelic poetry, and reviews. Her most recent book is *A Burrell Tapestry and a Marion Burrell Sampler* (diehard 2017).

Sally has also published widely in magazines, anthologies, and e-zines and has had two e-books published which both reached No 1 in the Amazon women's poetry list. She started the webzine *Keep Poems Alive International* in August 2015.

Sally says, 'Publishing and writing are not about "more of the same." If you are not a radical, you are just wasting ink. I've thrived on a degree of exclusion that came from not being Scottish, from being a woman (in early days), and from being an outsider.'

King's Bookshop in Callander is the continuation of Old Grindle's Bookshop in Edinburgh, which Sally and her husband started in 1987. It is from here that they run diehard publishers.[2]

In an interview for *New Linear Perspectives* (2011), Sally said:

'We moved our home and our bookshop to Callander simultaneously and it nearly killed us. It certainly wrecked my car, taking the lead type and printing presses our van man refused.

'At a time when other booksellers were moving into the Borders to be nearer the English supply lines, we decided to go further out into Scotland. We have a garden and a bindery, both of which we really needed for the sake of our sanity. We are on the edge of the Highlands, an hour from Edinburgh or Glasgow by road and among the lochs and landscapes that have inspired my writing. I love it here. It is a delight to be constantly visited by poets and book people and have conversations that are often more open and relaxed than those in the cities. We run an annual poetry weekend which has helped to shape other festivals, with its friendly atmosphere, inclusiveness, food and fun. We could hardly have started all this without the initial period in Edinburgh getting to know the scene.

'As for surviving, the top end of the trade is an international market and our bindery is establishing a quiet reputation of its own. You can't fail to survive if you can take a fifty quid burst book and turn it into a £700 full morocco and gold leaf masterpiece. You have to know your books to be able to do that.'

Unfortunately, due to an accident while hill-walking, I found myself confined to my house and unable to visit Sally in Callander, but she was kind enough to send me written answers to my questions:

What brought you to Scotland?

Living in Scotland was my destiny. It happened. I had moved around for jobs before that and Scotland is where I settled down, although I came because of my former husband's job and spent my first years in Scotland with my children very young. I was comfortable with the Celtic fringe — my father was Welsh. I was 37 when I arrived here so I have now spent half my life, and three quarters of my adult life, in Scotland. I'm pro-independence.

You have done a great deal to support and nurture emerging Scottish poets. Please say a bit about why you have done this.

I began by gaining from the support of others. In my early life in England, I did not discover the poetry community. It existed perhaps in the universities, and in London and elsewhere, accessible in certain pubs but not easily accessed by young women. There is a public network everywhere now, but there wasn't then. You had to find your way in, and I didn't. But coming to Edinburgh in 1980, I immediately found things happening here. I joined in and began to learn from the poets who seemed to be everywhere, and the process is two way. Then as now the scene was fractured and varied and often enlivened by clashes of personalities, but it was there and I became part of it. Learning from the old lags and passing on what I could to others behind me in the fight.

It was not long before I met Ian King who became my husband and business partner when we decided to open a bookshop. It opened in 1987. We now had a venue where poets could come and they did: beginners and pros, wannabes and moths to candles, crowds from the pubs and after important readings by Sorley Maclean, Norman MacCaig, and many others. There were the *Chapman* crowd, the crowd from the new Poetry Library, the Glasgow crowd and the annual jamboree that was poetry on the Edinburgh Festival Fringe. After ten years of this I knew hundreds of poets — Elizabeth Burns and I collected a communal 'Poem for Peace' with manuscript contributions from 120 poets, by going round the pubs.

Ian and I started publishing poetry books, and plays — our very first book was a play by Bill Dunlop which won a Fringe First. In 1997, with fifteen years of this melee behind us, and an established bookshop, we started the broadsheet *Poetry Scotland*.

Everyone probably thinks they have handicaps as writers seeking publication. For me it was that I was a woman (a disadvantage in poetry before 2000) and I was English in Scotland (a political drawback), while Ian wrote in Scots, refused to ape the middle class, and was regarded as a fiddle player rather than a writer. It seemed irrelevant that Ian had met all kinds of writers and publishers in London, had a grasp of the set-up, and could write like the wind in Scots. Irrelevant all I had done previously in England, too. I couldn't understand why I became known as a disestablishment writer, but I now realise it was because I supported so many other disestablishment writers. I believed in the word on the page, in the book, and I still do.

Since you first started helping other poets has the kind of help needed changed?

Nothing ever stays the same. When we started *Poetry Scotland*, poets had a desperate need to get their poems read, and quickly. The Internet has resolved this. Websites, e-zines, Facebook all allow poems to be published quickly and plentifully. Self-publishing, so frowned upon in my early days, is now acceptable to all but the most elitist and blinkered. New problems have arisen though. Reviews are almost impossible to get, in or outside the establishment media, to the extent that most poetry is driven underground.

The world of poetry readings in the cities has expanded hugely. Amateurs flood out serious beginners when book printing to a good standard is available to all. The universities have muscled in, supporting their new poetry graduates with all the clout they can muster. And politics weighs heavy, for poets are dangerous and many interests conspire to control and confuse us. In many aspects, poetry looks like a mug's game.

Several well-known figures were first published by you in Poetry Scotland *or diehard before they became high-profile. Could you please mention some of these people and say what satisfaction you derived from their later success.*

We published books by Richard Price and Elizabeth Burns and we brought Angus Calder back to poetry with a book after a long break. I realised Angus Calder was a poet because he had so many poet friends. We did him a book from 18 years' work. Less than a year later he came into our shop with three separate MSS and said, 'Publish them!' I wouldn't — I said he had too much new stuff and should take more time. He dumped the MSS on my desk and went off in a huff. I still wouldn't publish them. I was actually wrong — they were all good poems. He was a pro and got the books all published by different small presses. He even dedicated one, *Deepa's Bowl*, to Ian and me.

With the magazine, there was an era when so many of the known poets in Scotland appeared in *Poetry Scotland* that those who never appeared became almost conspicuous. Today, I don't know so many of the younger poets, and the role of *Poetry Scotland* has had to develop and change with the times.

It was good to see our poets do well and progress, but I am equally proud of all the good poets who are unknown or too little known who have graced our pages. Many dedicated and able poets who make poetry their lives may never reach the limelight. I describe these people as good disestablishment poets and I like to support them. So we've done books by Richard Livermore and Margaret Gillies Brown, for instance, poets who can hold their heads up with the best. And many others.

What are you working on at the moment? And what are you planning to write in the future?

I'll continue to write short poems, though I'm rather exhausted emotionally by the books I have already written within the last year. Making books is the thing that matters and I'll almost certainly be back with more poetry when I'm ready.

However, not long ago I decided I wanted to write a substantial novel containing much of what I know about poetry. Realising this would be a difficult assignment, I applied to a university to take a PhD in Creative Writing so that I could undertake this challenge with academic advice. The result is that I'm now embarking on an entirely new adventure at the university of my choice, 52 years after I took my first degree and 50 years after I took my post graduate degree. This will keep me pretty busy but I am used to working hard, and there will be little time for worries on the age front.

Your book The Bees *has quite a lot to say on themes of life and death. As you get older do these themes become more and more significant for you?*

Life and death are always significant. Death comes to many before age, and hits us with loss, especially when we have loved and depended on people who die on us. By the time we are older, we should be more used to this. It's not so much life and death, but the shortage of time remaining to us, that affects older creative people and writers. Unlike other people, we don't usually retire from our jobs and try for an easy few years before conking out. Writing is not something you retire from. At least, poetry isn't.

The Bees is arguably my best book and that could be why themes of life and death seem prominent in it. It was witty and light-hearted but serious — 'a light poem to enlighten'. As an object, with Reinhard Behrens' illustrations, the book was a triumph. People treated me with a bit more respect after *The Bees*.

How do you define creativity and has your definition of it changed over the years?

Creativity is not different from what it was when I started. I now know so much more about the craft but it is still about exploration, curiosity, delight, compensations and so on. At school, I told my (Scottish) headmistress, 'Yes, I do sit and make up poems, but I never like them when I've finished.' The difference is that I sometimes, even fairly often, like them now.

It is making a thing that exists — Dylan Thomas said something like that. A poem is there to be read again and again and it makes the world bigger.

Creativity is rather like sexuality. It is seeing a tree and wanting to hit it. It is wanting to get close and be a part of the world, to belong; it is seeing the new moon not through glass. It is being said no to. I have never actually tried to define it before.

Has the nature of your creativity changed as you get older?

Creativity plays a greater part in my life now I'm older. I have two very clever adult children but no grandchildren. I don't have the physical strength to do so much gardening. I still drive a lot, to Stirling, Edinburgh, Glasgow (the Highlands not so much nowadays), and between Scotland and Cumbria. Reading and writing is most of what I have left, and writing is the active part of that.

I've come to realise that writing has always been the most important thing. I often had to do other work from necessity when younger, and it was usually interesting work, but it was not my reality. I would always be writing overnight or on my days off or in odd hours whatever work I was doing.

You've described yourself as a poet and a gardener. Is there a connection between these two?

I'm a poet and a bookseller, the connection between which needs little pointing out. I always loved the countryside and wild plants and trees, and I have enjoyed making gardens especially our present one. I also love looking at other gardens large and small — garden watching could be the equivalent of reading, doing one's own garden like writing. Really when you plan and make a garden you're making a world.

Does religion or any form of belief system play a part in your life?

If so, has this changed over the years, and does it influence your creative work?

I'm not at all religious but I love life and I'm an optimist. I can't make any capital out of being regretful or fearful, although I could find many regrets. The "miserable sinner" approach to Christianity had a negative effect on me when young. There's much for me to admire in Quakerism and Buddhism, but I'm too old and too self-reliant for any of that now. I'm very self-reliant. Except when I crack up.

To what extent does reading inform or stimulate your creativity? Are your reading habits changing?

I've always read huge amounts, since a teenager. I used to relate to writing styles. These days I like reading books by people I know.

Apart from serious novels, poetry and light reading, I've had some funny interests over the years. I will read any book about survival at sea. I totally adore the mixed gardening and essay books of Beverley Nichols. I like books about London in the twenties and thirties. I read fast, usually a book in a day. Reading keeps my mind going and can therefore stave off the need to write. My parents used to read every evening, one on each side of the fireplace. Neither of them ever raised a pen to write creatively, which puzzled me, but they were very scathing of a schoolteacher they knew who, when asked what he read, replied, 'I don't read, I write.' So I was brought up in the habit of reading, but never encouraged to write.

The other thing I do is reread my favourites, quite a lot. If a book really impresses me on first reading I will read it again, straight over. That's something I don't remember doing when younger. I used to think I should read different books to complete the canon.

What, from your personal experience, have been the most negative aspects of ageing? How have these impacted on your creativity?

I miss people who've died, not only parents and other people who were older, but colleagues and writers who were friends. I miss Angus Calder and Sandy Hutchison and Elizabeth Burns, and Sebastian Barker in England. I miss talking poetry with them. I miss getting indecipherable letters from Maurice Lindsay, and I miss being glared at by Norman MacCaig and Sorley Maclean.

What gifts and joys have come to you in later life and how have these impacted on your creativity?

Some are private, but one I can talk about is how my brothers and sisters and I have reclaimed our family home from fifty years ago. It is a beautiful old vicarage in the south of Cumbria. When you have grown up in a vicarage, a glamorous tied cottage, you never expect to see it again, but one of my brothers bought it back for all of us, about five years ago. It has meant so much to me in terms of understanding my whole life, and I've written a huge lot about it, not all of it publishable by any means, but that doesn't matter. It all feeds in. This circumstance has also helped me to reconcile my two countries, Scotland and England — the north of England, that is. I have put so much into my work in Scotland and thrived so much from it, that now I am older it is relevant to make sense of two colliding parts of my life, and to express their separate characters if I am able.

How do you envisage the remaining years of your life? Do you see yourself continuing to be actively creative into even later life?

Moving out of the city to Callander was an 'oldie' thing to do, and we did it when the time was right for us. I will continue to live and work in our home and bookshop along with Ian, operating our cultural outpost for poets, writers and other free thinkers, as long as we are fit to do so. It has been a very productive lifetime — you see I am now beginning to think in terms of 'has been'. It may prove more difficult further down the line, but that could be true of any arrangement. The logistics of giving up, as all people have to give up in the end, are always a problem to be solved.

We've got it slightly under control with the bookshop. We rarely go to auctions any more — we used to enjoy their rough and tumble and excitement, sometimes several times a week. But the work of buying many books at auction has become too heavy for us. We have other strings to our bow and are now well enough known that we sometimes get calls from houses etc., and are able to purchase good lots of books without too much hassle. I will go on driving around the country while I have eyesight and a driving license.

I'm not likely to climb high mountains or go outdoor swimming again. I cannot imagine recharging an electric car. I probably won't drive large white vans again — I found out recently that you cannot hire a car or van if you are over 76. That's standard with all hirers. But beyond all that, I cannot see myself ever without a sheet of paper nearby and one of my disposable fountain pens at my fingertips, and having some reason to write.

Of all the things you have produced as a writer since passing 70 (not necessarily published), what gives you the most satisfaction and pride?

One of my most interesting recent pieces is a very intense story I wrote when I had run into a crisis. The story turned out to be all about my relationship with my father, starting in the earliest years of my life. It followed through as though to explain the whole of my personal life. It took a week to write, and I read it through every night for a month afterwards and it got me out of the bit. I may well never publish it but it is one of the best things I've written in terms of its therapeutic magic, a power in my writing that I exercised on myself. I was also very pleased with the two poetry e-books about the Scottish countryside. *Tormaukin* (winter) and *Drip Road* (summer) which I wrote very fast in the first half of 2017 when invited by Tony Lewis-Jones of Firewater Press, Bristol, to send him an e-book of poems. I derived great satisfaction from how well they did on Amazon, commercial success not being a feature of mine or most poets' books. These poems were also love poems and are among the best things I have done. Again, I re-read them a good deal at the time. Tony is very busy and so am I, but I hope I will do some more e-books as time goes on, for his Firewater Press. Like Maurice Lindsay, I don't want to stop writing poems.

I also get huge satisfaction from working on books for other poets, and I have done several of these in the last few years though my work in that area will be drawing to a close.

Do you have any role models as regards continuing to be creative and productive in later life?

I knew Maurice Lindsay when he was very elderly. He kept producing his 'last book' of poems, time and again, and I did two 'last books' for him after others had had enough. But I wouldn't do his 'very last book' — there were still some lovely poems but not enough for a book. It was not long before he died but he wouldn't let go. He was a very good poet. That taught me to recognise that the day will come when you have to stop.

Margaret Gillies Brown, a friend in her late eighties, is still an active writer. She's recently published the sixth of her well known biographical books about her family in Scotland and Canada, as well as her latest book of poems this year. She holds an annual gathering for poets at her home in Perthshire where she is deeply involved in her family's farm and winery and the daily lives of her grandchildren. Similarly Ian Blake, a retired school housemaster, who lives in a croft on the coast of Wester Ross, still writes, and drives south several times a year to his many friends in England, sometimes calling at Callander on his way, with no sign of giving up. If your health allows it you are lucky.

What advice would you give to young writers who aspire to continue to be productive into old age?

There's always the sense that youth matters. If you want money or fame out of writing, it probably does. But people who have to write will write, nothing will stop them.

Many writers notice as they move through the decades that new writers always seem to threaten those already active. The media support youth and newness and there is a sense that you will be deluged by the new, and even as you are gaining ground you are losing it. If you have a regular publisher they may offer you books less often. You see a social whirl of writers meeting to hear each other's work, or praising their friends on social media and you think, 'Where do I fit into this circus? How can I possibly contribute? Do they need me anymore?' Well, they do, and you need yourself.

Younger people have the opportunity of doing creative writing degrees and I would probably encourage that, though perhaps as a postgraduate study as with teaching or librarianship, for there's nothing like having a good grounding in a real subject. People with the new writing 'qualifications' already receive preferential treatment from publishers and promoters, so if you want to be a professional, go for it. But at the same time, the value of writing for all and sundry is being emphasised as never before. And really good gripping writing will make out in the end. It will stand you in good stead. In your seventies and eighties it will keep you content and alert, though it is not proof against dementia, viz. Terry Pratchett. I do believe that writing is a way of negotiating life for an individual, and that this is more important than outward functions.

The other small thing, but very important, is, don't be afraid to declare yourself as a writer. It is a kind of 'coming out' which I failed to do for far too long in my youth. (It didn't help that in that era, women poets were widely made out to be oddities, recluses and bampots.) Making others believe in you is as necessary as believing in yourself. If you have friends and family who vociferously do not believe in you as a writer, make some space between you and them. Move away. Change your job. Get some writer friends.

What haven't I asked you that you hoped I would ask you? Is there anything else about creativity in later life that you would like to say?

This doesn't really fit in as a summing up, but it's something else I've thought about, mainly because our bookshop and publishing house has a literary archive of its own.

'End of life planning' is a concept now used by accountants and others, and I think writers should think about dealing with their papers and archives. Some have universities queuing up for the chippings from their studios, but most of us had better think things out. Is there a family member who can be trusted to take charge? Many writers' families do not believe in the creativity of their eccentric relatives. Do we have a young literary friend who might become our executor? Have we tidied up our journals and note books, destroyed whatever is incriminating and shameful, or just too rough, dated remaining notebooks and poems, left our own archive neat and manageable? Can spare books be distributed to relatives or second hand bookstores? Could poetry libraries or university libraries offer a home for our papers, which may contain letters from eminent writers, or offer perspectives on history and events?

Writing is not a normal career and it has no career structure. You either succeed in various public or private ways, or you don't. Your books are circulated and read, then gradually disappear from view. Between higher profile writers and those less feted it is simply a matter of degree. After each publication, of poem or book, you are back to square one, every time. High profile exposure may seem like a career for some but it is not typical. In any other profession than writing, there would be more sense of consolidation from a lifetime of dedication to its skills, and some recognition from within, more than simply inclusions on lists of writers, which don't occur uniformly across the country in any case.

Speech is a part of our humanness and there is no easy solution to becoming older and having less clout: we have taken part in something exciting to the best of our ability, and if we can bow out knowing that a few people have understood us or are close to us, we are lucky.

Notes

1. Conceived as a broadsheet for current poetry, *Poetry Scotland* quickly found its place among poetry magazines. It is poet led, with a circulation which has grown to include many poets in England and Wales as well as the Scottish core. It will move to a Third Series with a different format after Issue 100 — like ourselves it has to accept that time moves on.

2. diehard publishers have been independently publishing since 1990 a range of poetry books in Scots, Gaelic and English, in paperback, hard back and pamphlet form. It has also published plays.

In the next village

In the next village I went to work
in the hotel's smart restaurant.
They knew I wasn't there for long,
they knew I couldn't fry an egg.

The locals in the bar would laugh
and watch me try to pour a beer
and watch me scuttle round with brooms
and wash the chintzy ornaments.

I'd have to set the tables out
and polish cutlery and glass.
I was a decoration too —
they knew I couldn't fry an egg.

I walked between the villages
through honeysuckle and wild rose
on the back lanes in summer time.
They knew I wasn't there for long

and did not much affect their lives
as I did what was asked of me —
to tidy rooms and make the beds,
to sweet-talk awkward visitors.

The waiter put a fiver in
a pewter tankard, said, 'You win
that if the horse I've backed comes in' —
I would not gamble, would not sin.

So, prim as well as privileged
I served my weeks of summer sun
for pocket money for my term
away at university.

If I was ever in their world
again, at table I would sit,
with wise, well-educated folk,
and eat and talk and give good tips.

Though honeysuckle frames the lanes,
the past is hollow and has gone
and no-one now recalls the girl
who couldn't even fry an egg.

Sally writes: This is a poem from Cumbria. It is distinctly an older person's poem. I am looking back many years, and seeing with humour an episode of my life long ago. Despite the fact that 'the past is hollow and has gone' I take pleasure from the memory. It is a true and honest portrait of someone about to disappear into her life — by the person she ended up as! I wonder how I would have reacted if I had known the paths through which my life would lead.

You may also wish to consult http://amzn.to/2F1L0uf

3. OLD FRIENDS

David Donnison
Larry Butler
Alison Prince

This grouping of writers contains the two oldest writers in the project — David at age 92 and Alison at 86. David is the only person in the project to have taken part in World War II as an adult. David, Larry and Alison have known each other for a long time.

DAVID DONNISON (Age 92)

David Donnison is an Emeritus Professor and Honorary Senior Research Fellow at the University of Glasgow in the Department of Urban Studies. He previously held the Chair of Town and Regional Planning at Glasgow. Before coming to Scotland he lectured and conducted research at the London School of Economics. David's professional interests, passions and areas of considerable influence cover urban planning, urban poverty and inner city regeneration, social policy and administration, social exclusion and the quest for social justice and equality, and the advocacy of health and social care. In addition to his many publications on these issues, David also wrote three critical essays for the Fabian Society on the Ingleby Report (1956) into the prevention and treatment of delinquency amongst children and young persons. He is a former chair of the Supplementary Benefits Commission and was a member of the Labour Party for 67 years.

David was married for twenty-three years to Kay Carmichael until her death in 2009. Kay trained as a psychiatric social worker before taking up a lecturing post at Glasgow University. She was an unflagging champion of the marginalised, and embraced such causes — then unfashionable — as gay rights, prison reform and the decriminalisation of prostitution. Kay became an adviser to Harold Wilson on social policy and was deputy chair of the Supplementary Benefits Commission. Her highly influential work contributed to the creation of children's panels and the special unit at Barlinnie for violent offenders, but perhaps her most famous work was her spell living on a breadline income in Glasgow's East End close to where she was born and brought up.

My plans to meet up with David were postponed because he had blacked-out and fallen down some stairs, damaging his head, breaking a collar-bone and suffering concussion. I had thought 'postponed' meant for at least several months. Not so. Within days he was out of hospital, back home looking after himself, feeling bored and eager to have our meeting. He had even managed to write a poem since his accident. Previously, I had been impressed when, at a public reading, David had recited some of his poems from memory. Now I was impressed all over again by the fluency of his answers to my questions.

'My father, Vernon Donnison, was in the Indian Civil Service. I have vivid memories of Burma (then part of the Indian Raj) from the age of 3–6 before I was sent to England. And then I went back at the age of 14 for a couple months during the school holidays.'

David has described his memories of Burma and much else besides in his book *The Last of the Guardians: A Story of Burma, Britain and a Family* (Newton, 2005), published when he was 81. A review of the book has this to say:

'Interlocked with the story of one family's fortunes is the story of an empire — how the British came to be in Burma and its consequences and legacy. Donnison is to be congratulated on his masterly and reflective presentation of Burmese history and society from the establishment of British rule through Burma's "journey to independence" via the gathering storm of World War 2: the Japanese invasion and collapse of the British administration, the drama and suffering of the retreat from Burma — including his parents' own experiences — and the "Pyrrhic victory" of the reconquest of Burma and the emerging new world that is the ending of an empire for some and a beginning for others. Out of the many questions that Donnison poses in his thought-provoking account of imperial guardianship, his final one is: "Did Vernon and Ruth throw away their lives — abandoning their country and their children for no great purpose?" He thinks that Vernon's answer would be that: "you can only do your best in life — drawing on the knowledge, the opportunities and the traditions of your own time." Donnison's own conclusion is that: "Living now in a society that is in many ways as deeply divided and as unfair as the one my generation inherited — a society engaged yet again in wars of conquest against brown skinned people — can those of us who have tried to create a better world claim that we have done anything more than pass on to a few people some of the kindness, hopes and the ideals that others gave us?"'(Patricia Herbert, The Britain-Burma Society).

I asked David to tell me more about his earlier life.

'I left my boarding school at age 17 in December 1943 and by March 1944 was in the Royal Navy until being demobbed in 1946. I was in the North Atlantic fleet on a cruiser as a sub lieutenant.

When the European war ended we brought back King Haakon to Denmark after his wartime exile in England. We were then sent to be part of the Pacific fleet, based in Sydney. When the Japanese surrendered, there was nearly a year to wait before I could take up my place at Oxford University, so stayed in Australia before working my passage back to Britain on a merchant ship.

At Oxford I read PPE (Politics, Philosophy and Economics). I graduated in 1950 with a First Class Honours degree. Shortly afterwards, I married a fellow student and we went to Manchester where I had been offered a lecturing post at the university. After three years there I moved to Toronto University in Canada where I lectured on the subject of Government, specialising in social administration.

I was at boarding school from the age of eight. There, I learned to control my feelings. When living in a closed community it's important to be able to get on with other people and to remember that others are going through the same sort of stresses and need friendship and support. Quite soon you find a group or "gang" who will protect and support you. That has continued throughout my life — in the Navy and in the academic world. My career could be described as the recurring creation of a gang: a group of colleagues who supported and learnt from each other. I have several gangs at the moment: the small community on Easdale Island; my music gang; my writing group; good friends who live nearby and who all know each other, many of them former colleagues.

My first marriage broke up in 1979 after 27 years. We had four children together. The first two, both now in their sixties, are solicitors and recently retired. The third, also retired, was a primary school teacher; and the youngest heads a small unit analysing statistics about children for the Education and Social Work departments in Islington. Seven years after my divorce I married Kay Carmichael and we were together until her death in December 2009.'

In addition to his considerable output of academic writings, his memoir of Burma and his poetry, David plays the concertina in a ceilidh band every Monday night; and he paints and draws. I asked him if these were different kinds of creativity or whether they all came from the same source and the same mental process.

'I'm very much an amateur as a musician and an artist. I began trying to draw and paint and play music fairly late in life when I was no longer in a paid job. I think they're all rather similar at a fundamental level. Music, singing, acting and other performing arts are great builders of friendships — they're shared activities. Writing, on the other hand, is a rather lonely task and quite a private thing. The painting is tailing off a bit now because it's more difficult in the sense that it needs a working space and there's a lot of cleaning up involved. I have rented part of the studio of an artist who lives nearby. He's a great help because he's much better than me and can give me advice. I still draw and carry a sketch book with me wherever I go. I like sketching animals and people. I usually make Christmas cards and postcards from my drawings. The common feature in these different types of creativity is that they are about conveying and sharing feelings. Even in academic writing there's a good deal of feeling, although it's not the main thing. The main thing in academic writing is employing analytical skills to find the truth, then presenting it clearly.

Some of my academic writing has creative elements in the sense that I was drawing on feelings, my feelings about the situations I was describing and conveying them to whatever one's readership was and trying to do this well and attractively. I think several of my academic books had this kind of creativity. Probably the most widely read was *The Government of Housing* (Pelican, 1967); also *The Politics of Poverty* (Longman, 1981) which is still in print. Both these books had elements of creativity. My job necessitated contact with some of the poorest people in the country and it was a radicalising experience. Trying to convey some of that and the character of the country and my feelings about the deprived people I met was as important to me as the academic content.

For me, creativity is about responding with feeling and emotion to all sorts of things and reflecting back to other people what those experiences meant to you. I think old age frees you to express things without the pressure to prove anything or meet the expectations of other people. It frees me to do my own thing and attempt new forms of creativity which I previously wouldn't have attempted. When I got older I realised that if something is worth doing, it's worth doing badly. Having said that, I must add that the weight of expectation is still there in doing academic work where I have built up a reputation over the years; also, the thought is there that this may be the last time I do something and I want to give of my best.

Some of my best writing was done in Kerry in the far corner of Ireland where I felt I was among friends in an uncompetitive atmosphere and where I didn't have to prove anything. Back at the LSE (London School of Economics) which was where I did my longest spell of academic work, it was very different. There was the ever-present hazard of intruding on other people's territory and a very competitive situation. Our work was under constant evaluation by professional colleagues and we were also in competition with the top American universities. These days my "get away from it all" place is a cottage on Easdale Island.

In later life I have developed greater emotional intelligence and this has benefited my poetry.'

I reminded David that, in his 80th birthday lecture, he had quoted from the Spanish poet, Antonio Machado (1875–1939): 'Traveller there is no path. Paths are made by walking.'

'Yes, it seemed to express an idea both Kay and myself had that it was our responsibility to test out our own moral principles and, although you can learn from others, you don't learn them from sitting at the feet of some philosopher, you have to make your own path.

The motivation for forming the Die-a-logue group, which meets here in my flat was that some friends and I felt the need to reflect on our own deaths. We had found it difficult to talk about it with those closest to us. We wanted to talk about our priorities in later life and the things we hadn't done that we still wanted to do; also about practical things to do with funerals: should one leave one's body to a medical school, or make notes that would help someone who had to write your obituary — and what would you say? Younger people — and all of us in the earlier stages of our life — are reluctant to talk about those sort of issues. It's probably a necessary characteristic of the human race, part of our survival. Otherwise, what woman would willingly have had a baby?

I have been working on a book since 1950, a collection of the writings of my wife, Kay Carmichael. I'm concerned to get that done as quickly as I can. It's the main thing I haven't done which I still want to do before I die. I don't want to die with it unfinished.[1]

I abandoned membership of any church when I was about fourteen, but I take spiritual life seriously. In the Navy I was officially recorded as a 'Freethinker.' It's important to think about these things because, if you don't believe in God, where do your principles come from? In a world where confessions and absolution and all the rituals evolved by church no longer mean anything to most people how does one deal with questions of sin and failures of that kind. Kay wrote a whole book about it — *Sin and Forgiveness: New Responses in a Changing World* (Aldershot, 2003). She argued that a lot of things that used to be regarded as sins are no longer sins, but that there are new sins for which we have a collective responsibility, such as abuse of the environment, nuclear weapons, pollution, poverty and inequality — issues which are profoundly important to all of us both individually and collectively.

I try to find a balance between solitude and comradeship, between individual creation and the need to collaborate, to find an audience. There's always a need for collective action of some sort and for learning from other people. I belong to an expressive writing group that meets once a fortnight during term time. We produce work in isolation but then come together because we need a response to it.

The most positive aspect of ageing for me has been the freedom to try new things and not feel that I have anything to prove; and finding that I can still make new friends. The most negative things are the obvious physical frailties. I may have to give up driving and that will change my life significantly and not for the better because it will make a lot of things I do impossible.

I feel my most important achievement — and one which continues to give me pleasure and satisfaction in later life — has been to produce a family of four children and six grandchildren who are such good, kind people, doing useful things well and always happy when together. Which is probably more their mother's achievement and their own than mine. Also my small book of poems, *Requiem for*

Kay (PlaySpace Publications, 2011) has been hugely important to me. Poetry has an economy and a frankness about it that made it the appropriate medium for this. I hadn't written much poetry before then. I find I can't write prose and poetry at the same time. If I'm doing any serious prose writing, I tend to skip the poetry. But, normally, I try to produce a poem once a fortnight to bring to my writing group. It's usually about things that are going on in my life and things I am thinking about.

My role models were teachers and senior academics. I have been very fortunate in having worked with some remarkable people. They taught me by example about attitudes and outlook and priorities.

My advice to younger writers who hope to continue being productive in later life would be: Have a go; write what you really want to write; express your own feelings; learn from other people's responses to your work, but don't be deterred by negative criticism or the fear of it.

Note

1. This book, edited by David Donnison, has now been published: *It Takes a Lifetime to Become Yourself* by Kay Carmichael (Scotland Street Press, 2017).

A sample of writing done since passing 70

At 91 years of age, 70 seems a long time ago; almost in my youth! And your request for something written since then may be less revealing for someone like me who has been writing all his life than for someone taking off as he/she ages into new possibilities.

If you are looking for creative new projects for which advancing age provides new opportunities and incentives I would pick the playing of music on my concertina, a revived interest in drawing and painting, and — if it has to be in written form — the writing of poetry, which I had never seriously attempted in earlier years.

Since I think it is writing you want I will offer a couple of poems. I had begun these soon after my normal work began to fade out — somewhere around the age of 75 I guess. I found this attractive for various reasons. I no longer felt I had to do things really well in comparison with other people. So long as I did my best, did a bit better than before, learned something... I also enjoyed getting to know the group — originally set up by Larry — with whom I did what could best be called 'expressive writing' (not 'therapeutic' or 'creative', though it had elements of both).

But it was the death of my wife that really drove me to poetry. I was going through the most powerful experiences of grief that seemed to demand written expression of feelings in poetic forms. I think the poems I wrote at that time were better poetry than anything I have written since that storm passed over. Larry, as you probably know, published 22 of these in a little book called *Requiem*.

I offer two of the shorter ones: one of the first and the last in this series.

As Death Impends

As death impends self-centred I become,
battening down the hatches
as the roar of loss approaches.

Grief seeps deep through my bones;
the busy crowd irrelevant —
citizens of a distant half-heard world.

time disintegrates. This tea and toast,
so carefully carried, fills all eternity.
Next week? Next month? Who cares`?

Postscript

Thought you wrote some poems?

You were wrong.
Powered by pain,
half-scream, half-song,
they kept your head to wind,
drove you through the storm.

The poems wrote you.

A couple of months after the interview with David, he sent me a poem he had written for Burns Night. I include it here because it sums up so much about his wit and his attitudes and insights into his own ageing:

Self Portrait

O wad some power the giftie gie us
to give not a toss how others see us!
What others? And what self?
Ancient prof, left lonely on the shelf?
Father figure? Scholar revered?
Friendly neighbour? Neighbour feared?
Elderly fellow, tottering down the street?

Former athlete shaky on his feet —?
each a relic of his long lost youth.
Each containing a bit of truth.
If there's work worth doing, get out, stir about!
You haven't long before the lights go out.

David's next book will be called Living Our Dying *and he wrote this poem after a visit to his oncologist:*

Deadline of Death

I join the queue to see my oncologist,
waiting the usual forty-five minutes.
(But do not complain: he's giving each patient
the time they need.) The man ahead
is wearing his funeral suit: dark serge,
silk tie and shiny white shirt,
his worried wife escorting him.
(This doctor may give us sentence of death.)
When my turn comes he gives me warning
of rising test scores. No point in asking
"How long have I got?" So I put my question
in a different form. "I'm sending my publisher
"my latest book. Planning the next.

"Should it be brief? Done in one year?
Or will I have time for a longer work?"
"Two or three years" he replies with a smile.
"But do remember: at your age
anything can happen at any time."
So I'd better get started. No time for rhymes.

You may also wish to consult his book *Last of the Guardians* (Superscript, 2005).

David Donnison died peacefully at his home eighteen months after this interview.

LARRY BUTLER (Age 73)

I was born in Southern Illinois, pig farming country, then spent my childhood in Northern California. I wasn't a model child or teenager; failing every subject in high school partly because I was dyslexic (not diagnosed until well into adulthood) as well as having Attention Deficit Hyperactivity Disorder. At 18 years old, I still didn't know how to read, and most of my best friends had gone off to university. That's what suddenly motivated me to want to learn how. Having just finished high school, I started changing fast, which disturbed my parents who thought I was going mad so they sectioned me to three months in a mental hospital. I had to drop out of my first year of junior college (for high school flunkies who were illiterate as I was.)

I ended up going to Bakersfield College where I studied a General Humanities curriculum — economics, film studies, social psychology, sociology, political science. While at Bakersfield I was an activist in the Civil Rights Movement. Soon after I learned to read, I started working in a Saturday school helping Hispanics, Mexicans, Native and Afro Americans learn to read and write so that they could register to vote. My first interest in writing deepened when I was asked to be the editor of a Civil Liberties magazine, which included interviewing migrant workers; and I did a research project on racial prejudice. My first attempts at poetry were slogans for posters on protest marches; my interest grew by sharing a house with my political science professor and a DJ who loved reading poetry aloud to me at night.

After doing well at Bakersfield, I was accepted by University of California at Santa Cruz as a third year student. But, the campus wasn't finished, which left me in limbo. So I went to Paris to study social psychology under Otto Kleinberg. I had some money saved from selling encyclopaedias in Idaho and Montana (even before I had learned how to read!) and had invested in a small unknown firm called Polaroid and an airline whose shares had fallen because of an accident over New York City, I predicted they would rise dramatically in price. And they did. I sold the shares — against my parents advice — and had the money to go to Paris, and enough to live on for a couple of years. There I met an English art student who said, 'Let me take you to the Louvre.' (She eventually became my first wife.) I had never seen paintings before. I had grown up with no interest in art. I didn't think human beings could do that sort of thing. I wandered through the Louvre with my mouth hanging open, stood in front of a portrait of Chopin by Delacroix and wept. I wanted to learn how to do this, so I enrolled in the Beaux Arts and decided not to go back to California to finish my degree in social psychology. Instead, I hitch-hiked to Valencia to attend a masterclass in landscape and portraiture, and to write a novel about my grandfather who had recently died. This was my first big writing project — never published. One of my lifts was from a laundry owner from Dusseldorf, who sparked my first interest in movement and meditation. A few years ago I wrote this poem about our meeting:

First teacher

Sechzig Jahre alt. Erste
Reise nach Spanien, Fahrt
Durch Cezanne's Land.

In der Naehe von Lyon
Biete einem jungen Mann
An mitzufahren.

Er spricht Englisch und
Franzoesisch. Ich spreche
Deutsch und Russisch.

Er hat einen Franzoesisch /
Spanisch Reisefuehrer.
Ich einen Deutsch/Spanischen

Reisefuehrer. Zwischen
langen Pausen, versuchen
wir's in Spanisch. Ich

Nehme ihn den
ganzen Weg bis zur
Costa Brava mit.

Twenty years old, hitch
hiking from Paris
to Spain, June 67.

I get a lift from
a German man who
owns a laundry in

Dusseldorf. I speak
English and French. He
speaks German and Russian.

He has a Spanish/
German phrase book. I
have a Spanish/French

phrase book — between long
pauses we splutter
in Spanish. He takes

me all the way to
Costa Brava. We
sleep that night on a

Fuer die Nacht
halten wir am Strand.
Er schlaeft fuer eine Weile

Ich sitze die ganze
Nacht auf einer Duene.
Er erwacht um 3 weil

er muss. Zum Fruehstueck
am Morgen fragt er
mich in Spanisch:

?Algama vez duermes?
Und ich antworte — No
Solumente me

siento, dann erzaehle
Ich ihm von Yoga
und Meditation

und beim Ueben von
Pranayana Atmen
aufzupassen

Zureuck in Duesseldorf,
Schicke ich ihm drei
Bucher uber Mantra,

Hatha und Raja
Yoga. Habe seitdem
nichts von ihm gehoert.

beach. Well I sleep, he
sits on a sand dune.
I wake at 3 to piss.

He's still sits staring
at the sea. In the
morning he's still up-

right — alert — awake.
At breakfast I ask
in Spanish: *?Algana*

vez duermes? And he
said: *no solamente*
me siento. Then

he told me about
yoga and meditation
and to be careful

when practicing pran
ayama breathing.
He asked me for my

P.O box in Spain.
I forgot about him,
till three months later

I received recorded
delivery — three books
all in English on

raja, hatha and
mantra yoga. I've
practised ever since.

Now I'm his age.

Back in Paris an American artist friend, Myron Barnstone, saw
my paintings and recommended I apply to the Ruskin School of
Drawing in Oxford. He helped me put together a portfolio and

I was accepted. Around this time, the English woman I'd met in Paris agreed to marry me so that I wouldn't be extradited back to the USA to serve a five year prison sentence for committing treason. In Paris I was part of a small group of radicals based at the bookshop *Shakespeare & Company*, plotting to help American servicemen desert and find safe homes in Europe.

After a year at the Ruskin, the foreign student fees rocketed so I couldn't afford to continue, so I chose to study at the British Museum in London, where you could register at no cost. I studied Chinese calligraphy there as an independent student. Through the Ruskin and the British Museum, both with splendid collections of Oriental art, I became interested in Taoism which eventually led me to Buddhism. To earn a living I worked on adventure playgrounds in London as a community artist. Sometimes I would get kids referred to me who had been expelled from school because of their behaviour. I worked with them, playing games, getting them to help me with pottery. They loved smashing the cracked biscuit fired pieced into grit I could re-use. After several months their psychologist would say they were ready to return to school. Teachers started asking me to teach them what I was doing. Through these workshops, I developed an interest in education and took a degree in Movement Education through London University, which led me into a whole world of movement and dance and choreography. This, in turn, led me to Tai-Chi.

While at Sidney Webb, along with fellow students I started an organisation called Playspace. My first publication was a book of co-operative games with a training manual for teachers: *Games Games*. A lot of the games we invented ourselves through improvisation, others were from the Games Foundation in America. Through Playspace I began to be employed training staff in hospitals and prisons. I worked all over England running workshops in creative play, and co-founded a touring company called Matchbox Theatre, staging our own plays. It was during this period that I divorced my first wife partly because she didn't want children and I did. Eventually I re-married — to Mary Troup (music therapist and a performer with Matchbox), and within a year we had our first child Ossian. At this time I was working part-time as a drama therapist in prison and probation services, and teaching communication skills courses to NHS and social care staff. We were living at the Diorama Arts Co-operative — probably the poshest squat in London — where I was warden and manager. That's another story!

Partly because of the stress of living in a squat, we decided to move to Scotland where Mary was from originally. We worked and lived at a community arts centre in Glasgow called Steppingstones and our second son (Colum) was born at home. The only person I knew in Glasgow at the time was Kay Carmichael — we had met in London. Our friendship grew and she became my 'guide dog' to Glasgow introducing me to the political, social and art scenes in Scotland. This led to work in the Gorbals at an addiction centre, prison visiting in the Barlinnie Special Unit, and starting ProjectAbility through Manpower Services Commission at the Third Eye Centre (now the CCA). Around this time I started leading therapeutic writing groups with Glasgow Association for Mental Health, which eventually became Survivors Poetry Scotland (SPS),[1] and Lapidus Scotland (LS)[2] which promotes creative words for health and wellbeing. In the last 14 years I've been leading writing groups and tai-chi classes at the Maggie Cancer Care Centre in Glasgow[3].

In the late 1980s I ran a research project called 'Better Health for Men (BHFM): Men, Emotions and Relationships' for the Health Education Board for Scotland. We looked at what needed to be published about men's health — almost nothing existed at that time. I followed up BHFM with an Arts on Prescription feasibility study (AoP), funded by the Greater Glasgow Health Board (GGHB) to research and gather evidence on how the arts benefit people's health.

At Survivors' Poetry, we started Survivors' Press and I edited the first three issues of their magazine: Nomad, and small books written by survivors of the mental health system. More recently I unearthed the name Playspace and started a small press called Play-Space Publications which raises money for various charities (each author I publish chooses the charity they want to support) including Friends of the Earth, Freedom from Torture, Maggies Cancer Care Centres. *Autumn Voices* will raise money for *Age Scotland*.

More and more the arts are shoved to one side, often the first victims of funding cuts. The arts for wellbeing are crucial. I am also passionate about a new Lapidus Scotland project — *Words Work Well for All*: a partnership between the Scottish Story Telling Centre, the Poetry Library and NHS Education Scotland (NES). Our current website *Words Work Well Scotland* is a toolkit for facilitators of creative words for wellbeing.

My first paid commission as a writer was in the 70s when I was working with a puppeteer who was carving life-size wooden puppets of the characters in *Beowulf*. We produced a play which went on a short tour; then Sir Peter Hall came to a workshop on puppetry and masks at the Central School of Speech and Drama where we did a few scenes from *Beowulf*. Hall commissioned us to produce a new version of the play for the first show in the Cottlesloe Theatre — part of the National Theatre in London's South Bank. *Beowulf* then went on tour with forty performances all over the UK.

Three major influences on my writing have been: Buddhism and Taoism, dance and movement, with playfulness still at the centre of my mandala. I had been studying Buddhism and Buddhist scholars and poets from the late sixties onwards through Chinese and Japanese paintings and through poets like Gary Snyder and more recently Jane Hirshfield. Ratnadevi, my partner for the last twenty-two years, is a Buddhist who teaches yoga and mindfulness and we co-lead retreats with titles such as Mindfully Moving Through Pain & Loss, Earth Rituals, Everyday Mindfulness. She also loves to play and is trained in the Dalcroze method, also known as Dalcroze Eurhythmics, used to foster music appreciation, ear-training, and improvisation while improving musical abilities. Students listen to the rhythm of a music piece and express what they hear through movement. She also plays piano and cello. For several years, we co-led improvisation workshops.

There are various places where I like to write. Often I go to my allotment. I need simplicity around me. I need to withdraw from the bustle of everyday life. I need to sit and do nothing or go out for a walk in order to get into a creative mood, I usually need all day. I can't just switch it on. Midweek I might go to the hut at Carbeth owned by my friend Gerry Loose (he and his partner Mo use it more at the weekend). I spend the first hour or two just chewing my pencil or going for a walk, foraging mushrooms or brambles — then I'll do some writing for a couple of hours, then go for a swim in the loch or another walk, do some more writing. I need that sort of leisure in order to write.

I also teach Chi-Kung (Qigong) to cultivate energy. You can also do it in groups of people and that has a strong effect. I encourage my students to feel where their energy is blocked, then to create flow through movement. In relation to my poetry, I look for flow and release blockages. Sometimes I can't see them and that's when I need feedback from my friends.

The Buddhist poets, Manjusvara and Ananda, have had a big influence on me. They invited me to be the organizer on a retreat with them and others at the Dhanakosa retreat centre[4] by Loch Voil in the Trossachs. We worked together for eleven years. One of their mentors was William Stafford, an American poet laureate. It was through them I became influenced by Stafford. Manjusvara died from a massive stroke in my arms while we were leading a retreat. Realising I wanted to continue his work, I started developing the 'Poet's Way', a monthly event at the Glasgow Buddhist Centre looking at how poetry enhances spiritual practice. You don't have to be a Buddhist to participate, it's open to anyone. One of the many wise things Manjusvara wrote was: 'Have the courage to work with what is happening, rather than wishing it was not there.' He also said: 'Always do your writing in the wilderness,' by which he meant — explore unknown territory. I try to do that, too. And I look for pattern and meaning in life, which is why I'm attracted to studying Buddhism. It asks what life is all about. A lot of the Zen and Chan masters of the past were also poets and painters, doctors, politicians. One modern Buddhist teacher — Joanna Macy[5] — has had a big influence on my way of thinking and acting in the world. I first came across her work in late seventies through a peer network called InterHelp which supported political activists. She wrote a book called *Despair and Empowerment in the Nuclear Age* which eventually led to what is known as 'The Work That Reconnects.' I facilitate this workshop process and train others in how to do it. The basic question we address is: How do we move from an industrial growth economy that is trashing the planet to life sustaining culture? Joanna call this 'The Great Turning.'

Since the earlier 70s when I set up Playspace, dance and movement have continued to be an important element in my life. I'm currently involved with an Authentic Movement Group[6] which is a form of dance movement therapy and meditation; we meet once a month. I also do one-to-one peer counselling which often involves movement and strong emotion, and I dance most nights in our living room before I go to bed, sometimes with music, sometimes without; sometimes with Ratnadevi, sometimes alone. My movement is influenced by Tai-Chi and also by contact improvisation. My paid work these days is teaching Tai-Chi and Chi-kung, Physical fitness and mental fitness definitely go together. Every morning, I play Tai-Chi and Chi-Kung, do a few yoga stretches and meditate before breakfast. It's like brushing my teeth. Many of my poems have come out of movement. I often mull over ideas as I walk.

Last Summer I organised a writing walk around the Gartnavel Hospital complex. There were six of us. Each person had a turn leading the walk and then stopping where they felt like it. We then wrote for two minutes, something inspired by where we had stopped — all in silence. The walk ended in the walled garden where we read out what we'd written, stop by stop, to one of the gardeners, rather like a renga. This is typical of how I work with a range of groups. Playfulness is very important in my life. It's how I survived as a child — playing the fool, the classroom clown. Johan Huizinga's book *Homo Ludens* inspired me and still does. I play on the page. That's how I write — I play with words and sounds. I love the Japanese tradition of renga which is simply people in groups playing with words. I'm not a solo writer. I enjoy collaborating with others and writing together. It creates that tension I need for the creative energy to flow. It's seeing conflict as an opportunity for creativity. The craft of writing is important as well, but I don't want to lose the playfulness — which doesn't mean that you can't also be serious. Huizinga says 'to children, play is deeply serious.' Play is about flow and if you're in the game and in the flow, to be interrupted is extremely upsetting.

My poetry and my writing in general have changed as I've got older. My early poems were much more political. Then my writing shifted more into theatre writing influenced by fairy tales and folk tales with audience participation built into them. I have improved largely through contact with other writers such as Tom Leonard, Linda Chase, Linda France, Gerry Fellows, Sandy Hutchison, to name a few. Donny O'Rourke on the Scottish Poetry Library website, when asked how to improve your writing, he replies with three words: READ READ READ. I'm a founder member of SPL and check-out books regularly.

Inventing a dance is quite close to poetry — getting into the rhythm of it. With dance there's a mind-body integration. With painting or making sculpture or pottery it's like a mandala, there will be a focal point and there's a stillness about it as well; whereas, with writing, it's more of a flow, a movement through to a beginning, middle and end. The end may take several drafts — Mary Oliver's minimum is 8 drafts (*Poetry Handbook*). In my first draft I try to bypass my head, writing from belly to heart to hand to pencil to paper.

I do an exercise with my writing groups called 'Dialogue with your inner critic.' I ask: What is your inner critical voice saying to you? Then write down three projects, things you'd like to do with your life. What came up for me was to go on a long retreat next year. I need more spaciousness in my life and more time for solitude to do more inner work, which will also include writing. I have a collection of 300 notebooks that go as far back as the 1960s. Part of what I want to do on my retreat is to go through them and see if there is anything worth keeping. One of the fruits of ageing is that you've had a lot of creatively stimulating input over the years and in my notebooks there's much material. Going through them might throw up all sorts of treasures.

Another growth point for me is supporting the *Autumn Voices* project. I want my autumn voice to be heard. I endorse the notion that ageing is the last great adventure as Ken Jones describes it[7].

The most positive aspects of getting older, for me, have to do with grandchildren and legacy and also having a quieter and deepening relationship with the woman in my life and other people who I am close to. And witnessing my sons grow up and establishing themselves in the world. My older son — Ossian — set-up his own business as an arborist and called it 'Tranquillitree'; and my younger son — Colum — is a care worker for the Richmond Fellowship.

And now the joy of being a grandfather for the past five years, and two years ago Ratnadevi and I were asked to be 'Buddha parents'. So we now have the joy of two little ones in our lives.

Getting older has increased my curiosity about death. For the past six years, I've been part of a small group, a sort of co-operative inquiry about death & dying. David Donnison is our scribe and we plan to publish a book this year called *Living Our Dying*. An acknowledgement of death increases my appreciation of life: On my shrine in my bedroom, where I meditate, are photographs of more than 50 people I knew who are all dead. At least three or four times a week at the end of a meditation, I speak their names... then a flash of memory will come of what that person gave to me.

Role models as regards ageing — Cid Corman,[8] author of *Livingdying*; David Donnison, who is almost 92 now; John Heron aged 89, Robin Lloyd-Jones who is 83. I like having people in my life who are older and staying creative. I love gazing at Rembrandt's late self-portraits — he had such a curiosity about ageing. I seek that out in people.

My advice to people aspiring to maintain their creativity into later life is keep going, don't stop. Stay open to what you really want to do. Keep asking the question, 'What am I doing with my life? Is this what I really want to do? Am I doing what is true to my heart and to those around me?' Those questions, for an artist of any kind, are the vital ones. Never stop asking them.

Notes

1. Survivors' Poetry Scotland is an arts group led by survivors of mental distress and the mental health system to help combat their effects in creative and empowering ways. By using poetry workshops, readings, publishing, and various other arts activities, Survivors' Poetry provides survivors with a means to explore wellbeing, artistic perception, and contribution to society. http://www.survivorspoetry.org

2. Lapidus Scotland holds and facilitates a wide variety creative words for wellbeing practitioner events throughout Scotland. It

is aimed at users of bibliotherapy services, and anyone interested in writing/reading/storytelling for wellbeing, whether healthcare or library professionals or simply members of the public: http://wordsworkwellscotland.co.uk/ http://www.lapidus.org.uk/index.php/whats-on/in-your-region/lapidus-scotland/

3. The Maggie's Cancer Care Centres are a network of drop-in centres across the United Kingdom and Hong Kong, which aim to help anyone who has been affected by cancer. They are not intended as a replacement for conventional cancer therapy, but as a caring environment that can provide support. The original Maggie centre was founded by and named after the late Maggie Keswick Jencks, who died of cancer in 1995. https://www.maggiescentres.org/

4. Dhanakosa Buddhist Retreat Centre offers a wide range of retreats including yoga, hillwalking, Tai-Chi, arts and alternative health, all complementing a programme of introductory meditation teaching. Additionally, there are meditation and Buddhist study retreats designed for those with a more regular practice. https://www.dhanakosa.com/

5. Joanna Macy is a political activists and a Buddhist scholar. She offers the Work that Reconnects, also called the Great Turning: https://workthatreconnects.org/history-of-the-work/#

6. Authentic Movement assists participants in developing kinesthetic awareness, gaining access and giving creative expression to the inner life through an approach in which 'movement is the personality made visible. Originally called Movement-in-Depth by its founder, Mary Starks Whitehouse, the method grew from her roots in Jungian studies, and pioneering work in dance/movement therapy. Building on Jung's method of active imagination, she saw symbolic meaning in physical action. http://www.embodiedtherapy.org.uk/authenticmovement.htm

7. Ken Jones (1930–2015) was founder of the Engaged Buddhist Network, he wrote a pamphlet called *Ageing, the last great Adventure:* http://www.kenjoneszen.com/buddhism-and-social-engagement/ageing_the_great_adventure.

8. Cid Corman (1924–2004) was an American poet, translator and editor, most notably of *Origin*, who was a key figure in the his-

tory of American poetry in the second half of the 20th century. A critic described *Livingdying* as 'Stunningly lean and spare modern poetry that sometimes appears as a form of Western haiku.'

A sample of writing done since passing 70

I recorded my dying mother's last words and transposed them into a series of short sketches.

Here a few of them:

we planted a tree in the children's park for Nadine's mother

when she died in that accident   I don't have a favourite tree

                I like all trees

you can't plan on anything   you plan something

then something else happens   I take care of what I can take
                    care of

     what I can't take care of

          I just leave

John's parents insisted on staying with us and I didn't have guts enough to tell them to find their own place   I regret that   we were buying all the groceries   and it was kinda tough trying to stretch it   so when we were moving from San Leandro to San Jose   I bought the smallest damn house I could find   it was a little log cabin   it had porch all enclosed in the front with doors dividing it   that was perfect for Pat & Larry   they each had an end   I bought it cause I didn't want them living with us   there wasn't any room for his parents   John didn't have guts enough to tell them   we were feeding them and taking care of them in

San Leandro   John could not say "no"   he was the youngest
so he felt obligated   I don't think he should have   cause his
brothers and sister wouldn't have given it to them.

Chris Ebe was John's best friend
he lived near us in 5th Street
and when we moved to Cottle Avenue
he bought a one-bedroom batchelor's house next door
he often came to dinner
I think the man was so lonely
he just wanted to be with family

I always had somebody apart from the family
at the dinner table

                there's something in the air that will happen

                    that I wouldn't even dream of

                    something will happen

                someone's gonna have a disaster

                there's so many weird people in the world

                and so many things

                 no one's even thinking

You may also wish to consult www.scottishbooktrust.com/profile-
author/2690

ALISON PRINCE (Age 86)

There is no better place to find out about Alison's background than her own website:

'I'd always thought I was going to be an artist, due largely to the fact that the Art Room in my very formal girls' grammar school was the only place where any self-expression was permitted. So, ignoring all entreaties to try for Oxford, I won a scholarship to the Slade School, which is the Fine Art department of London University. They taught me to draw by pointing a stern finger at work in progress and asking, "What is the purpose of that line?" It was a tough approach, but it taught me to see as well as to draw, and that has been immensely useful in writing. I still "see" things happening first, and write about them afterwards.'

For a couple of years Alison worked at fairly low-paid jobs then she did a post-graduate teaching course at Goldsmiths College:

'That went rather well, and I got a job as Head of Art at the newly-formed Elliott Comprehensive School in Putney — and loved it... Rather recklessly, I married the PE master at the Elliott and had three children in five years, which stopped the teaching career. However, it started a lot of journalism, as I turned my hand to writing art reviews and features, and managed to lever one or two stories into anthologies. We were constantly broke, largely because my husband was having a merry affair with the whisky bottle and various expensive ladies. I needed a miracle.

Then I met Joan Hickson, with two pairs of very young twins, in a park. Joan was an ex-theatre designer whose husband had fled at the sight of the second pair of twins, and we instantly agreed that we needed to do something to make some money. I wrote a story about a small boy who lived in a transport café, and through a weird series of interested people, bankruptcies and luck, it fetched up as a *Watch With Mother* series called *JOE*. It's just been redis-covered after 40 years, and people are excited about it, since it is now a relic of the classic age of children's TV. *JOE* plunged me into seven years of writing for children's comics, and an appearance on *Jackanory* led to the publication of my first book. I've been writing them ever since...

Trumpton came about casually. Monica Sims was Head of Children's Broadcasting by this time, and she asked if I'd like to write the scripts for a puppet programme about a fire station. I went to see the puppets, which were like bendy toys, and was shown the opening sequence, where the wee men slide down the greasy pole into the fire engine. They all looked rather alike, so the first thing was to give them names. There could be a pair of twins, to deal with two at one blow, and the rest would have to get whatever characters I could dream up. So there they were — Pugh, Pugh, Barney McGrew, Cuthbert, Dibble and Grubb. Freddie Phillips, who wrote and played the music, put them into that order, but I invented the names...I never thought *Trumpton* would become a classic. I was paid £15 per story, no repeat fees. It seemed OK at the time.

Meanwhile I'd written and narrated a week's *Jackanory* stories about being at school during the war. Adults were a bit shocked — it was before any kinds of reality hit the children's market — but kids loved it. So did Marilyn Malin, editor of Methuen Children's Books. She phoned to suggest a book arising from the TV series, and that was the first of many.

Writing is my reason for living. I wake up in the morning thinking about what I'm going to tackle in the current book, and go to sleep dreaming about it. Writing is like playing an endless, fascinating game, and I can't imagine what I'd do without it.'

Alison's cottage, just past Whiting Bay on the island of Arran, is exactly how I have always imagined a country cottage should be. The small garden is in touch with the wild. Steps lead down to a burn before it flows under a bridge and enters the sea. When I arrived on the bus from the ferry terminal, Alison, who has suffered from ill health in recent years, was on the point of being taken shopping by her support worker. So, accompanied by her three cats, I had half an hour or so to browse through her packed bookshelves. Alison's interest in travel and in art was evident. Several shelves were filled with her own books, including translations into Russian, German, French, Swedish, Danish and Spanish; and there were shelves full of her research for her biographies of Hans Christian Andersen and Kenneth Grahame. On the living-room walls were some of her own paintings. They had a dream-like quality, reminiscent of Chagall [1].

With several breaks while a care-worker came to see if she needed anything (Alison has three visits a day), and friends dropped by, Alison and I talked:

'There is no lack of ideas coming to me, but my imagination is becoming more scrupulously looked at because you have less time left and you have to be hard-headed about how you use that time and how important the various ideas are.

The different kinds of writing I have done — screen, fiction, non-fiction, poetry — are very different things. The basic process might be the same. Although the sounds made by a double base and a French horn are very different, you still need to know the principles of music to play them. The difference between writing for children and for adults is mainly technical. You have to strive for a greater clarity of meaning and avoid long, complicated sentences. You have to be able to hear the words that come off the page into the reader's ear. Writing, after all, is only a way of notating a spoken system.

The kind of readers' letters about my books I value most are from adults who have read one of my books as a child and write to say that they have never forgotten it. I like that because it has become part of their emotional equipment and maybe helped them in some way.

Arran is very much part of my background because I came here as a child. I had wonderful holidays here. It was everybody's dream childhood. I always planned to come back. When I did, it still smelled the same as I remembered it. I have now been here thirty-six years. I try not to be too specific about the setting of my books, but a lot of the settings of my children's books are, in fact, on Arran.

I sensed that my children don't want me talking about them in interviews. I have tried to respect their privacy, so I won't talk about them today. One of my poems, 'Miracle,' is about a mother having to give away a baby. I had a child when I was just out of college. My parents were very supportive, but there was really no other way ahead than for him to be adopted. I never forgot him. I was sitting here one night when the phone rang and a very nervous voice said, "Hello, I think I am your son." I knew at once that it was true. There was something very familiar about the voice. We met at the Gallery of Modern Art in Glasgow. He ran up the steps and we embraced. We have kept in touch ever since.

The aspect of ageing I fear most is becoming a nuisance to other people. There are health issues, too, but I can accept those as part of life. Last year I had a heart valve transplant, which made me breathless and playing the clarinet difficult. In the mid 1950s, I travelled around Europe for three months on seven pounds. And I then went to India. But I don't travel much these days.

You don't have the power to choose what things in your life influence your writing. They either lodge in your mind, or they don't. I think my creativity has changed over the years. The physical energy is less. I used to be able to keep going almost without a stop. I am writing far more poetry than I used to, partly because I work in shorter, but more intensive bursts. Also, I no longer want to do that huge output thing. A lot of my writing is by hand in notebooks, which I carry around with me.

Quite obviously I don't have the memory that I used to and I have just lost my driving licence which means a huge loss of freedom. There are moments, when the batteries are low, that I think, O sod it!'

Alison read a poem to me she was working on at the moment:

> 'They now write notes about me to each other
> And leave them on the table in full view
> It's kindly meant, but makes me feel like an item on display
> That must be checked at intervals
> In case a part should be absent or defective.
> This appears to happen gradually
> Though they're quick to say, She's not all there,
> The odd thing is, they never look for what's been lost
> You can't have everything, they say,
> But don't know what it is you haven't got.'

I don't read as much as I used to. Partly because so many books fall into recognisable and predictable categories — but not the classics, like Trollope, for example. They transcend categories. I love reading other languages. I can read in French, German, Spanish, Russian.

One of the positives that ageing has brought is grandchildren. And all that competitiveness with one's peers has dropped away, so that I'm not striving to prove myself anymore.

I am attracted to Hinduism and Buddhism. I find meditation extraordinarily difficult. I find it very hard to prevent the mind trickling off on its own little side-tracks. I don't think I am capable of deep meditation for more than a minute or two. I have a huge respect for the self-selected few who can do this, but it's always going to be just a few — society couldn't function on a practical level if everyone was like that.

Hans Christian Andersen is almost canonised in Denmark. My biography of him, showing that he was gay, was not well received over there. Hans Andersen and Kenneth Grahame were very different men. Kenneth Grahame's work is deeply touching. He speaks to me as one child to another. It was a sense of shared childhood experience which started me on the writing of his biography. His *The Wind in the Willows* was originally written as a series of letters to his son when Kenneth, the father, was away from home and his son was missing his usual bedtime story. Of all writers, Grahame is the greatest defender of the eternally young awareness that lives in those of us who acknowledge it. His early Golden Age stories, together with the first part of Hugh Walpole's *Jeremy*, are the most richly-flavoured evocations of childhood I have read. The effect of these powerful early experiences is long-lasting. I can stand again in the garden of our house in South London, one evening before the inevitable air-raid, and hear my father playing Chopin in the living-room. The sky was so clear. It still is, when I remember it, and the smell of dewed grass is as sharp. Such moments, though not understood, colour what comes afterwards, just as milk tastes bitter when you have been eating a grapefruit.

I have a brother, five years younger than me. He was a more orthodox child than I ever was. He's an Oxford graduate. He is still alive

— technically. He believes he is a helper at his care home. He has always wanted to be helpful. At one time the Medical Authorities asked if I would have my brother to stay with me for a fortnight so that I could observe him closely and write a detailed report for them. This started me on writing his biography. I am still, from time to time, working on it. I am trying to do an insider view of Alzheimer's disease. It is such a debilitating disease. Both for the patient and the carers there are so many pitfalls and humiliations. There are lots of books looking at it from the outside, but not from the viewpoint of someone who has it. I want to get to the centre of someone with this problem. There is a lot that hasn't been said.

My collection of poetry, *Waking at Five Happens Again* (Mariscat Press / Happen*Stance* Press, 2016), has given me a lot of satisfaction. It caused me to work with an excellent editor and to revise some of the poems. It got good reviews. I would like to do another collection, using the poems I wrote while in hospital. You see a lot of drama unfolding in hospitals. People reveal so much of themselves when they are in pain, particularly at night. Conversations in hospital at night are so interesting.

The first baby I had died at three days old. A nurse came in — she was Malaysian — and we talked for about two hours. There was a contact with another human being that was wonderful and which I never quite let go of afterwards. There was one night when a patient had died and the doctor had to come and fill in all the forms. I was only a patient, but I was awake, so I got up and made him a cup of tea and we talked, with no barriers between us.

I moved on from working with and writing for children when my own children grew up. The period between that happening and having grandchildren was when I started writing poetry and when I went back to painting. You can only react to circumstances and use them as usefully as you can.

I quite often look at the news bulletins from Médecins Sans Frontières [2]. If I had my time again I think I would train in medicine and go out and do the sort of things they are doing. My mother was a nurse. By coincidence, I ended up having to nurse her. I am not worried by injury or the sight of sudden death. It just seems part of the scope of things. If I could start again I would rather be a doctor than a painter. We did do a course on anatomy as part of my art training at the Slade and I found that very interesting. Surviving as a freelance painter is tough, very, very tough. You are at the mercy of reviewers and you have to spend so much time taking your work to galleries and trying to arrange for exhibitions.

I think the remaining years of my life will be much the same as now. I love it here, close to nature. My physical energy varies. I tend to write at night because I am quite busy during the day. But I always have my notebook with me. I have done about one hundred pages on my autobiography, but not starting at the beginning, just the memories as they come back to me. And then there is the book about my brother I want to finish. Writing for children is in the past. I have other things to do now. My grandchildren are too young at the moment. When they are old enough to read, I might find a renewed interest in children's writing.

Serious writers have usually been writing since they were young and nothing is going to stop them when they are old. So I'm not sure that any advice from me is needed. Keep on using what you've got, whatever it is, because it's all you've got. Grumbling is a waste of time.'

Notes

1. Marc Zakharovich Chagall (1887–1985) was a Russian-French artist of Belarusian Jewish origin. An early modernist, he was associated with several major artistic styles and created works in virtually every artistic format, including painting, book illustrations, stained glass, stage sets, ceramic, tapestries and fine art prints.

2. Médecins Sans Frontières, also known as Doctors Without Borders, is an international humanitarian non-governmental organization best known for its projects in war-torn regions and developing countries affected by endemic diseases.

A sample of writing done since passing 70

These poems are taken from Waking At Five Happens Again *(Mariscat Press/Happen*Stance *Press, 2016). 'Common stuff enchants me,' Alison once said, and it still does despite the shadow of illness cast over her recent years.*

Newborn

The windscreen wiper on the left-hand side
has picked up a dead leaf.
The breadknife
is newly well-known to the hand.
Waking at five happens again
and seems for the first time. The days
are numbered now, so their component parts,
their nanoseconds, come as miracles,
shining.

Reckoning

There is no column in which to enter
sudden rainbows, and the purred credit
of a cat that used to run away.
No auditor will ever scrutinise
the totals, no unhappy creditor
is going to get paid for moments seen
as marked in red ballpoint on debit page.
It doesn't work that way. This reckoning
weighs the years of non-accountancy
and absence of all tangible profit
against a small blue marble, trowel-turned
from the cold earth of spring and finds
a perfect balance.

You may also wish to consult www.alisonprince.com/

http://literature.britishcouncil.org/writer/alison-prince

4. SECOND WIND

Douglas Dunn
Diana Hendry
Vicki Feaver

Douglas Dunn, Diana Hendry and Vicki Feaver were the focus of Second Wind *(Saltire Series No. 9, 2015), a joint publication by the Saltire Society and the Scottish Poetry Library for which they were commissioned to write about their own ageing process. As the Introduction to this excellent booklet says: 'Here are poems that spark fresh thinking and challenge the orthodoxies surrounding ageing.' These three also had a 15-minute slot each on the BBC Radio 3 broadcast,* Late Style *(May 2017), talking about writing in later life.*

Photograph by Gerry Cambridge

DOUGLAS DUNN (Age 74)

Douglas Dunn's work, which includes fourteen collections of poetry and two of short stories; and a translation of Racine's *Andromache*, has been the object of much academic attention. He has been extensively translated (there are editions in French, German, Spanish, Czech, Polish, Italian, Norwegian, Slovak, Armenian and Japanese, at least). He has edited anthologies of poetry from Hull, Scotland and Ireland, and has regularly reviewed books for a range of publications.

Douglas grew up in Renfrewshire in a part-rural, part-urban community. At school, he excelled in English, but, uninterested in maths and science, left without the breadth of qualifications needed for university entrance. After working for Renfrew County Library, he attended the Scottish School of Librarianship in Glasgow, and in 1964 secured a librarian's post in Akron, Ohio, where he lived for 14 months with his new wife, Lesley Balfour Wallace. The stay ended when Douglas received a demand from the local Selective Service Board to attend a medical examination prior to possible enlistment in the U.S. Armed Forces — and a prompt return to Scotland.

He applied to study English at Hull University (where the entrance criteria were more flexible than at Scottish universities), and moved there with Lesley in 1966. He graduated with a 1st-class degree in 1969, by which time he was working in the university library under Philip Larkin, another decisive influence on his career, and with whom he shared a love of jazz. In the same year his first collection, *Terry Street*, was published by Faber (on Larkin's recommendation). Long working hours, and Larkin's refusal to allow him time off for reading engagements, encouraged him to become a full-time writer in 1971, subsisting on reviews, readings and part-time teaching. The couple stayed in Hull, with Lesley becoming Senior Keeper at the Ferens Art Gallery. Her death from cancer in 1981, at the age of 37, overturned this settled life. After a brief spell as writer-in-residence in Dundee, Douglas returned to Hull to complete what has become his best-known book, *Elegies*, a series of poems about his wife which won the Whitbread Book of the Year Award for 1985.

Douglas then settled in Fife with his second wife, Lesley Bathgate, who gave birth to their two children. His son is now a painter and his daughter, mother of his two grandchildren, a puppeteer. In 1991 Douglas was appointed Professor of English Literature at St Andrews University. He was a founding Director of the St Andrews Scottish Studies Institute in 1993. That same year he founded the School's MLitt in Creative Writing. He and Lesley separated in 1997. He was awarded an OBE in 2003 and the Queen's Gold Medal for Poetry in 2013. He retired from university life in 2008 [1].

Douglas was kind enough to shorten my journey from Helensburgh by suggesting we meet in a café in Edinburgh. In case I didn't recognise him, Douglas had modestly emailed me a description of himself.

He began by saying that a feature of retirement and of the ageing process was that he had more time to write, but less energy for it. This, however, was offset by two young grandchildren who had brought back a stimulating element of play into his life. On the other hand, he missed the stimulus of being around his young university students.

I asked Douglas if taking up a post at St Andrews University had been creatively liberating, in the sense that it gave him the security of a salary, thus reducing the pressure to write what would sell.

'I thought it would bring freedom,' he told me, 'but it didn't work out that way. University life had its own set of stresses.'

What about the feeling of being overtaken by younger poets that he had commented on before?

'It's just the way it is. Older poets simply don't have the energy and the stamina to undertake tours abroad, or tiring events that involve multiple appearances on the platform. In my case, ageism is self-imposed. Styles and fashions change, too.'

Douglas recalls that, as a young poet himself, he had spoken disrespectfully of older poets.

In his poem, 'A Teacher's Notes,' [2] Douglas wrote, 'But there's a price to pay.' Working with the imagination so much, he explained, is hugely stressful. Recent research has shown that it can cause neurological damage which leads to mental illness. Another aspect of the price to pay, he says, is that many poets, particularly from the older generations, adopted a lifestyle that had self-destructive elements to it in a kind of hangover from romanticism and Bohemianism.

'Undoubtedly there is a negative side to ageing,' he says. He doesn't fear dementia as he once did, because it is much more widely and openly discussed now.

In researching for his section of *Second Wind* he read quite a lot about age-related conditions and this has made it easier to contemplate them. He found Oliver Sacks and Kay Redfield Jamison especially helpful. What he fears most about ageing, he says, is being dependent on other people. Death itself, he does not fear and he does not expect to find that there is an after-life. His mother wanted him to be a Minister of the Kirk. However, despite growing up in a family steeped in the kirk, he is now a non-believer.

Douglas holds that openness to sensory experiences is important to a poet and that all five senses should be invoked. These, he says, have been declining as he ages, particularly the sense of smell and of taste. Poems don't come as readily to him as they once did.

'You can't write a poem unless you've got a poem to write. You have to be visited by something,' Douglas says, quoting Philip Larkin. In a broadcast for the BBC Radio 3 programme, *Late Style* (May 5th 2017), Douglas expanded on this: 'It could easily be the case that the older poets get, the fewer the poems that visit them. Or, in T.S.Eliot's words, "the desperate exercise of failing powers."'

Douglas found it difficult to adjust to retirement — a difficulty he expressed in his poem 'Leaving the Office' with lines such as:

> Permit no tears, but still, allow a sigh
> Closing a door on what was once my life,
> My days, my work. Farewell, and so goodbye
> While haar is forming over North-East Fife. [3]

He suffered bouts of depression. However, as one clinical psychologist told him: 'You are not clinically depressed, but you *are* bored.'

What, for Douglas, have been some of the negatives of ageing?

'It's not only retirement, it's all the physical things, all the discomforts that were not there before. I am now beginning to write about these things. And then there are the deaths of friends, relatives, colleagues. These days I make sure my funeral suit is kept clean and my black shoes polished.'

Douglas says his access to memory is diminishing. He finds himself fumbling for the right words — something he writes about in 'Remembering Friends Who Feared Old Age and Dementia More than Death'[4]:

> Even when just the other day
> From Then to Now feels decades away.
> The name at the back of the mind...
>
> What can I say?
> That memory's fickle, that fretting
> Over a lost name or forgotten month
> Makes you feel guilty, mindless, and blind,
> That it's perfectly natural to fear the labyrinth
> Where 'the ageing process' might one day take you
> Into the land of forgetting?
> You said it, friends. Too true.

Currently, Douglas is finalizing a new collection of poems: *The Noise of a Fly* (since published by Faber & Faber).

'When I was younger, I had more ambition. Not that I was ever looking for fame, and even less so now. Would I write a poem if I knew it would never be published and would remain unread? Yes, I would.'

Douglas tells me he will certainly continue writing for as long as he can, 'Although I know I'll become less and less productive and probably start repeating myself.' His role models, the writers who give him hope are Robert Browning and Thomas Hardy, both of whom managed to make a virtue of longevity.

I quote to Douglas an extract from an interview he did with Gerry Cambridge,[5] for *The Dark Horse* in Autumn 1999 when he was fifty-six:

'GC: So do you hope for what John Berryman called 'that mysterious late excellence / which is the crown of our trials / and our last bride'?

DD: Berryman didn't really give himself much chance. I've got this funny feeling, you know, that I've done my poetry, written my poetry; been there, done that, don't want to go back. I think we'll see what happens to my two books to be published next year.'

Eighteen years on from making that statement, how does Douglas feel about his answer? 'Needlessly pessimistic!' he replies.

Old age has its positives too, he says. Douglas elaborates on this in his *Late Style* broadcast:

'Growing older might not add to one's sagacity, but I've found that it heightens my awareness of the transcendental, or sacramental, dimensions of poetry. Far more than was the case when younger, I find myself living in a constant state of preparation to witness what Philip Larkin called "celestial recurrences" —

> The day the flowers come,
> And when the birds go.

Do we perceive these seasonal sensations differently when older?

I think I do. First snowdrops, crocus, daffodils, the greening of one's garden and the countryside, the first swallows... These feel more significant, more demanding of attention. They alert me more than ever to the rhythms of life and time, to the pleasures of being alive. It used to be the case that the cries of geese and duck flying overhead in early winter sounded like an urgent, desperate, melancholy, and dissonant music, like a piece by an unmelodic, contemporary composer. Now it strikes my ear as a heartening, and exciting, note of continuity.'

Douglas tells me that he thinks he has a deeper self-knowledge now, but that is not something that suddenly came with age. It has been slowly developing all his life.

'You begin to see how you fit into a much wider picture, to see yourself in proper scale.'

'What about the internal censors,' I ask. 'Are they easing up a bit?'

'There never have been internal censors,' Douglas replies, 'Just a struggle between reticence and candour, with which every poet has to contend.'

There have been two or three poems he has written since passing seventy which have given him particular satisfaction. One of these is 'Wondrous Strange' which is shown in full at the end of this chapter.

Douglas' advice to poets who wish to continue being productive in their later years is to give up smoking and drinking. I am not sure whether or not this is an example of Douglas' well-known dry sense of humour.

Has the nature of his creativity changed as he gets older? 'I'm not sure that it has, but there's less of it. For example, I seem to have dried up as a writer of short stories, but I'm trying to get that back.'

He is fearful of the world in general, he says: wars, suicide bombers, the prevalence of prejudice and hatred and the amount of suffering it causes. In his poem 'Recipes and Refugees' from *Second Wind* he writes:

> How can a man be good and kind, and true
> While knowing he's got more than many have
> In hot, dry countries? What can I do?
> Or you? Or you? It isn't very brave
> To keep on shopping, though to stay alive
> Means buying drink and dinner. I'll survive
>
> Even worse torments of guilt and conscience.
> Everyone else does. So, then, why can't I?

These lines illustrate something Gerry Cambridge said in his tribute to Douglas on the latter's 70th birthday: that he was full of empathy for the dispossessed, full of social responsibility and of a *caritas* which avoids sentimentality and does not preclude at times a straight-speaking anger. (Scottish Poetry Library Blog, October 2012).

As we emerge from the café, Douglas pauses and lights up a cigarette. With the death of Seamus Heaney, Douglas is now the oldest poet on the Faber list. Long may he remain so.

Notes

1. This opening section draws heavily upon the biography of Douglas Dunn provided by the Scottish Poetry Library website.

2. The original title of this poem was 'Older Poet to Younger Poet' and it first appeared under this title in *Second Wind* (Saltire Series No. 9, 2015).

3. One of Douglas' poems in *Second Wind*.

4. As for note 3.

5. Gerry Cambridge is a poet, essayist, editor with substantial interest in print design and typography as well as a background in natural history photography. His publications include five full poetry collections and several poetry collaborations with schools. The long poem pamphlet *'blue sky, green grass: A Day at Lawthorn Primary'* won the Callum Macdonald Memorial Award in 2004 and was revised and reprinted in a limited edition for Canadian events with the cellist Christine Hanson and guitarist Jamie Philp in autumn, 2017. Since 1994 Cambridge has edited and published *The Dark Horse*, a transatlantic poetry magazine with an international reputation.

Like many poets, I've found myself from time to time acknowledg-
ing a consciousness of sensations that never quite break through into
the land of clarity. Such events — if that's what they are —can begin
with something heard, or felt, or smelled, or tasted, or something I
think I've seen, but always with a degree of uncertainty.

There are more things in heaven and earth, Horatio,
Than are dreamt of in your philosophy,

says Hamlet to his friend, in the presence of the unseen ghost of
Hamlet's father, and after Horatio, having just heard the ghost ex-
claim, has said 'O day and night, but this is wondrous strange!'

'Wondrous Strange'

Now it can almost be heard. But not quite
Almost. Still on the far side of nearly,
It is the melody of a floating feather.

A spiderweb tickles my cheek in the dark garden;
A briar plucks at my sweater.
Wind on a windless night wafts through my hair.

Or the aroma of sandalwood soap
When that's impossible. Or of fenugreek,
Or the scent of one who is no longer here.

Or something I half-believe I've seen,
A glisk of movement on the hill's horizon,
An ominous shadow cast by nothing at all.

Then there's the taste of zero-flavour,
Not even the taste of my own mouth,
Neither sweet and delicious, or bitter or sour.

Or the taste of strawberries Romanov
(That restaurant in Bonn!) or stolen plums
Remembered on a January night when snow's falling.

Is this just dream-stuff, or is there enough
Sense in the senses for the mystical
To prove itself real as any truth?

Yes, it's "wondrous strange"; but I must ask
My Muse to save me from contriving
A forger's touch of moonlight on the page.

You may also wish to consult Margitta Rouse, The Self's Grammar:
Performing Poetic Identity in Douglas Dunn's Poetry *1969—2011.*
(Heidelberg. Universitatsverlag Winter, 2013).

David Kennedy, Douglas Dunn. *Writers and Their Work,* (North-cote House/British Council, 2008).

Photograph by Gerry Cambridge

DIANA HENDRY (Age 75)

Diana lives in Edinburgh with her partner, Hamish Whyte[1]. On her website this is what she has to say about herself:

'Diana Hendry was born in the Wirral and grew up by the sea. She did very badly at school — falling in love at 13 being rather a distraction — and spent a long time catching up, which included becoming a mature student at Bristol University and later studying for an M.Litt.

Primarily a poet, Diana also writes short stories and is the author of many children's books. She's worked as a journalist, English teacher and a tutor at the University of Bristol, University of the West of England and the Open University. She has tutored many creative writing courses for the Arvon Foundation and for a year was writer-in-residence at Dumfries & Galloway Royal Infirmary.

She is a honorary member of Shore Poets, Edinburgh, and from 2008–2010 she was a Royal Literary Fund Fellow based at Edinburgh University. From 2015 to 2017 she was co-editor of *New Writing Scotland*. She writes the occasional book review for *The Spectator*.'

'A commission's a wonderful thing,' Diana says in her BBC Radio 3 broadcast, *Late Style*, speaking of her Baring Foundation commission to contribute to *Second Wind*. In this broadcast she goes on to say:

'It's akin to being desired. Somebody wants you, likes what you've done, wants you to do more. And joy of joys, is willing to offer both a generous fee and publication. It's also a terrifying thing. What if you can't do it? What if the muse pricks up its ears at the very word *commission* and makes for the door? And then the subject, age and ageing, was more than a little daunting. It meant looking back on one's whole life. It meant thinking about death...

...The first poem I wrote that made it into the collection was sparked by Philip Larkin's 'The Old Fools', a poem that presents a grim view of the old 'crouching below/ Extinction's alp.' But the lines that lit the match for my poem were 'Perhaps being old is hav-

ing lighted rooms/Inside your head, and people in them, acting.'
I recognised those lit rooms! Often, on the edge of sleep, or day-
dreaming in the bath, I hold an imaginary conversation with someone I know or have known. It struck me as one of the pleasures of
age to be able to live in both the past and the present.'

Callers

Well yes, maybe I *am* an old fool
For there is a lighted room inside my head
Where folk I know — alive and dead — come to call.
It's like the foyer of a grand hotel,
And though I'm out of sight I watch them all.

Often it's my children, as they were when small.
Yesterday a friend I haven't seen for years,
My brother-in-law who died last spring,
And a girl I used to know quite well at school.

None of them stays long or knows they're here.
I watch them look about then hurry on.
It pleases me to think I might appear
As guest or ghost in lighted rooms elsewhere.

On a beautiful day in May I (Robin) took a taxi from Waverley
Station in Edinburgh to 'the Colonies,'[2] with their terraced housing and rows of small, colourful gardens. Over tea and biscuits Diana told me about her family. Her son, Hamish, lives in London.
He's a leading teacher of Ashtanga yoga. He's married to Anna,
and they have a little girl, called Talia. Diana's daughter, Kate, is
also a writer and lives in Edinburgh. Kate's Happen*Stance* Press
pamphlet, *The Lost Original*, was short-listed for the Callum Macdonald Award this year[3]. 'She is my reader and my critic,' Diana
said. Kate has two children, Ruairidh, age thirteen and Freya, age
nine — they spend most Friday afternoons with Diana and Hamish. 'They certainly keep my imagination alive and they've been the
source of several story ideas. My grandson is an enormous reader,
which is very pleasing.'

RLJ: In your introductory section in *Second Wind* you quote Muriel Spark: 'How nerve-wracking it is to be getting old, how much

better to be old!' Please expand on what these lines mean to you personally.

DH: Some women tend to spend quite a lot of time and effort trying to look young. I've done it myself. So actually it's a bit of a relief to relax into being old!

RLJ: You call this introductory section 'Off/On Joy'. Which brings out the best poems in you — off or on?

DH: I think it's when the two come together and that, despite there being a downside, I am able to reach some kind of joy. If I may quote from the section you mention:

'Working on these poems I've counted up my losses of friends and family (most recently a sister) and pondered other losses, of looks, physical strength, expectations. But as hunger sharpens the appetite, so age intensifies one's awareness of the beauty and wonder of the world, of love and of blessings. Mixed with grief and sorrow is kind of off/on joy.'

RLJ: What a wonderful passage! In the same introductory section, you quote lines from the American poet, Alicia Suskin Ostriker: 'I want to live/said the old woman/like a flame in flight.'[4] Could you please say how 'like a flame in flight' applies to your poetry and your present life.

DH: I would love to be like that. It's a wish, rather than how I do live, although I have quite a temper, which might be a bit of flame. Rather than mellowing, I think I'm probably getting a bit more irritable.

RLJ: Your poem 'Beyond' [given in full in Note 5 at the end of this chapter] seems to be reaching out for something. It's an intriguing poem. Please tell me more about it.

DH: A dream provided the spark for the poem. This dream was prompted by the haunting sound of a train going by in the night, a sound I remembered hearing as a child. And the poem that grew out of the dream was a kind of meditation on mystery. My notepad recorded a favourite quotation from one of Emily Dickinson's letters — 'The unknown is the largest need of the intellect although for it we never think to thank God.' The need for mystery, the unknown, for whatever is beyond, became the poem that spread out in irregular lines across the page as if searching. I do think there is something beyond, not necessarily an after-life, but some kind of spiritual life.

RLJ: Do you think that taking part in the *Second Wind* project has contributed to your poetic development and your personal development?

DH: Yes, it has contributed to both. Vicki and I had quite a few workshops together, commenting on each other's drafts. It made me think about ageing and try to process it, which I probably wouldn't have done otherwise.

RLJ: Are writing for children, writing short stories and writing poetry different creative processes for you? Has the amount of time you spend on each altered with the passing of the years?

DH: The poetry is more intense than the other forms. But I enjoy writing for children and it's really been my way of earning a living. I had some early success with children's books — back in 1991 I won a Whitbread Award for *Harvey Angell*. I write for all age groups from picture books to young adult, but mostly for the 8–12 age group. I have been writing since I was twelve, but I didn't get published until I began writing for children, which was when I was coming up for forty. I started a late university degree at Bristol University. I wanted to keep writing and do something in contrast to academic essays, so I began writing for children. My professor's wife was the well-known children's author, Diana Wynne Jones [6]. She read some of my stories and put me onto a publisher and I struck lucky. I have an eight-year-old in my head. I have strong memories of being that age. I grew up by the sea and I was an avid reader at that age. I belonged to four different libraries. There was the Public Library, Boots Library and two sweet shops which had libraries.

RLJ: Which form of writing is most important to you?

DH: The poetry. I care more about it. It's always been my first love. Sometimes I have blank periods when I'm not sparked. Nothing comes. I belong to a poetry workshop. There are four of us: myself,

Hamish Whyte, Christine De Luca and Ian McDonough. We set each other a theme and bring two poems to the workshop — one on the theme and one free choice — and that can keep me going through a dry time.

RLJ: For quite a lot of writers in later life the loss of people close to them has been a theme, a stimulus. Is that true of you?

DH: I wrote about my sister when she died. There are elegies I'd like to write for friends I've lost — but there has to be an initial spark, a line or phrase that starts off a poem.

RLJ: What sort of things encourage that spark?

DH: Often, when I've sent something new to a publisher, I can't get going on anything until I've heard one way or another about it. I'm in that position at the moment as regards poetry having just sent out a new collection. In the meantime, I've become hooked on essays — partly because the *Late Style* radio broadcast was an essay and I really enjoyed doing that. I did an essay recently for the Royal Literary Fund on the topic of my early days in journalism. Various RLF Fellows — of whom I was one several years ago — write essays which they put on the RLF website under the heading of 'Collected.' I think the essay is a fascinating form. If a poem strikes me I will stop whatever I'm doing for it, but otherwise I'll get on with what I'm doing, which is essays at the moment.

RLJ: And you write short stories as well. In fact, you have had a collection published this year by Postbox Press: *My Father As an Ant & Other Stories*.

DH: I like a variety of forms of writing, as I've said. I think each form helps to illuminate and add to the other forms. And music as well — I hope there's musicality in my poems.

RLJ: Tell me more about *My Father As an Ant*. Do the earlier stories differ from the later ones?

DH: I hope they are better! And sharper, the language is sharper, the craft more honed. And I also hope that the reader can't tell which are the early ones and which the later ones. A good half are relatively new. There are family stories, fantasy ones and quite a few to do with escape and rescue. Do you know that feeling when you think somebody will come along and whisk you away to a more exciting life? Not that I'm trying to escape from Hamish! I'm told that God appears rather a lot in these stories — not just the later ones. God has been on my mind since I was eight. There's an autobiographical element in a lot of the stories. My father used to get obsessions about various things. One of them was oil paintings. He would go off and buy, at whatever price, a painting and bring it home. My mother would try and bring him down from his grand fantasies by saying, 'Remember, you are only an ant. In the grand scheme of things you are insignificant.' Hence the title of the book.

RLJ: You have twice mentioned the age of eight as a key period in your life. Why is that?

DH: It might be a bit arbitrary. My grandmother died then — the first time I'd been close to death. I think it's the age of coming to a consciousness of self. Becoming aware of being an individual — or that's how it was for me at 8. Also I didn't go to my grandmother's funeral and her death wasn't really spoken about. So it was as if she'd just vanished. Where had she gone? I think that's how God 'arrived' in my eight-year old head!

RLJ: Has religion been important in your life?

DH: My mother was Jewish and married out. I was always very interested in her past, because she was cut off from her family. She was one of six living in a Jewish area of Liverpool, I was aware of a lack of faith. I couldn't have articulated it, but I missed belonging. There was my mother with a whole history of faith and religion from which I was cut off. My father became Jewish in order to marry her, but he never practised it. I think I might have been the only child who chose to go to Sunday School!

RLJ: How do you define creativity?

DH: I probably wouldn't define it. I think it's tuning into yourself and the world around you. Often for me it's two ideas coming together — like they say that rubbing sticks together produces fire. And it's a bit magical — a kind of given grace. Creativity comes in all sorts of ways, from gardening to painting.

RLJ: Has your creativity changed as you get older? And have your motives for writing changed?

DH: The way I work has changed. I used to do a lot more brainstorming than I do now — warm-up exercises and things like that. There's always been a conflict between wanting success and wanting to write well. The two don't always go together. Overall, I just want to write as well as I can. I'm motivated by wanting to be able to release something that is in there waiting.

RLJ: Have your reading habits changed?

DH: In my thirties I read a lot of psychology and philosophy and books by Jung and Kierkegaard. I don't attempt that these days. I read more biographies than I used to. I like finding out how other writers have lived and worked. When I was younger I would have an obsession with a particular novelist and read everything by that person in a concentrated period. I find it harder to do that now, though I have read almost everything by Amos Oz. Currently I'm reading the biography of Robert Lowell[7]. I'm interested because he suffered from manic depression, as I did in my early to late thirties. The author of the biography suffered from it herself. She writes about both Lowell's manic episodes and his depression.

RLJ: What treatment did you have?

DH: I was sectioned twice, on one occasion for a month. Then I was prescribed lithium which puts you on a very flat, even keel. I didn't like that. But then I went to university and it was like a convalescent home for me. I got divorced and I weaned myself off lithium. I had two young children and I wanted to be well enough to look after them. I worked very hard at getting myself back on track. At my worst, I thought I was going to be fat, mad and lose my children. I have been drug-free for a long time now, but I am aware of being someone who lives near the edge. There's always that fear that it might come back. I know the warning signs. I'm sure some of this must have fed into my writing, but I don't think I could tell you how. I do have a folder of poems written when ill. I had a look at it the other day. There are a couple I might be able to use. The rest are rubbish, really. That was my mid-life crisis. I've had the very opposite of a late-life crisis, because when I moved to Edinburgh, I met Hamish and my life took off. It's been a late life happiness.

I moved from Bristol to Edinburgh after spending a year as Writer-in-Residence at Dumfries & Galloway Royal Infirmary. I couldn't quite settle back in Bristol and at the time my son was living in Edinburgh and my daughter doing a degree in Glasgow. Visiting the Book Festival perhaps clinched Edinburgh as the place to be.

RLJ: Have there been any negative aspects associated with later life?

DH: Well, physical appearance does matter to me and I'm sorry I don't look as good as I used to look. I feel bad about caring about it, but I do. And I don't have as much energy as before — physical energy, though I try to maintain it. There's a swimming pool across the road, so I swim twice a week and I do some yoga and Hamish and I play table tennis.

RLJ: What, for you, have been the joys accompanying ageing?

DH: Hamish and late love; and becoming part of Mariscat Press with him. My grandchildren have been a great joy. The essays I'm writing allow me to be more reflective. I'm sure I know myself better than heretofore. Since moving to Edinburgh I have found a couple of close friends. Really good friends are quite rare, so that's been a joy. Some of the gifts of old age that other people talk about I'm still unwrapping. I'm working at being more accepting of myself and of life as it really is. I struggle with trying to accept my limitations. I think I'm less patient with people than I was. Life is short and I want to spend it with the people I love. I would like to be a bit more useful than I am, but I can't quite think how.

RLJ: Do you think you will go on writing until you drop?

DH: I've done a lot this year. I was co-editing *New Writing Scotland*, I've brought out my short story collection, I've a collection of poems coming out with Worple Press this year (2018) , and two children's books in the pipeline. A few months ago, I thought, 'Diana, your life's work is done.' To an extent, that's true. I mean, if you look at the list of my publications, obviously most of my output is behind me rather than ahead of me. Anything from now on is a bonus. I hope there are poems still waiting to be released, but I can't guarantee that. A part of me wants to take some time off, but I find that quite hard to do.

RLJ: In the nearly six years since you passed seventy, what piece of writing has given you the most satisfaction?

DH: Somehow that's very hard to answer. I've written a lot in the last five years but 'satisfaction' is often rather fleeting! One or two of the poems in *Second Wind* are ones I hope might survive a while — so I'm pleased you liked 'Beyond', which is my favourite. I'm looking forward to the publication of my next junior novel, *Whoever You Are* — because it seemed to come from some very authentic part of — dare I say it, my 8 year old self! Lastly, I'm excited about essays.

RLJ: Have you had any role models as regards ageing well?

DH: Muriel Spark was writing well into later life. Elizabeth Jane Howard was still writing in her eighties (I read all the Cazalet Chronicles recently). I think. Margaret Atwood is going strong. Ditto Edna O'Brien.

RLJ: On your website you quote the psychologist, D. W. Winnacott as writing about 'the urgent desire to communicate and the still more urgent desire not to be found.'

DH: Yes, I particularly chose that quotation. I like to be outgoing — but there's a core of reserve.

RLJ: Do you still feel that inner tension, the grit in the oyster that produces the pearl?

DH: Yes, I still feel that. Recently at my poetry workshop, the choice of subject was 'Rage.' Sometimes rage can accomplish something good and sometimes it can be destructive. I wrote a poem about that conflict within myself. Also, quite recently I went back to an old haunt. Everyone there was just the same and I felt I wanted to escape. So there was that conflict between wanting to be loyal and steadfast and wanting something new.

RLJ: What advice do you have for those who want to go on writing into old age?

DH: Write every day, even if it's only for an hour.

Notes

1. Hamish Whyte was born near Glasgow where he lived for many years before moving to Edinburgh in 2004. He has edited many anthologies of Scottish literature. He runs Mariscat Press, publishing the poetry of Edwin Morgan, Gael Turnbull, Janice Galloway, Stewart Conn and A.L. Kennedy among others. He has worked as a librarian, reviewed crime fiction for *Scotland on Sunday* and is currently an Honorary Research Fellow in the Department of Scottish Literature at the University of Glasgow. His latest poetry collection is *Things We Never Knew* (Shoestring Press).

2. Situated between Glenogle Road and of The Water of Leith, the Stockbridge colonies were built between 1861 and 1911 by the Edinburgh Co-operative Building Company. Their purpose was to provide owner occupied low-cost housing for, and organized by, working people. Over a third of the shareholders were stonemasons and other tradesmen. At the end of each of the eleven parallel terraces are the original artisan crests portraying the different trades of the workmen. The colonies are often considered to be a small village in their own right.

3. The annual Callum Macdonald Memorial Award is for the publisher of an outstanding example of pamphlet poetry that has a connection with Scotland or Scottish culture. In rewarding a publisher, rather than a poet, it is a unique award in Scotland.

4. *The Old Woman, the Tulip and the Dog* by Alice Suskin Ostriker (University of Pittsburgh Press, 2014)

5. 'Beyond':

    Nothing so lovely as   the hoot
                  of a distant train
       running through your dream.

                    Is it childhood
you're listening
to, worlds going off the map,
or infinity?
        Always you liked views that spoke of beyond —
        those seascapes stretching out that didn't stop at sky but went
            on...

        What is it about the need for it? The why
        of flight,   mountaineering the gift of grace.   How dire

        if ours were the only galaxy!

        How happily the word sits in the mouth, satisfying
            as a communion wafer.

        This is the sound of the distant train
                            running through your dream —

        be-yond be-yond   be-yond be-yond

6. Diana Wynne Jones (1934–2011) was a British writer, princi-
pally of fantasy novels for children and adults. Some of her better-
known works are the Chrestomanci series, the Dalemark series;
the novels *Howl's Moving Castle* and *Dark Lord of Derkholm*; and
The Tough Guide To Fantasyland.

7. The biography of the American poet, Robert Lowell (1917–1977)
— *Robert Lowell, Setting the River on Fire: A Study of Genius, Ma-
nia and Character*, Kay Redfield Jamison (Alfred Knopf. 2017).

This is a prayer/elegy written for my mother and published in *The Seed-Box Lantern* (Mariscat, 2013). Kaddish is a hymn of praises to God found in the Jewish prayer service.

Kaddish

Lordy lord, pick up this little troubled Mama of mine,
Swoop her up in your arms as if she were a toddler,
For a toddler she is at heart and I cannot know what wounded
      her
Or stopped her growing or held her mind in such narrow straits
That it couldn't escape and left her always on the main road
That was not a main road at all but a kind of dead end
When all the off-the-beaten-track places should have led her
      astray
Into the highways and byways of joy.

Dust the disappointment off her. Shake her up a bit.
But gently. Remove those bifocals through which she never liked

The look of the world and borrow a little of Puck's magic
That she might see deludedly yet properly. And laugh.
Brook no complaints about Your House (or whatever Mansion
You have in mind.) Dress her in your bestest green. Attend
To her heart. Pump it up a little. Have you a piano?
Is Sophie Tucker with you? Introduce them.

Let her feel at home who never truly felt so on earth
Even when the babies came and the money
That bought fitted carpets, a washing machine,
A cheque book of her very own. The holiday in Capri.

Fish her wedding ring out of the ashes
And put it back on. Re-unite her with the husband
If you think this is a good idea.

May she be dumbfounded by love.

You may also wish to consult www.dianahendry.co.uk

Photograph by Chris Park

VICKI FEAVER (Age 73)

Vicki Feaver studied music at Durham University and English at University College, London where she was awarded a Henry Morley Medal and the prize for the Best English First. She taught English and Creative writing at the University of Chichester where she is now an Emeritus Professor. She is the author of three poetry collections: *Close Relatives* (1981), *The Handless Maiden* (1994), winner of the Heinemann Award and shortlisted for the Forward Prize for Best Poetry Collection of the Year; and *The Book of Blood* (2006), shortlisted for the Forward and Costa Prizes. *The Handless Maiden* includes the poem 'Judith', winner of the Forward Prize for the Best Single Poem of the year. In 1993 she was awarded a Hawthornden Fellowship and in 1999 a Cholmondeley Award. Vicki moved to Dunsyre, South Lanarkshire in 2000.

In addition to her home in South Lanarkshire, which she shares with her second husband, a retired psychiatrist, Vicki has a small flat in Leith, which is where I met her. Her kitchen and sitting-room overlook the Water of Leith. Across the road, a couple of boats were moored at the quayside.

Over a cup of tea, Vicki told me about her family. 'Jane, my eldest child, is a novelist and short-story writer. Emily is a painter. Jessica is a cellist and Silas is a consultant anaesthetist. I'm so proud of them, not just for their achievements, but for surviving a fairly difficult childhood to become kind and responsible adults and wonderful parents of their children. I'm incredibly lucky to have such lovely children and grandchildren. It's a great positive in my life: undeserved because I was too preoccupied with studying and writing to be the ideal of a devoted mother and I live too far away to be a hands-on grandmother.'

We then turned to the questions I had sent her in advance.

'Teaching is one way for a poet to make a living, but probably not the best way. I envy archeologist, doctor, or gardener poets, or any poets who belong to a world outside poetry. One of the things on my list of blessings, now I'm retired, is not having to teach large groups of students, especially students who think creative writing is an easy option. I enjoyed working one-to-one, or with small groups of highly-motivated students, though I hated having to grade work. I used to wake in the night worrying about it. I still teach occasional courses: always beginning with a reading and discussion of a related poem, or poems. I am convinced that you can't write good poetry without reading it.

Studying for a degree in English Literature in my late thirties certainly enriched my poetry, sometimes directly. For example I used the argument from George Herbert's poem 'The Flower', about his recovery from spiritual despair, for my poem on the same subject, 'Ironing'. On the negative side, in developing my critical mind, it has increased my tendency to relegate poems to the rubbish pile before they have a chance to get going. The syllabus consisted mainly of male, pre-twentieth century English poets. I love the work of Donne, Herbert, Marvel, Blake, Wordsworth and Keats, but found it, mostly, too daunting to inspire my writing. It was reading later male poets, like William Carlos Williams and Theodore Roethke and a whole line of women poets including Emily Bronte, Emily Dickinson, Sylvia Plath, Stevie Smith, Elizabeth Bishop, Adrienne Rich and Sharon Olds, that encouraged me to write and had a more immediate and freeing effect on my writing. I found the poetry and prose of Adrienne Rich [1] particularly inspiring, especially for her distinction between her early, anonymously-voiced formal poetry, written with 'gloves on', and the poetry where, with 'gloves off', she wrote about the experience of being a woman. Stevie Smith, [2] who I worked on for a PhD, was also a major influence: not in the style of her poetry but in her use of characters from fairy tales and legends to write about her own concerns and predicaments.

How to write a poem ought to be, as I get older, a question to which I know the answer. I have published three essays about the process of writing poems [3]. However with every poem I write, I seem to have to go back to the beginning and discover how to do it all over again. Recently, preparing a talk for A-level students and their teachers on my poem, 'The Gun', I gained more insight into my process. Talking about the form of the poem, I explained that there are two ways to write a poem. One is to fill a jar — that is to write in an existing shape like a sonnet, or villanelle. The other is for a poem to grow organically like a tree. This is mostly how I write: the shape of the poem emerging gradually from the sound and rhythm and meaning of the words and vice versa. It's about finding a voice for something inside me. I can't write at all unless the emotion behind the poem is strong enough to carry me through the process of trial and error, of growing and pruning and growing and pruning again, that it involves. Quite often at the end of this process the poem is dead. Reading Sylvia Plath's poem 'Stillborn', I immediately identified with her despair over poems that she's laboured over and almost brought to life, but that in the end, as she put it, 'are dead, and their mother near dead with distraction'.

Though I was thrilled to be one of the three writers invited to contribute poems about ageing to the Saltire pamphlet, I almost turned down the commission for fear of failing to write anything. The impetus to say "yes" was provided by the words of the ninety-year-old Scottish artist Wilhelmina Barns-Graham [4]: "Do it now. Say it now. Don't be afraid". I found the quote while preparing for a workshop in her house as part of the StAnza Poetry Festival. I wrote it on a post-it note that I stuck over my desk. Fear, I think, especially fear of failure, is the chief thing that stops people who want to create something from getting on with it. It is certainly what inhibits me.

'Riding a Wave', the title I chose for the short introduction to my poems, derives from a poem I wrote, inspired by one of the paintings I saw in her house. In my memory — because I couldn't find a reproduction of it either online or in one of the illustrated books about her — it consisted of

> a single brave
> upwards sweep with a wide
> distemper brush so loaded
>
> with paint the canvas filled
> with the glistening blue wall
> of a wave before it falls.

I was also thinking about my experience of body-boarding with some of my children and grandchildren. It's so lovely, when you are old, being able to join in some physical activity that you can still enjoy. If you catch a powerful-enough wave at exactly the right moment, it carries you all the way to the shore, without you having to do anything except hang on. It did feel for a while, as ideas for poems kept coming, that I was 'riding a wave'. There are two kinds of 'riding a wave'. One is when ideas for poems keep on arriving. The other, and best kind, is when you're in the process of writing a poem and get the feeling that the poem is writing itself, carrying you with it. It happened in my poem 'Judith' with the lines 'I rolled in the ash of the fire/just to be touched and dirtied / by something'. It happened again in the final lines of 'The Gun' when the image of a 'gun sprouting golden crocuses,' in my notes for the poem, became 'the King of Death/had arrived to feast, stalking/ out of winter woods, / his black mouth/ sprouting golden crocuses'.

On my fiftieth birthday, I sat on the kitchen counter at Lumb Bank (where I was tutoring an Arvon poetry course) and said, 'I'm half way through my life'. My fellow tutor replied: 'You'll be lucky!' — or something equally dampening, but , of course perfectly true. At the age of fifty, I considered myself more or less immortal.

'The Gun' was written in 2001, when I was fifty-eight, long before the poems for *Second Wind*. But I see now that the poem was in part a vehicle for writing about my difficulty in dealing with death. One of the first drafts began: 'Bringing a gun into a house/ is like bringing in a skull'. At the end, by equating the gun (instrument of death) with the king of death, 'his black mouth/ sprouting golden crocuses' — flowers of the spring, symbol of the new life that grows from the frozen winter earth — an image of death is transformed into an image of life. My imaginary vision of preparing and cooking a feast for him is a way of domesticating death, of disarming him, as Stevie Smith does again and again in her poems, calling him in one her 'friend at the end of the world'. In mythology, the Greek god, Hades, became the Roman god, Pluto, worshipped not only as the God of Death, King of the Underworld, but also as provider of seeds for earth's harvest. It's this god I imagine inviting to a feast: the god and his cold kingdom that Stevie Smith claims, writing in the voice of Persephone, she loves more than life on earth with her smothering mother: 'in this iciness / is my happiness.'

A key element of Freudian theory is that we contain both the instinct for life (eros) and the instinct for death (thanatos). I recognise both in me. In my childhood and early womanhood and at the end of my first marriage, there were times when I momentarily courted death. Sometimes I think it's a miracle I survived, which is why I personified death in the poem 'Death and the Maiden', as a figure prepared to wait, and even actively keep us alive, until the moment when he chooses to take us. Now I've reached a point where I can't ignore the fact that death is closer, 'creeping behind me in velvet slippers', as I put it, I cling fiercely to life. 'The Larder', another of my poems in *Second Wind*, is about filling every day, while I still can, with a store of memorable sights and tastes and scents.

The invitation to write poems for the Saltire pamphlet arrived at the point when I'd reached an impasse with a collection of poems about childhood that was supposed to come out to coincide with my 70th birthday. Still nowhere near finished, I was glad of an excuse to stop digging into mostly painful memories of childhood and consider ageing instead. My initial title for the childhood book, *Like a fiend hid in a cloud*, is a line from Blake's poem 'Infant Sorrow':

> My mother groan'd! my father wept.
> Into the dangerous world I leapt:
> Helpless, naked, piping loud;
> Like a fiend hid in a cloud.

It describes a child, at the mercy of the adult world, who, in possessing a voice strong enough to challenge its beliefs, is regarded as anarchic and dangerous. I think it is Blake's vision of himself as a child. It's also a vision of how I see myself: as a child wanting to be a poet — to 'pipe loud', to speak out against injustice — to others and to myself, to describe the turmoil of my feelings, but if I did, immediately censored and silenced.

There are no poems about my childhood in my first collection. I didn't think of writing about it until I read the work of Sharon Olds[5]. As a child of abusive parents she saw it as a political act to break the silence imposed on her and speak out in her poems. I never suffered sexual abuse. No one intended to harm me. Yet, as a pawn in the war between my mother and grandmother (her mother who lived in our house) I was torn apart and my kind and loving but nervous and frightened father was helpless to stop it.

I emerged from childhood under a black cloud of guilt: for disloyalty to my mother — for not, as my sister did, always taking her side; for not being able to protect my grandmother who'd looked after me as a baby; for not sticking up for my father when he was attacked as a failure; for my lies and disturbed behaviour, for failing to fulfil my mother's ambitions for me and repay her for the sacrifices she made to give me a good education. So powerful are the taboos against a child from a middle-class family spilling the secrets of what happens behind its closed doors, that even when I tried to express my misery, no-one wanted to hear. When I took an overdose of pills, I was rushed to hospital to have my stomach pumped out, then sent home. Nothing was done. No-one spoke about it again. Everyone carried on as if it had never happened. I learned to hide my misery. I wanted to be liked. I put on an act. I told anecdotes about my life that made people laugh.

It wasn't until my forties, living alone, that I discovered the suppressed voice of the child: 'piping loud, like a fiend hid in a cloud'. The title poem of my second collection, *The Handless Maiden*, is based on the fairytale of a girl whose hands are cut off by her father to save her from being sold to the devil. She is given silver hands by a king who falls in love with her. Her own hands regrow at the moment that she plunges them into a spring to save her drowning baby. The feminist psychoanalyst Marie-Louise von Franz[6] interprets it as the story of a woman who has lived through her husband's achievements eventually finding the courage to create for herself. The baby she saves from drowning is her own creative work. I recognised this immediately as my story. Wanting to write but fearful of failure, I had first fallen in love with and married a writer and painter. All my creative energy went into having babies and supporting him in his work. As the marriage fell apart, I began to write poems. But soon after it ended I met and fell in love with another successful writer. He was very encouraging of my work; but that didn't stop the pattern being repeated. It wasn't until this relationship ended, and I read the 'The Handless Maiden' story and its feminist interpretation (ironically in a book my former partner had lent to me) that I found a powerful voice of my own.

I'd like to claim that in my seventies I still possess this voice. My second husband is a retired psychiatrist, not a writer. I don't squander my creative energy in supporting him with his work. He is very willing to take over domestic tasks to leave me free to write. Yet I still find it difficult to produce poems that satisfy me in the way the poems in *The Handless Maiden* did. My dilemma is that living on my own, I long for a close relationship. When I am in a relationship, I wonder if I'd find it easier to write if I was alone.

One of the very first poems I wrote was 'The Coat':

> Sometimes I have wanted
> to throw you off
> like a heavy coat.
>
> Sometime I have said
> you would not let me
> breathe or move.
>
> But now that I am free
> to choose light clothes
> or none at all
>
> I feel the cold
> and all the time I think
> how warm it used to be.

I still feel the same ambivalence: wanting to be held and wanting to break free; wanting security and independence. I've found a sort of solution in spending a few nights a week away from my husband in my flat in Edinburgh. But I am always glad to go back to the house that I think of as home where we live together.

The other reason for my difficulty in accessing the 'piping loud, like a fiend hid in a cloud' voice, must be that in setting out to write a book of poems about childhood I chose the one thing most designed to suppress it. When my mother was alive, I didn't want to write anything that might hurt her. That taboo has gone now, but I still worry about upsetting my sister. We have completely different versions of our childhood: hers happy, mine deeply unhappy. Combining the childhood poems with poems about old-age will, I hope, enable me to finish the book. There are similarities between the experience of childhood and old-age. Both the young and the old engage in the act of dreaming and fantasising. Both can feel completely powerless and at the mercy of people and events outside their control. To write a poem in the voice of a child or an old person is to give them power.

My new title, 'I Want! I Want!' is the caption to Blake's etching of a child with one foot on a ladder reaching to the moon. Wanting the moon isn't only confined to childhood. The ideal may be to live out a peaceful old-age in a state of serenity, accepting things as they are. But I don't think I can be the only writer, or artist, or musician over seventy who wants to achieve more and better and who is always striving for the unreachable. The etching is from Blake's book *The Gates of Paradise*, a collection of scenes from life designed 'for children'. Another, with the caption, 'Help! Help!', shows a man drowning in the sea waving an arm above the waves. I wonder if Stevie Smith, a big fan of Blake, was thinking of it when she wrote 'Not Waving But Drowning'? I can identify with both images: the child wanting the moon and the drowning man calling for help.

Twenty years ago, I was censored for writing about menstruation in my poem 'Woman's Blood' and considered 'brave' for writing about sex and violence from a woman's point of view. Now, except for writing negatively about family members, I can't think of anything that might be subject to censor, or earn me the epithet 'brave'. Death and disease and dying have always been subjects for poetry. The ageing body, once a taboo subject, has been written about in intimate detail by Sharon Olds, first in poems about her dying father, and, in her newest book, *Odes*, about her own body. My poem on the subject, was inspired by Alasdair Reid's 'Weathering', a meditation on his dead father that compares the ageing of a body with the weathering of wood. I titled my poem 'Bone House', after the kenning Anglo-Saxon poets used to refer to the body. A sort of self-portrait, I described how my body has 'weathered': my 'hunched shoulders and stiff neck' evidence 'of hours spent battling with words', my 'belly-skin, stretched by four babies,' resembling 'the rippled sand on a beach/when the tide retreats'; 'my face's fretted lines' betraying 'a lifetime as a worrier'.

In my poem, 'Prayer at Seventy', I put the anxiety that has grown worse as I age, into the images of 'a tiny spider, launching into the unknown on a thread of gossamer' and 'a polar bear leaping between melting ice-flows'. Another poem, 'Forgetfulness' was a vehicle for my fears about memory loss. It's words I lose, not events. But it was easy to imagine myself as the old woman at the end of the poem who kneels on the floor, in a library of film-clips from her past life, 'pale and worried as a ghost, rummaging in a tangle of shiny black ribbons.'

Recently, I've discovered that there is a Tibetan Buddhist Centre very near my flat in Leith. I go there sometimes to meditate and also to a Qigong workshop given by the nun who runs the centre. I'm hoping that in time this will have the effect of making me calmer and more accepting. A person who was and still is a source of inspiration to me, in this respect as in many others, was my friend, Norman Kreitman, [7] the doctor, poet and philosopher who died a couple of years ago. He went on until the end, writing poetry and philosophical papers, and debating new work and ideas.

My ideal in the future is to go on writing, and also to start painting again. If I could do both, and the work was going well, I think I would be entirely happy. If I couldn't do either I would be completely miserable. I find it comforting to think that even confined to bed it is possible to have a pencil and paper and, of course, books to read and look at: art books as well as literary books. I've just been looking again at Morandi's etching and paintings, another body of work that is about objects, though very different from my gun, in that his interest is in their harmonious relationships with each other. I've also been rereading Mark Doty's collection of poems, *Deep Lane*, Gaston Bachelard's *The Poetics of Space* (hoping to find inspiration for a poem about the houses of my childhood) and Van Gogh's *Letters*. Opening this randomly I found a wonderful quote that I immediately transcribed in my notebook. He has quarreled with his artist friend Mauve because, as he explains: 'Mauve takes it amiss that I said, "I am an artist", which I won't take back, because it's self-evident that what that word implies is looking for something all the time without ever finding it in full. It is the very opposite of saying, "I know all about it, I've already found it." As far as I am concerned, the word means, "I am looking, I am hunting for it, I am deeply involved."'

That expresses perfectly what I feel about writing poetry. I don't know what I'm looking for until, in the process of hunting, something strikes me. I've always remembered Mathew Sweeney[8] saying to me, 'Nothing comes of nothing'. My advice to myself, which I'm not very good at taking, is to write down quickly, by hand, the first thoughts that come into my head. I can go back to revise them later. Nothing beats the satisfaction of having found something and put it into words, or paint, of having 'saved it' from being gobbled up by time. There's a poem in *The Handless Maiden* about my mother boiling up crab-apples that would otherwise have gone to rot, to make the most wonderful clear jelly. My husband does the same with rowan berries. Writing a poem is the nearest thing I can do to preserve something. It stops the panicky feeling of time running out along with the guilt at wasting days and weeks with nothing achieved that is for me the most negative aspect of ageing.

The most positive feeling I bring to old age is the sense of having survived. The story of my life that when I was younger I often thought of as a series of mistakes and wrong turnings, now appears to be a chronicle of survival. Some of this, as well as the pleasure of being close to nature, came into the poem 'I have chosen for my sample of something written since passing the age of seventy — the poem I like best in Second Wind, 'Old Woman in a Forsythia Bush.'

Notes

1. Adrienne Cecile Rich (1929–2012) was an American poet, essayist and radical feminist. She was called 'one of the most widely read and influential poets of the second half of the 20th century', and was credited with bringing the oppression of women and lesbians to the forefront of poetic discourse.

2. Florence Margaret Smith, known as Stevie Smith (1902–1971) was an English poet and novelist. Her best-known poem is 'Not Waving but Drowning'. She was awarded the Cholmondeley Award for Poets in 1966 and won the Queen's Gold Medal for poetry in 1969. She published nine volumes of poems in her lifetime (three more were released posthumously).

3. The three essays were: (i) 'The Handless Maiden', in *How Poets Work*, ed. Tony Curtis (Seren, 1994); (ii) ' "Judith", The Making Of A Poem'. in *Creative Writing Course Book*, ed. Paul Magrs and Julia Bell (Macmillan, 2001); (iii) 'Head Wars: Finding a Voice for a Poem' in *In their Own Words, Contemporary Poets On Their Poetry*, ed. Helen Ivory and George Szirtes (Salt, 2012).

4. Wilhelmina Barns-Graham CBE (1912–2004), painter and printmaker, was one of the foremost British abstract artists of her day, a member of the influential Penwith Society of Arts.

5. Sharon Olds (born 1942) is an American poet. Olds has been the recipient of many awards including the 2013 Pulitzer Prize in Poetry, the 1984 National Book Critics Circle Award, and the first San Francisco Poetry Center Award in 1980. She currently teaches creative writing at New York University.

6. *The Feminine in Fairy Tales* (Shambhala, 1993, first published by Spring Publications, 1972).

7. Norman Kreitman (1927–2012) was a psychiatric researcher and academic, based in Edinburgh, primarily known for coining the term parasuicide. He was also a published poet of some distinction, and wrote perceptively on the philosophy of art — in particular, on the psychology of metaphor.

8. Mathew Sweeney (born 1952), an Irish poet.

Old Woman in a Forsythia Bush

Bright bush of yellow stars,
reaching out to me with long
bowed wands, among fields,
ringing with blackbird songs;
where lambs, licked into life
by sheep's rough tongues,
leap like ballet dancers,
impossibly high, as if hung
on strings of a great puppeteer
who also dangled me when young,
exciting me to strip off vest
and bra to celebrate spring;
and, now I'm old, whose arms
have dragged me through the long
dark corridors of another winter
to sit on this sunny seat, among
starry stems of forsythia,
buoyant again, as if sprung
from my body and floating
above it, like a seed flung
from the grey head of dandelion.

You may also wish to consult https://www.poetryarchive.org/poet/vicki-feaver and https://literature.britishcouncil.org/writer/vicki-feaver

5. TWO GLASGOW WRITERS

Alasdair Gray
James Kelman

Although their writings differ, these two friends, Alasdair Gray and James Kelman, have quite a lot in common. They are both Glasgow based, with left-wing views and champions of those who are victims of injustice, inequality and oppression. Professor Willy Maley, of the Department of English and Scottish Language and Literature at Glasgow University commented: 'They [he included Tom Leonard] have shown that Scotland is capable of great literature by producing it. They have done much more than put Scotland firmly on the map of world literature. They have changed the critical climate as well as shaping the literary landscape.'

ALASDAIR GRAY (Age 82)

Alasdair Gray describes himself as a 'self-employed verbal and pictorial artist'. He was born in Riddrie, Glasgow, on 28 December 1934, and trained as a painter at the Glasgow School of Art. He worked as a part-time art teacher, muralist and theatrical scene painter before becoming a full-time painter and playwright. Later he wrote fiction, illustrating many of his own books.

His highly-acclaimed first novel *Lanark* was published in 1981. It won a Scottish Arts Council Book Award and the Scottish Book of the Year award. A complex and at times surreal mix of fantasy, autobiography and social realism, the book provides a vision of contemporary society through the story of art student Duncan Thaw. This novel led to Alasdair being acknowledged as one of the most innovative figures in contemporary literature and culture.

Painter, novelist, playwright, poet and editor, Alasdair often combines his diverse artistic talents within single works (some of his murals have words in them, some of his fictions have illustrations) to challenge existing forms. Blending satire and tragedy, realism and fantasy, his work has been credited with spurring a renaissance in Scottish literature.

Alasdair became, with Tom Leonard and James Kelman, joint Professor of the Creative Writing programme at Glasgow and Strathclyde University. A staunch socialist and supporter of Scottish independence, Alasdair's activism extends beyond the covers of his books, protesting against nuclear weapons at Faslane and against the second Gulf War in 2003.

In June 2015, Alasdair fell down the outside steps to his basement, seriously injuring his back and spent seven months in hospital before being allowed home in a wheelchair.

When I visited Alasdair at his ground floor flat in Marchmont Terrace, in January 2017, the door was opened by his dentist who was there on a home visit and was in the middle of taking a mould of Alasdair's mouth. I am not sure that Alasdair had remembered I was coming. He was in his wheelchair and had a heavy chest cough. He was not the ebullient, excitable person I remembered, but fairly quiet and subdued.

RLJ: How are you? How is your recovery progressing?

AG: I would like to recover the use of my legs, but it may not be. It does inhibit my ability to work on the murals, but I can work on small drawings and pictures.

RLJ: Do you think your accident is likely to steer you away from painting and back to more fiction?

AG: No.

RLJ: (nervous laugh)

AG: The Antibookclub is bringing out a collection of my later verses this year. And I've completed the text of a paraphrase, rather than a translation — I don't do Italian — of Dante's *Divine Comedy*, which Canongate will be publishing in three books. *The Inferno* will be coming out this year before Christmas. What I've to do is to design my embellishments. It's totally a hundred cantos or chapters over the three books. I've been thinking of this for a long time. I've collected various translations. Some of them annoyed and displeased me because, although I admired them, I felt that, as English, they did not read easily and were rather stilted, with too many archaisms. What got me started on it about three years ago was that I had absolutely no ideas for anything original of my own. My wife, Morag, who was still alive then, thought it was a great waste of time.

RLJ: You once said that artists should continually surprise themselves, otherwise they can't hope to surprise their audience. Did you surprise yourself with Dante?

AG: Yes, I did. I was even more surprised when I found that somebody would publish it!

RLJ: I believe that, several times, you have sworn to give up fiction.

AG: Yes. It seems that fiction isn't in me anymore. I would be delighted for a new fictional idea, but I don't think it is very likely now.

RLJ: The last fiction you wrote was *Old Men in Love*, three or four years ago, wasn't it?

AG: Yes.

RLJ: Do you think this fiction drought is an aspect of ageing?

AG: It just isnae there. In the past, fiction ideas just came to me. In the case of *Poor Things* I had a dream. I thought I could make a short story from the dream. Then, when I started work on it, to my amazement, it turned into quite a big novel. That sort of thing doesn't seem to be happening these days. I've never suffered from what is sometimes called writers' block, in the sense of it being like constipation, where's there's a mass of stuff waiting to come out, but it won't. I just feel there's nae anything there.

RLJ: Do you think your accident will prevent further work on the Oran Mor [1] murals?

AG: I would like to complete the auditorium upstairs in the Oran Mor and might be able to do that with the help of Nichol Wheatley [2]. I've got many unfinished works [pointing to a large canvas on the wall] — that's one there: *The Northern Birth of Venus*. I may be getting a friend of mine who is a painter to do the foreground and a few modifications. I'm a slow worker. I started painting that in the 1960s.

RLJ: You said you don't get writers' block, but do you get painters' block?

AG: No, I'm just a very slow worker.

RLJ: What is it that makes you stop what you're working on, then start again later?

AG: One thing is that, in the past, not many people wanted my pictures and, therefore, there was no particular reason to complete them. Then I got a dealer, Sorcha Dallas, who got me several public exhibitions, for which I worked to finished paintings.

RLJ: Tell me about the Glasgow Museum's commission which you had started on before your accident.

AG: It's a picture of St.Mungo[3] for the Museum of Religion. It's in my bedroom at the moment. I've finally stopped feeling guilty about working slowly. [Before I left, Alasdair showed me into his bedroom — like an exhibition room in an art gallery, but with a bed in a corner — and pointed out the painting. It was propped against the wall behind a spare mattress.]

RLJ: Have you felt guilty about it for most of your life?

AG: Oh, yes. If you've been commissioned for a work and partly paid for it. I have a horror of owing people anything.

RLJ: Do you think that no longer feeling guilty about it is part of a wider thing that often comes with old age — becoming more accepting of yourself and who you are?

AG: Yes, I'm afraid so.

RLJ: What do you see as the most positive things about ageing?

AG: I'm not sure that I see many positive things. I feel loss: loss of my wife; loss of friends. My wife, Morag, died in May 2014. We had been married for twenty-five years. I would have preferred to die before she did. I live alone now — except for the relay of helpers and care-workers, of course, who come at regular intervals throughout the day, and lots of friends call to see me. One positive has been that my appreciation of colour has increased. Colour was always something I wrestled with. I was very fond of bright colours and admired post-impressionists like Gauguin and Van Gogh and was keen on the Primitives — that is, before the development of oil painting, when they used colours almost like stained glass. I enjoyed doing these, but I could not do a huge painting in nothing but bright colours. Harmony is required, and the use of more subdued colours.

RLJ: What belief system lies behind your work? And have these beliefs changed as you get older?

AG: No, they haven't changed. The Oran Mor murals were influenced by Gauguin's *Where Do We Come From? What Are We? Where Are We Going?*[4] These are questions that human beings have asked themselves from the year dot and most religions and sciences and many arts have been created to provide partial answers to them.

RLJ: What are your own answers to these questions?

AG: Our lives are rooted in Death's republic. What are we? Animals that want more than we need. Where are we going? Our seed is returned to Death's republic. I have no belief in the immortality of my soul. I am not frightened of dying. Artistically, I've been very lucky, because I've done most of the things I wanted to do. But I do fear physical and mental decline. I do notice unexpected holes in my memory. Things I thought I knew well that I can't recall. Memories suddenly disappear — but they do come back.

RLJ: What other negatives do you find in ageing?

AG: The absence of walking. I hadn't expected to start doing without that so soon. I find it sad to think that I'm not likely to climb a hill again.

RLJ: You have described *The End of our Tether* as being about the physical, social and moral decrepitude of people. Did you include yourself in that?

AG: Yes. Many of my books and stories have been imagining myself a little older and more decayed than I actually was. It has been a natural progression for me to write about older people as I age myself. When I was younger my health was poor. I was asthmatic and, therefore, I found it easy to imagine myself being much older than I was.

RLJ: If I may quote a question put to you by the *Scottish Review of Books* three years ago: 'Your new collection, *Every Short Story*, covers more than sixty years, which is a remarkable span of creativity. What was your motivation? A sense of completeness? A desire to bring between covers stories that can only be found in disparate collections? Or to show how your work has developed and matured over that period? In a sense a portrait of the artist throughout all stages of his life?' Your full reply, then, was: 'All these three'. Now that you have passed eighty, do you have anything else to add?

AG: In writing *Old Men in Love* I was partly looking for some sense of completion, or a summation and drawing together of things. And I was doing the same with *My Life in Pictures* and my collected short stories and collected verses. I suppose I'm still doing this to some extent. My agent organized an 80th birthday exhibition of my work at the Kelvingrove Art Gallery. I'm glad the show pleased so many people, especially those in my own family. I used to think that one day Glasgow's public gallery would think well of my work, but I didn't expect to survive to see it.

RLJ: In the last twelve years, that is, since passing seventy, what has given you the most satisfaction in terms of creative work?

AG: I suppose finishing things that have lain unfinished for a long time. I was very pleased to have some public exhibitions of my work because I had not been expecting to get public appreciation of my paintings. And one of the things I was most pleased with was the Hillhead Subway mural. I always wanted my work in public buildings and to be enjoyed by as many folk as possible.

RLJ: Some of the buildings in which you have done murals have now been pulled down. Does that hurt?

AG: Yes, it does a bit. My first big mural in Greenhead Church of Scotland, Bridgeton — the building was demolished to make way for a motorway extension that never happened. That hurt.

RLJ: Rodge Glass in his biography of you said: 'He still hopes for one major artistic work before the end of his life.' In your opinion, has that happened yet?

AG: Yes. Oran Mor. That would be it, I think; and if I finish the St. Mungo painting... Oh, dear, dear, dear!

RLJ: Do you have doubts about finishing it?

AG: It's a possibility. I think I probably will. I'll just keep pushing on with the unfinished things.

RLJ: You said in your 70th birthday interview for the BBC that recent years were some of the happiest in your life. Would you say that now, in your 80s?

AG: When I said that, Morag was still alive. I miss her immensely. Her absence is still a grief to me.

RLJ: Does your grief for the loss of Morag find expression in your work?

AG: No, and I don't suppose it ever will. I don't seem to be able to express it.

[At this point we were interrupted by a group of social workers who had come to discuss the provision of a ramp down the front steps for Alasdair's wheelchair.]

RLJ: How much do you see of your son, Andrew?

AG: He lives in Connecticut in America. He's a physiotherapist. He came over for three months when I had my accident. We speak on the phone regularly. And my married sister, who lives in Northumbria comes to see me about once a month.

RLJ: To quote from your biography again: 'Alasdair makes a financial arrangement to secure some income, is set a timetable, then, every time is surprised to find he can't work to it. All this would not be so serious if the worry, stress and pressure of providing were not making him ill. Illness then necessitates a break from work, which puts on more pressure when he returns from it. And so on.' Do you recognize that as accurate?

AG: No, I don't think I do. Not now. I suppose I worried more when Morag was alive. Well, I didn't want to cause her worry. She was always afraid that we might not be able to pay the mortgage on this house, which she had bought. I never worried about money on my own behalf. Actually, she left me quite a bit of money when she died, so now there is even less reason to worry.

[At this point, the phone rings and Alasdair makes a date to play chess with a friend]

RLJ: Are you a good chess player?

AG: No, a very bad chess player, but I enjoy it.

RLJ: In a way, you have come full circle in that your early creativity was as an artist and your late life creativity is mainly as an artist, with the other things, the plays, short stories and novels in the middle. Any reason for that?

AG: Drawing and painting was what I was good at as a child and my parents and teachers encouraged me in this. Making pictures and telling stories were ways of getting affectionate attention and I hoped to make a living by it and that eventually came about.

RLJ: Quite a few years ago, when you gave a talk, I asked you if the mental processes were different for you when painting and when writing. You replied that painting was an exploration of space and writing an exploration of time. Would your answer still be the same?

AG: Yes.

RLJ: In your biography is the sentence, 'All work bleeds into all other work, all the time.' Would you still agree with that?

AG: I can't remember whether I said that, or Rodge Glass did, but, yes, I suppose I would agree with it. I was always impressed by Rudyard Kipling's *Just So* stories in which he magnificently illustrates them and had a poem attached to each story, or a little essay attached to each illustration, explaining it. I found something very beguiling and very entertaining in this approach. I've never seen these things in a very grandiose way. Mostly picture-making and story-telling and other things have been ways of entertaining people and that's what I hope to have done.

RLJ: Tell me a bit about your political views and activities.

AG: I don't see that you can entertain people very thoroughly without developing ideas. I have never seen politics as separable from my view of the world. Everyone has a conception of what is fair and what is just. My father was a socialist and a Labour Party supporter. In the Second World War, when I was growing up, a Coalition Government, in order to fight the war, had nationalized the whole country — out of which came the Welfare State, which was a better form of socialism than Russian communism.

RLJ: You have written quite a number of political pamphlets over the years. Are you still doing this?

AG: My wife was a very convinced Scottish Nationalist. I'm not very pleased with the Scottish Government. The fact that they have been reducing the number of police stations and courts has galvanized me into writing another pamphlet and complaining about the direction the Scottish Government is taking. I am working on that at the moment... Oh dear, I suppose I'll get it done.

RLJ: Has the nature of your creativity changed at all as you get older?

AG: I only meant to write one big novel — *Lanark*, which I started when I was about seventeen or eighteen and it was published when I was forty-seven. And I also only meant to write one book of short stories. But one of the stories grew and grew until it developed into my second novel, *1982, Janine*, which I think is a better novel than *Lanark*. I found myself coming to write more than I intended. That was surprising and quite pleasant.

RLJ: Do you have any role models in terms of staying creative in later life?

AG: There are many artists. Edward Burra is one. He is one of the few artists, I think, who has painted modern landscapes, with motorways and things like that. His range is immense. Thomas Hardy's later poems were the fruit of a really great novelist. [Alasdair quotes the opening lines of Hardy's poem 'After a Journey']: 'Hereto I come to view a voiceless ghost; /Whither, O whither will its whim now draw me?/Up the cliff, down, till I'm lonely, lost, /And the unseen waters' ejaculations awe me.' Marvellous! 'Ejaculations awe me.' The way it conveys the tide coming into a sea cave and bursting, then subsiding. 'Ejaculations awe me.'

RLJ: Are you able to quote quite a lot of poetry from memory?

AG: Some. Mostly frivolous stuff — 'The Hunting of the Snark', for instance.

RLJ: Do you think that, as you become more accepting of yourself and as the inner quarrels are quietening down, that your creative spark is doing the same?

AG: I wouldn't be surprised if it were!

RLJ: What advice would you give to those who hope to remain creative into later life?

AG: Get hold of a house and let some rooms to ensure yourself a small but steady income. The problem is always to get enough money to develop yourself along the lines that you wish — especially if you can't get somebody to pay you to do it. I remember when I was in my teens, I did hope I would meet a patron who would give me money to work at exactly what I wanted to do. To some extent, The Scottish Arts Council filled that role. And the Royal Literary Fund has helped me at various times of my life when I was getting short of money.

RLJ: Is there anything else you would like to say about your creativity in later life?

AG: Not a thing!

Notes

1. Oran Mor: Formerly Kelvinside Parish Church, Òran Mór, Gaelic for 'great melody of life' or 'big song', is a thriving arts & entertainment venue in the heart of Glasgow's West End, in Byres Road, opposite the Botanic Gardens.

2. Nichol Wheatley: Nichol Wheatley is a Scottish artist mainly concerned with painting. He started and ran Perfect Circle Art, Scotland's largest commercial art studio, for more than a decade. He was also a co-founder of Maryhill Art School. He makes paintings, mosaic and murals and is well known for his collaborations with other artists and organisations. He mainly works in Europe but does consultancy work elsewhere.

3. St. Mungo's Church: A Roman Catholic church in the Town-

head area of Glasgow, built in 1841 in the Gothic Revival style by the architect, George Goldie.

4. *Where Do We Come From? What Are We? Where Are We going?*: Painted by Paul Gaugin in Tahiti in 1897. The original title in French had no question marks.

A sample of writing done since passing 70

I suggested to Alasdair a passage from Old Men in Love *(Bloomsbury, 2007) and he asked me to pick something from it myself. The blurb, by the spoof critic, Sidney Workman (invented by Alasdair himself) states: 'Old Men in Love exhibits those faintly preposterous foibles for which Gray is loved. The bulk of the text constitutes the posthumous papers of a recondite retired, schoolmaster, John Tunnock, seemingly edited and collated by Gray himself.' In the Epilogue to this book, Sidney Workman (of 17 Linoleum Terrace, Kirkcaldy), after tearing Alasdair's work to shreds, says: 'This book should therefore not be read, or if read, swiftly forgotten.' The selected passage is taken from Chapter 15, 'Wee Me'.*

But I stopped enjoying the Sunday Schools held by a church elder in a comfortable part of the undercroft. She was a retired school teacher as kind as my aunts. She told us simple Bible stories, chiefly about Jesus first, but at the age of seven started teaching the early history of mankind and God's chosen people with straight readings from *Genesis, Exodus, Numbers, Deuteronomy, Joshua, Samuel* and *Kings*. She omitted dull *begat* chapters and sexually explicit ones like Abraham's fraudulent prostitution of his wife in chapters 12 and 20, but did not censor the genocidal wars by which the people of Israel replaced the original inhabitants of Palestine. I thought the Lord God who ordered the Israelites to *"smite them and utterly destroy them and make no pact with them, nor show mercy unto them"* was cruel and unfair. I said so. The teacher was a gentle soul. She told me the war was not a fight for land between Jews and those earlier settlers the Ammonites, Midianites, Canaanites and Philistines; it was "a life and death struggle between truth and falsehood for the cultural development of God's people." I asked what that meant. Becoming a little flustered, she said God *needed* to order the slaughter of men, women and children who did not believe in Him so that the Jews had a homeland where his son Jesus, Prince of Peace, could be born to preach the religion of peace for everyone.

You may also wish to consult www.alasdairgray.info/

https:// literature.britishcouncil.org/alasdair-gray

JAMES KELMAN (Age 71)

James Kelman was born in Glasgow in 1946. He left school at fifteen and began a six-year apprenticeship in the printing trade. In 1963 he left the trade and emigrated with his family to California. He later worked at a variety of jobs.

During a period of unemployment in London, England he began writing. He was then twenty one years of age. He met a girl from Swansea, Wales by the name of Marie Connors. They married in London in 1969. Back in Glasgow he drove buses for a living but grabbed time wherever possible for writing. In 1972 through mutual friends Philip Hobsbaum and Anne Stevenson he met Texan writer Mary Gray Hughes. With Mary Gray's support his debut story collection, *An Old Pub Near The Angel*, was published in Maine, USA in 1973.

Writing about himself, James says: 'Since 1976 he has fumbled around trying to live as a writer, supported financially by Marie who has supplied the daily bread, he the occasional chocolate biscuit.

Kelman has published novels, short stories and essays, and has written for stage, film and radio. In past years he taught at the University of Texas @ Austin and briefly at San José State University, California. For a short period he held jointly, with friends Tom Leonard and Alasdair Gray, the Chair of Creative Writing at the University of Glasgow. It was tough going and ended after two years. Nowadays he and his wife live most of the time in Glasgow, not far from their two daughters and two grandchildren.

Despite James' willingness to meet up with me for an interview, a combination of ill health and full schedules on both our parts made it too difficult. In the end, James suggested that I email him my questions and he would reply in writing. Here is the resulting dialogue:

In an essay for the Scottish PEN website you said that the marginalisation of your work continues. Could you expand on this, please. Do you think actual hostility to your work is at the level it was? — the hostility is nowhere near the same level although it would be inaccurate to say that it does not continue. A general marginalisation occurs anyway at the Brit level for Scottish writers who fail to assimilate. And not only Scottish writers. A recent example is the level of hostility directed towards the tennis player Andy Murray when as a young fellow he identified as Scottish. He had to learn to identify as British in the first instance, and allow his Scottishness to remain secondary. This frees the media and establishment, and allows them to push the oneness of the 'one nation' argument, by inference its unity, its indivisibility. What's new?

A lot of criticism you received in the past was vicious and personal. Were you hurt at the time and what are your thoughts about it now? — not so much hurt as dumbfounded. So much of it was obvious nonsense, these peculiar, anti-literary notions trotted out by established literary authorities. I thought it instrumental that one of the more vociferous was quickly promoted to higher editorial positions within quality newspapers, and later selected to chair a Booker Prize panel. In 1989 I was on the Booker short list and awarded the prize in 1994, yet none of my last five novels has even made it onto the long-list never mind the short-list! Another unprecedented achievement.

*In '*The Red Cockatoo*', Mitchell & Rodger have a diagram 'The Network: Kelman's Political & Intellectual Firmament.' To what extent has this network changed since then?* — I don't know about 'The Network' which appears to be an imaginative construct by the authors. I had no involvement in writing the book. People do move on, move away, give up, burn out, expire, drap deid.

The same authors comment that the 1980s and 90s were the most intense period of your political activism. What are the reasons for the level of intensity dropping since those two decades? — as I said, I had no involvement in writing the book, and can say little about the authors' perception. However, very few people ever get paid for these forms of activism, although those who police or punish the activists typically do earn a wage.

I was an unpaid full-time worker in the struggle against the British State's abuse of people suffering asbestos-related diseases. I relied on my wife as bread-winner, and also an advance from a publisher. Eventually I had to stop it all and earn some money. I needed to be writing, needed to repay the advance.

These economic pressures remained. Eventually I couldn't find a way to earn a living in Scotland. In 1997 I applied to a university in USA which I knew was teaching my work and I was given a job in their Department of English Literature. I was offered the chance to continue there but was tempted back to Glasgow University in 2002, working with Alasdair Gray and Tom Leonard in a three-way split of the Chair in Creative Writing. The universities of Glasgow and Strathclyde were involved jointly in the Creative Writing set-up.

After I arrived it dawned on me that we weren't being welcomed with open arms! A wee while later I realised it was worse than that. Altogether it was a lousy experience. I resigned in 2002–03 and haven't set foot in the place since. But one day I'll tell all!

Do you still call yourself a Libertarian Socialist? — forms of anarchism are the only way ahead.

You have written in the past about the essential working class experience being intimidation, provocation, sarcasm and contempt. To what extent do you still experience this personally? — to a certain extent.

An article in The Guardian *(July 2016) says of you: 'Being a professional irritant is at the heart of how he describes his creative development.' And you are on record as saying, 'Good art is usually dissident.' Do you intend to continue being an irritant and a dissident into old age? Have your motives for writing changed at all as you grow older?* — I do my work as best I can. The only motivation is survival.

You are currently campaigning for the Kurdish people. What led you to this? Of all the injustices that exist in the world today, why did you choose this one to campaign for? — I'm not currently campaigning at all. I don't look for campaigns. I reject that way of looking at it. We learn to deal with injustice in our own individual ways but most of us learn to live with it. The ruling elite and leisured classes come not only to live with injustice they value it as the cost of their own survival which is contingent upon survival of the State itself.

Injustice affects the lower orders in a different way. I use the term 'lower orders' very loosely here; referring to working class people, immigrant groups and diverse minority communities; racial, ethnic, linguistic, religious, and groups such as single parents, people with health issues, learning disabilities. The question of 'choice' remains but the context shifts. Injustice is no longer indirect, but thrust upon us, it is happening to us or those closest to us. Each day is a minefield of exploitation and humiliation, not only for ourselves but for our families and friends. Allowances aren't made for writers. A working class writer is a working class person. In the United Kingdom the reality of class is thrust upon us.

On the situation in Kurdistan itself, perhaps you are thinking about a talk I gave in Edinburgh 2016, at the invitation of Scottish PEN. You should know that as far back as 1990–91 I was invited by Kurdish people to talk at the University of Edinburgh. I accepted the invitation. My interest extended beyond then, at intervals. In 1997 I attended the inaugural Freedom for Freedom of Speech assembly in Istanbul. I launched my novel *Translated Accounts* at a joint benefit night in support of the Stephen Lawrence Family Campaign and the struggle of Kurdish people. The situation in regard to Kurdistan is a nightmare for the political authorities in Europe, USA and beyond. Anyone can read up on what's happening but find your own way: disregard the propaganda, the disinformation, the lack of information, and the downright lies. Be creative and do the obvious: go and check out what Kurdish peoples are saying themselves ('peoples' plural).

How do you define creativity and has your definition of it changed over the years? — I don't think I define 'creativity' other than as an infinite set of activities pursued by any member of humanity. Perhaps in earlier times I might have attempted to find a way of 'arguing' that every human being is creative. It is now forty years since I first had to deal with the work of Noam Chomsky (1977) in a course on the Philosophy of Language. His stuff on 'creativity' irritated me at first. It seemed too constrictive. I realized that I just had to come to terms with reality, that I am a human being after all, and my 'creativity' is a function of that. Wittgenstein made the point that if lions could speak we wouldn't know what they were saying. Yet Wittgenstein's work on 'language games' is very relevant, how they cross boundaries yet remain sealed off — which leads me to field theory and so on. Yet in art...I remember a great short story by Doris Lessing, the South African writer, a rather brilliant story written from the perspective of an actual creature — so there ye are, logic and reason defeated by a good piece of art. Wittgenstein would have approved.

In general, has the nature of your creativity changed as you get older? — no, as with impatient non-swimmers, we just jump in the deep end and swim for dear life. Those of us with a little more patience lower ourselves into the shallow end and paddle about, wondering whether to risk it, but how do we define 'it' is an interesting question.

What aspect of ageing do you fear most? Has this found expression in your creative work? — I don't fear the ageing process itself but I'm kind of flummoxed by the idea of relying on other people, apart from Marie whom I've relied upon for the past 50 years. I accept the right to die.

What, from your own personal experience, have been the most negative aspects of ageing? How have these impacted on your creativity? — I don't find much that is 'negative' at all although younger folk might presume it can hardly be otherwise. Some older people despair, or simply bemoan the fact that things are not, after all 'changing for the better.' This suggests they could have done better themselves, or adopted a different outlook. It applies most regularly to people engaged in party politics from a moral or ethical perspective (rather than selfish or personal interest). They come to suspect they've been party to a fraud or hoax, and maybe discover they've engaged in the fantastic notion that the British political system will evolve, that it will come to alter itself sooner or later, if only we commit to the process in spite of all common sense — a kind of teleological, pre-enlightenment view of existence.

For you, have there been any gifts and unexpected joys that accompany ageing? What are they and have they found their way into your writing? — 'Gifts' and 'joys' relate chiefly, but not wholly, to my family, immediate and wider. I love to watch my grandkids take part in things with other youngsters. I realise that my last three novels have been influenced by them.

What have you been reading recently? — I tend not to read books

individually but as part of a field of interest, most recently trying
to understand some basic factors in the work of Immanuel Kant. I
delved in and around this area, beginning with about four books.
Obviously he was very aware of David Hume's work but he was
also aware of Hutcheson's work on morality. Thomas Reid's position on judgment and perception, and non-Euclidean geometry
would have been of great interest to him if he had known it. Later
Scottish thinkers have made important contributions to Kantian
studies, eg. Kemp-Smith and H. J. Paton. It was through William
Hamilton that Clerk-Maxwell and James Ferrier were introduced
to it.

Before delving into Kant I had been doing the same around Clerk-
Maxwell, enjoying the line back through the Scottish tradition in
philosophy, a tradition which includes seminal thinkers like Des-
cartes, Newton, Shaftesbury, Leibnitz, Spinoza and George Ber-
keley — not to mention George Buchanan, Plato and Pythagoras.
I'm here belabouring the point that the Scottish intellectual tradition is generalist by application, internationalist in approach.

It's not a massive leap to see a connection between Clerk-Maxwell's work, McLaurin's use of Newtononian method, and the
mechanistic implications of Kant's work on The Moral Law. It
occurs to me that this sort of leap may be evidence of advancing
senility. One area of interest from around five years ago concerned
my grandmother from Lewis. Reading into this side of my family
took me in all directions but for a so-called radical like myself it's
been interesting to see how little I knew about our own history. I
always looked forward to retiral age so I could read more. I forgot
that writers don't retire. Nor do we stop reading. If writers do retire it may not be a function of age. I should say that I never need
to stray beyond my own home for books. I have a decent collection,
plus broadband. And if I cannot access something in that way I
make it up, or leave it alone.

*How do you envisage the remaining years of your life? Do you see
yourself continuing to be actively creative into even later life?* — As
I've been suggesting, I see creativity a little differently, as an inseparable aspect of the thought process; in others words we cannot
help but be creative.

Of all the things you have produced as a writer since passing 70 (not necessarily published), what gives you the most satisfaction and pride? — I don't know about 'satisfaction and pride'. Every book is an issue to resolve, yet remains at issue during the editing process. Sometimes the work is never finished. A couple of my published works contain errors that will never be resolved. At the same time I don't wring my hands about it. It's a pity but it cannot be helped. The editorial process has altered drastically in the last fifteen or so years, with the advent of word processing systems. The areas of literary endeavour which appeal to myself have very little space to breathe. There is a lack of knowledge among writers that I find surprising. Many seem unaware of what is possible in literature or why some writers may have felt obliged to develop formally in particular ways, e.g. drama and the problems of time and space. It seems not to occur to some that the central issues of their epoch exist in their own areas. There is an intellectual passivity, a docility; a worrying lack of scepticism, suggesting the dangers predicted by George Davie on the push to specialisation.

What advice would you give to writers who aspire to continue being productive into old age? — there is the practical matter of doing the work: get the first hour or two in every morning "before the day begins". With luck ye might manage more later, but even if ye don't that one solitary hour — preferably two — will keep ye going till tomorrow. A close friend of mine — Chris Harvey — published his first book past the age of 70, and lately has published his second. He's lived fifty years in Scotland and retains his Berkshire accent, having failed abysmally to assimilate to Scottishness. We argued on philosophical points 50 years ago. Nowadays we tend to nod in agreement, but I'm waiting for one of us to double-click on the nod. Our children and now our grandchildren are acquainted; perhaps they argue on other matters.

What haven't I asked you what you would like to say in relation to writing/creativity in later life and the changes that ageing bring? — We just have to keep doing it. Creation is survival. Making art is life. There seems so much to do but I have to confess, it's exciting. Why is that 'confession'? Who gives a fuck, on we go.

Last February (2017) as the matter of 'downsizing' arose:. I began on the books. I have so many books. Get rid of the books, all the ones I don't need; hundreds of them — the other ones I'll keep, hundreds of them too. Plus the files and folders; the letters, the papers, pamphlets, documents. Then the electronic stuff cluttering up the computer! Forget the other stuff, concentrate on the unfinished projects, bring some of them to a conclusion. It applied to this project in particular, taken from the period I worked as a voluntary worker with Clydeside Action on Asbestos in the early 1990s.

Introduction

I began this project back in 1994. I thought of it as a sort of handbook for activists on industrial disease. Casework was at the heart of it. An immediate problem arose, how to deal with particular cases without naming individuals, not only claimants, but doctors and lawyers. Some I could, some I couldn't. I realized then that the project was unworkable and shelved it. Once in a while I opened the folders, looked over what I had and did a little work, then closed them again. Last February I reopened the folders, after how many years, I don't know. But I had turned 70 the year previously. This was it, now or never.

A couple of days later I heard Harry McLuskey had died. His was the first case ever I won, back in 1992. Not only had Harry survived more than twenty five years beyond diagnosis, he remained central to the struggle. As recently as 2015 and now into his 70s he was part of a delegation attending a meeting in the Scottish Parliament, one of a handful suffering asbestos-related diseases. Others present included politicians, lawyers and various interested parties. Harry's delegation was there to support a proposal by a research group that offered a way to help claimants, streamline Government practice and remain within budget. The politicians, lawyers and other interested parties listened attentively, and were respectful. Harry and the delegation returned to Glasgow. Days later word was received that the Scottish Government had rejected the proposal. Nothing much changes. The Scottish government operates like any other, akin to the 'defender' in a civil action, whose first move is deny any claim and reject all proposals to change. They will continue to do this until finally backed into a corner and with no place to turn. In the case of the people suffering the effects of asbestos abuse the Scottish Government returned the burden of proof to them, and their supporters. The unspoken dictat: 'Prove to us that we have no choice but to implement this proposal.'

The matter won't end there. People like Harry McLuskey never give up. He was an example in two basic respects: 1] Asbestos-related diseases aren't terminal unless so diagnosed. Mesotheliomas are terminal; others aren't. 2] People need your support, regardless.

While it is misguided to generalise on what is possible for the rest of us, one man so diagnosed with Mesothelioma played a prominent part in campaigning. Most so diagnosed were at the later stages. One woman down to less than five stone was unable to move from her bed, but managed to voice her support in the fight for justice.

And 'the fight for justice' is how most people see it. But it's a difficult fight. Whether Holyrood, Whitehall or Washington DC, the denial of justice is institutionalised.

You may also wish to consult https://en.wikipedia.org/wiki/James_Kelman

www.theguardian.com/books/2017/aug/05/james-kelman-my-writing-day

6. DIFFERENT AUTUMN VOICES

In the Introduction I pointed out that, as well as the established, full-time writers, such as those interviewed for this book, there are many more part-time writers. Throughout Scotland open mic sessions, poetry slams and performance poetry events take place. Similarly, writers' circles, clubs and workshops abound in Scotland. Typically, quite a high proportion of their members are either unpublished or self-published, or with a limited list of publications; and others have no interest in publication or in selling their work, but simply enjoy creative writing and the kind of discussion and friendships that being in a group of like-minded people offers. A significant proportion of members of groups of this kind do not start writing until late in life, often after retirement. Their creativity matters too, not only to themselves, but to society in general. The Autumn Voices *Over 60 Writing Competition was run with such people in mind.*

THE AUTUMN VOICES OVER 60 WRITING COMPETITION

It was planned from an early stage that part of the *Autumn Voices* project would be the *Autumn Voices* Over 60 Writing Competition. This was administered through the Scottish Association of Writers. Entries were received during June and July 2017 and the winners announced at the SAW event at the Westerwood Hotel, Cumbernauld in September. The competition rules asked for any form of prose — life writing, non-fiction, short story, with a maximum 2,000 words. The entry must not have been published before. In addition to small cash prizes, the winners would be published in *Autumn Voices*.

RESULTS of the *Autumn Voices* Over 60 Writing Competition, 2017:
1st Place: 'Morning — the Fishing Village' by Jeanne Dron
2nd Place: 'Travel with Theos Lines' by Morelle Smith
3rd Place: 'Love and Revolution' by Catriona Courtier
Highly Commended: 'Sixty Seconds in the Death of Henry' by James McPherson
Commended: 'Krakatoa' by Ellen Dickie

GENERAL COMMENTS BY THE ADJUDICATOR

The competition was adjudicated by me. There were 40 entries, all of a good standard. The entries demonstrated the same thing that the main interviews demonstrate — that sixty or seventy plus is a wonderful place to be if you are a writer. You have more material to draw upon than ever before, which you can write about from a wider perspective and with a more balanced judgment than when younger; and you can write about old age with an insider knowledge that those of fewer years do not possess.

In many of the entries the voice and viewpoint of elderly men and women, their thoughts, physical problems and worries, their losses and bereavements were recounted with a convincing authority, often with an accepting, self-deprecating humour, gently poking fun at their own infirmities.

Other entries were about none of these things, but simply showed that a late flowering of talent is definitely possible.

Jeanne Dron's winning entry was a wonderful description of an East coast fishing village, somewhere near Aberdeen, in about 1940 — Dylan Thomas meets Grassic Gibbon.

1ST PLACE: MORNING — THE FISHING VILLAGE

Jeanne Dron

Take a deep breath —

The air is crisp and salty with the smell of drying seaweed, rich with the warm earthy dampness of the distant moor. You can't see it in the dark, but the first hint of burning peat is seeping and swirling up from the cottage chimneys by the shore, mingling with the scent of purple heather on the hill and the sharp fresh sweetness of early spring.

Inside, people are awake. Lighting lamps, dressing, packing provisions and whispering farewells before, all along the steep passages and narrow streets, doors creak open, flashing warm yellow lantern-light as shadowy figures pass out into the still dark morning; feet clattering on cobbles, voices softly yawning.

Now, mumbling greetings as they gather in the glimmer of pre-dawn light down on the beach, the wool-clad men of the households set to work. Here, where there is no comforting harbour, but only the unprotected open shore, ruled by wind and weather, gulls rise screaming from their sleep, anticipating the morning catch, while worn boots labour, crunching wetly through sand and shingle, as the nets and lobster pots are thrown aboard.

Then, with knotted shoulders braced against salty timber and biceps burning at the ropes, they push and shove the heavy wooden boats, hulls churning from their settled bed of stones, down toward the sea.

So another day begins.

One by one, calling voices fade into the splash of feet on wet rippled sand. Water swirling around canvas-bound legs as they leap in amongst the creels, crushing the tang from fronds of crusty dried seaweed. Then, oars clunking into place, they're away; pulling, muscles straining, into the surf. Each boat finding its path through the tideline rush and tumble of waves and out into the deep, deep green-black, cold and cruel ocean.

And now the long haul while daylight creeps up over the horizon, hands thick and calloused from the grip and roll of the old smoothed wood as oars dip, backs bend and muscles tighten. Heave and creak, heave and creak: hauling the perilous wooden craft through the wild waters to the fishing ground day after day. And all the while their wives wash and cook and do the endless crofting chores, and needles flying, tightly knit the village pattern into the lifesaving warmth of their spouses' next woollen jersey.

There, on the empty beach an old man now stands alone. The sailor's shouts fading with the cries of wheeling gulls. But still he watches; until the clunk of oars and the power of strong back muscles working against the tide have left a shadow on his mind, against the gentle rush and rattle of shore bound waves.

His arms longed for the work they could no longer accomplish. His tired hands itched for the smooth roll of the oar and ached for the feel of the silk-worn wood. It was this time, when the sun crept up over the horizon and the sounds faded away, that were the best and the worst.

After a lifetime of longing to rest, away from the toil, the danger and the exhaustion; now, now that time was all he had, it was ironic how that slow, powerful rhythm of the oars pulled at his heart, how the very smell of the fishing wafted deep into his soul.

So, what was there left for a man no longer needed, a man whose tasks were complete; an empty home, a table bare but for a half drunk mug of cold tea? The boats were almost out of sight.

Breakfast held no interest for one without appetite: yet his memory was ripe with the longing for it, rich with the need for porridge and bacon, for thick slices of fresh baked bread, of yellow butter, new from the churn and hunks of precious cheese. And there it was again; the rock of the boat, the cries of the gulls, the cloth-wrapped piece in his salty fingers and that longing for site of the shore and the safety of home.

Yet now, with the safety and comfort of home all that Dougal Cameron had, he wanted none of it.

Up the street in the second house on the left, Mrs. Maclean was scrubbing the table, worn and scored by generations of thoughtless men and careless children. She knew every crack and scrape and stain. There, was where Rosie left the beet lying all night, and here, the score where Victor dragged that thumping great creel he was mending.

This was a table that worked for a living, the hub of their home. The scrubbing brush was old too, smaller than the one she used on the floor, its bristles worn almost flat over the years. But there was no need to get down on her knees to do the floor today. She would make the bed; just the one bed now the children had homes of their own. She would tidy and sort the washing, feed the chickens and then, when the table was dry, she would have her tea; her skeins and balls of wool spread across the time worn surface. Then she would cast on the first of a new pair of socks. The thought brought a smile to her round face. Last night had seen her sewing up the jumper she had worked on for many months, the complicated pattern denoting her man. And her thoughts turned to Molly Stevens further up the hill.

Molly was, at that very moment, running tentative fingers across the pattern of salt hardened stitches that had identified her husband's body when it washed up thirty miles down the coast. The men had buried him in his best, but this jersey, she had washed and dried as if it would be worn again, because she didn't know what else to do with it. Though it would take a week of soaking and soaping to bring it back to life. That was within her power. She knew exactly how to bring the empty sweater back. But not her Gordon; he was gone.

For now though, still stiff with the remnants of the sea, she folded it, pulling open the creaking, hefty oak drawer and smoothed the dark and lonely symbol of her life, down amongst the socks. Everything there, smelling of the wash she had been so proud of until now; now when she only longed for the smell of him. Gone, washed away. Her man.

Mrs. Mclean's needles were clicking now, four thin shafts to make the circle. The sound would accompany all her resting, waiting, even walking time. Because the weather ruled their lives, and the cold was their enemy. And she knew how to make the neatest, warmest, most watertight, life sustaining woollens to keep her husband safe.

The old man had left the beach, climbing the steep hill behind the village and looking out towards the horizon once again. This time he searched for signs. A tumble of clouds or a soft whisp; a shadow on the sea, a dimpling where a shoal of fish gathered; choppy waters or the shadow of rain heading their way.

His life no longer depended on the weather. Those others could see the signs for themselves. But how to change the things that made you, the thoughts and actions that had been your life?

Billy Turner was out and running, barefoot, hardfoot; running to meet his day. The cow would be waiting, anxious by the gate, udders heavy and sore for want of his pulling hands. And he was late. The cats would have gathered in the barn, mewling and hungry for the smell of the milk that squirted wet and warm, splashing into the pail. Hungry for a drip, dribble or spill. Sometimes, pointing a teat at one, he laughed at its look of shock mingled with satisfaction, as, with an impossibly long pink tongue, it licked itself clean.

Later there would be school, but he was happy there in the barn, where the smell of fresh hay mingled with the odd sweetness of cow; his forehead resting warm against her soft flank. Where the gentle sound of her munching mingled with the pleading of cats. Kittens running, chasing and tumbling. Outside, the cockerel crowing his importance to his chuckie hens.

In any weather, this was the place to be. Even on those days when the gales drove the cow to hide amongst the gorse on the hill and he had to trudge through the mud, leaning against the wind in search of her. Even then, slipping and skidding with her eyes rolling in fear, they knew the warmth and safety of the barn was waiting.

Recently though, his unruly thoughts had changed direction. Cows and hens, foxes, eagles and stoats, rabbits, traps, ropes and kittens had given way to one single image. A smile from Kirsty Morgan.

That smile, having been directed around the room and at no one in particular, Kirsty's thoughts were elsewhere; amongst the secrets sewn into the patchwork quilt on her bed, revealed mistakenly as her mother searched through Gramie's button box. The scrape of tin against wood and bone, ending with a sigh as she pulled one free, remembering. The look on her mother's face speaking to young Kirsty, of longing and romance.

It had been covered with a yellow cotton print. The same material as the patch Kirsty now ran her fingers across, stitched neatly into the bed cover. It must have been a summer dress, buttons at the neck perhaps. What memories might lie behind that sigh? And what other unknown memories lay silent in the many squares of faded fabric beneath her fingers, warming her through the winter nights?

Greer, grey hair wild on the windy moor, lifted the rabbit to her belt and reset the trap. There were another three amongst the trees, higher up. She tutted, seeing Dougal in the distance, still looking out to sea. With the cow milked, the hens fed and the tatties already hoed, she was impatient at such idleness. For her, time raced by. How could he waste it? She smelt the coming rain and still needed to get up the hill to dig the peats.

One trap was empty. But two rabbits hung from the low branch, supper in waiting, for collection on her return, as Greer trudged on up toward the diggings. The empty creel rubbing a sore on her shoulder. But for now, she needed the woollen head-scarf to protect her ears against the wind that made walking all the harder. With no man to help in the digging, Greer's limbs would be yellow dyed and mud splattered by the time she had filled the creel. Perhaps by then the wind would have lessened, freeing the scarf to pad her sore shoulder on the way back.

Then there would be soup. The smell, rich and warming as she opened the door. Her tiny croft welcoming her home, to rest before she started her day's work. At the weaving.

Jeanne, aged 70, lives in Fife. She worked as a photographer for the Ministry of Defence both in London and Rosyth Dockyard before having her two children, and later managing a conservatory design centre. A self-taught artist, she has been drawing, painting and creating for as long as she can remember. Jeanne then added creative writing to her repertoire, joining the Inverkeithing Writers' group and then the Southeast Scotland branch of the Society of Children's Book Writers and Illustrators. She is currently working on a children's novel, *Boodika Bron and the House of Horrors*.

'Any writing skills I have, I owe to the constructive comments and discussions held with other writers in the two groups I have belonged to. Am I inspired by this competition? Absolutely. Confirmation that you are on the right track is invaluable.'

Jeanne explained some of her thinking behind 'Morning — The Fishing Village': 'Simpler times and situations help provide a clarity that is confused in our complex modern lives. This piece is reflecting on our astounding human ability to adapt to different circumstances and make the most of them, however difficult. To form our own place in the world and create the symbols that comfort and support us. In the long term, those circumstances mould us into the person we become; like it or not. Flexibility fades with time.'

Jeanne believes strongly that, given the opportunity, older people have a valuable contribution to make to society.

'In the history of the world, how many devastating mistakes could have been avoided if lessons from the past had not been ignored or forgotten? Not to mention the skills that have been lost and those it is still possible to preserve. In our own lifetime we have seen too much wisdom entirely dismissed in favour of fresh new ideas. Perhaps the opportunity has come to combine forces. Your *Autumn Voices* project could be the start of a movement to bring that collective experience and understanding into the mainstream. I believe there are a lot of fine minds out there, just grumbling to themselves about the state of the world, when they have it in them to make a difference given a combined voice.'

2nd PLACE: TRAVEL WITH THEOS LINES
(where the management takes a personal interest in your journey)

Morelle Smith

Some dreams glow with a numinous energy. These are the ones that get me crossing my fingers, touching wood, making offerings of fallen oranges — for only their perfect ripeness is suitable for the gods. How after all do we make gestures of gratitude to the gods in the modern world? No it's not something we do too often, is it? So I revert to more ancient ways of giving thanks, because they feel authentic to me, though I draw the line at sacrificing a cockerel to Asklepios, the god of healing dreams. Somehow I cannot quite believe that any god would wish for the death of another living creature. Besides, I don't want blood on my hands.

Other dreams often deal with the go-betweens, the ones that transport or accompany us, from the waking to the dream or mythic realms — and back again — the guides, the ones that know the paths or straits that link the worlds. And, although we have to trust them, we also know there may be negotiations, deals, and bargaining. Charon is not the only ferryman who needs a coin.

In my dream last night, the bus driver turns on the charm, is almost flirtatious in that way, you know, where they're being helpful and accommodating, then put a slab of icing on top, or extra cream in your coffee, it's that rolling of the eyes, that — what wouldn't I do for you, lovely lady — kind of attitude. It's one I respond to with a smile and an inclination of the head at the same time both acknowledging the compliment and letting it run past me like water, not holding on to it, not taking it up like the end of a rope and winding it in. I'm nudged into a role I don't really want to play but feel it would be churlish to refuse outright.

When I was very young I used to take this kind of compliment quite seriously. It was the way I met my first husband, he was selling tickets at an open air event I went to. I was meeting up with friends inside the grounds, but I arrived on my own. The ticket-seller, a good-looking young man, said to me — I'll see you after the show. It was a simple compliment, a throwaway remark, but I believed both in the sentiment expressed and the power of words.

I went up to him afterwards. It's possible that he didn't even remember making that remark, never mind intending it to have consequences. Well, it did. My first husband's shyness was masked by a show of bravado which I took to be his authentic nature. What else could he have done, on seeing this young woman coming up to him after the show, except continue where his throwaway remark left off, and arrange a date with me?

In those days, banks — he worked in a bank — were bastions of tradition and security and upheld the status quo. Short hair was obligatory for male employees. He wore his hair as long as he could, with a thick fringe flopping over his eyes.

A bit like the bus driver's, come to think of it. After marrying someone as a direct result of an admiring but light-hearted comment, I'd been dismayed to discover the deep perturbations and the murky water underneath the sunlit surface. I don't mean that he was malicious, no, he was incapable of holding grudges, but he was deeply confused and this confusion tended to spill over into intimate areas of our contact, leading to a detachment which he did not mean as coldness but which was felt by me as a lack of interest. I much preferred it when the more sunny and light-hearted side of his nature reappeared — the side that had first attracted me to him. He was kind and self-absorbed. I too was self-absorbed. He talked about his career, where he wanted to go. When I thought of mine and the direction that it would take me in, it was clear that our paths would have to diverge. His job took him to a small town in the north of Scotland. I returned to my home town, to study at university. He stayed on in the cultural desert — as I saw it — where the newspaper he worked for catered to more traditional, straightforward prejudices.

This left me with a deep-seated suspicion of casual compliments and a belief that they covered over personal doubts that the speaker wished only to avoid. My other reason for wanting to sidestep the implied invitation of the bus driver is that I very much wanted to get on that bus. His invitation had been to do with the future — if you can't get a seat on this bus, then I'll personally drive another one for you, take you where you want to go — as soon as I can. But he knows it's this bus I need to get — I've already bought a ticket, so there has to be a seat for me. I have a connection to make — perhaps a flight home, I'm not sure, but whatever it is, this is the bus I need to take. I've no interest in 'some other time' just as I have no interest in personal favours, however well meant.

All these years ago, the remark thrown out by the young man with the floppy hair at the ticket desk took me away from my intended course — I'd been planning to go to university in a few months' time. Instead, we headed for a shared life in a tiny flat, taking whatever jobs we could get — for what did that matter, as long as it paid the rent and we could be together? In those days — ah those days! — it was possible to get jobs, rents were low and we earned enough to pay the bills. We lived in a lovely part of town with Georgian architecture and leafy gardens in the centre of curved circuses and cobbled avenues.

We enjoyed each other's company or so I remember. Having a companion distracted me from the boredom of my job and my lack of interest in the office topics of conversation. But I still had a nagging doubt that something important was being sidelined and neglected. It was not until his job relocation, when we had to leave the leafy grandeur and the Georgian architecture, that it came home to me that this was not, absolutely not, where I wanted to be in my life.

I realised I had to get out fast and I re-applied to university. I'd made a lucky escape. I had nearly sleep-walked into a life that would have been no kind of life at all. For your life needs to engage you, demand things of you, require that you face challenges and work with them, doesn't it?

We rely on bus drivers, train drivers, ferrymen and pilots, to get us where we want to go. They are all Hermes' helpers and they have very differing personalities, perhaps reflecting Hermes' quicksilver and ever-changing nature. Here in Greece, in the land of the gods, these mercurial assistants can be friendly and helpful, as well as curt or impatient with someone who does not speak their language and finds it difficult to convey where it is she wants to go. And sometimes this is because I hardly know myself. Would this be a good place or would that destination be better? When one is exploring, it's often hard to be decisive, with clear goals in mind. There are as many imponderables as there are possible routes to take. But that's not for Hermes to decide. The drivers simply want to know where you are going. Sometimes decisions have to be made quickly, despite uncertainty.

Last night's bus driver offered the possibility of a distraction from the route. Not from maliciousness or desire to lead me down a false path but from — as far as I could see — the very nature of the flighty god with winged sandals on his feet. His embrace of yes and no, his delight in crossroads, in quick decisions, never seen as irreversible, the separations in his nature are not of life or death quality, they are made lightly, in the knowledge that backtracking is always possible, that taking yet another turning may seem like going back and yet can still be going on and that sometimes going on will lead you precisely to the place you thought you'd left behind. For he is also the god of backroads and alleyways, of narrow entrances and unexpected turnings. He might ruffle the sea surface, giving a sly prod to one vessel, while holding back another, but he is not the ruler of the ocean's depths, he is not Poseidon, who knows currents and underwater waves and deep-sea monsters. Hermes plays with surfaces, he trails fingers in the water, and above all he loves movement. He is the master of the liminal realm where elements and textures, moods and relationships overlap and merge.

Last night's bus driver made a charming gesture — but only because there seemed to be a doubt that there was a place for me on the bus. In my experience, doubt is a reliable companion. All is going well — you have your ticket, you're about to get on board — and then there is some unexpected hitch that you did not foresee. How many times has this happened? To someone as maladroit as myself, when it comes to life's practicalities, whether wrestling with a door handle, trying to find my way from one place to another in unfamiliar streets, particularly when you do not know the language, it's so frequent an occurrence as to be customary, even comical.

So I am well acquainted with the hand of doubt slipping into mine. For Hermes has as much allegiance with no as yes, he has no prejudice, to tilt scales in one direction or another. But he spied division in me and exploited it. Then he saw that this time I was clear — this time, I knew where I was headed. This time, the enticements of dark hair and a sunny, appreciative comment, they were not the road itself. All these fascinating characters you may spend time with, they are not the roads you travel on. Even if you sometimes think — ah, here is a harbour in the sunlight, I could stay here, make a life here — you will always — at some point — have to raise the anchor and set off. Don't ask me why. That's simply how it is.

I'm not saying that there is no Ithaca. But it may not be as you remember it. After all these journeys made with Ithaca in mind, with Ithaca as your goal — when you arrive it confronts you with itself and you realise that places too, are on a journey.

There's controversy over the precise location of the real Ithaca, the home and starting-point and destination of Odysseus. This seems fitting to me for surely mythic contours have to be a little imprecise?

But when we leave this 'once upon a time' and return to clocks and Everyday — as it seems we always do — won't some other dark-haired ticket-seller catch our eye one day, won't we strike a deal with some dream bus driver, board another ferry, cross another wine-dark sea?

*

Morelle Smith studied English and French at Edinburgh University and currently lives near Edinburgh. She is a writer of poetry, fiction, essays and travel articles. Her poems, stories and articles have been published in magazines, periodicals and websites, and included in anthologies such as *Anthology of Scottish Women Poets, Scottish Literature in the 20th Century* and *Modern Scottish Women Poets*. She has won prizes for her poetry and fiction, and her poems have appeared on transport systems in Glasgow and Edinburgh as well as in exhibitions in collaboration with visual artists. She has lived and worked in various parts of Europe, with three Writers' Residencies in France, one in Serbia and one in Switzerland. Her work has been translated into French, Romanian, Slovenian, Bulgarian and Albanian.

Her publications include *Deepwater Terminal* (diehard, 1998), *Streets of Tirana, Almost Spring* (ORA Publishing, Tirana 2004), *The Way Words Travel* (UK Authors Press 2005), *Time Loop*

(Playback Editions 2010) and Gold Tracks, Fallen Fruit (Cestrian Press 2011). More recently, Morelle has published travel memoirs, *Tirana Pages* (2013) and *Every Shade of Blue* (2015, both Kairos Press), travel articles 'Open Roads' and 'Secret Destinations' (2016, Bibliotheca Universalis, Bucharest) and *Shaping the Water Path* (poetry collection, 2017, diehard Press, Callander). And in 2014 she received the Audience Award during the Terra Poetica Festival in Kyiv, Ukraine.

7. IN THE DORIC

Sheila Templeton

Sheena Blackhall

Sheila and Sheena were both brought up in North East Scotland and both write poetry in the Doric (as well as in English). They are working on a joint translation of Jane Eyre *into the Doric.*

SHEILA TEMPLETON (Age 76)

I had a nomadic childhood, ranging from Aberdeenshire to Dar-es-Salaam. My Dad was a railway worker. I wouldn't say we were poor. We got by, but with not much to spare. I remember my mother kept me off school one day because there was no jam to put in my pieces and she didn't want the family to get a showing up. My Dad first worked on railway maintenance at Dyce in Aberdeenshire, then became a ganger, in charge of a gang of maintenance workers and we moved around in various places in the north of Scotland. He saw an advertisement for a better railway job in what was then Tanganyika, applied for it and got the job — which was how we came to be in Dar-es-Salam. I was seven then. He was a clever man, but had to leave school at twelve in order to contribute to the family income.

In 1951, when I was nearly ten, we returned to Dyce to stay with my grandmother for my dad's six months of leave. At the end of that time, she asked me if I wanted to go back to East Africa or stay in Dyce. I said I preferred Dyce and she persuaded my parents that I needed to stay to get a proper schooling. Although it was what I'd said I wanted, I'm not sure that the ten year old child I was actually understood the full implications of that decision. It hurt me deeply that my parents agreed to it and returned to Tanganyika with my brother and sister, but without me. My grandmother was a very forceful woman, of course. Affecting me much more strongly than the colours, smells and excitement of Africa was this abandonment at an early age, or what I perceived as such. Yet looking back at my whole life, it probably was the right decision for me. I loved living in Dyce in that household, a big extended family where I felt safe and part of the place and its heritage. I think my grandmother knew me very well and intuitively realised that this was a better life for me. And there was no question that it was the right decision in terms of my education.

My mother, brother and sister returned in 1953 because of the Mau Mau crisis, although my father stayed on until his next leave in 1955. Then my family again returned to East Africa, leaving me still in Dyce. It has a lot to do with who I am. It wasn't until I was forty that I talked to my mother properly about it and learned how upset she had been and that she cried for most of the train journey to Southampton. Hearing that from my mother was very healing.

By the time I was in sixth year at school I loved writing and I used to hand in to my teacher extra pieces I had written. The idea that I could write poetry never occurred to me. Poetry was not something anyone I knew did; it was a sort of foreign idea and slightly pretentious to most folk in North East Scotland, not part of the culture. Even to my grandmother, who had been a primary school teacher and who loved poetry, the idea of anyone she knew actually writing it would not have crossed her mind. How Jessie Kesson managed it I don't know. She was from a very poor background and without much education. She must have been an extraordinarily strong and courageous person. The thought of showing anything I had written to a publisher was a completely alien notion. It never occurred to me.

When I went to Aberdeen University I planned to study English Literature, but I didn't like the course which was heavily weighted towards criticising texts. So I opted to do Honours History.

A thirty-year career in secondary teaching followed, based in West Lothian and Edinburgh. I became a History teacher, got promotion as a Head of Department and then did a 'side-ways' move to be a Principal Teacher of Guidance. During that time I had a son, Aleks. He is now thirty-eight and works in electronic music... his passion. His father and I separated when he was nearly nine. I took early retirement from teaching when I was fifty-one and signed up for a diploma course in Counselling at Glasgow University. In a 'light-bulb' moment I realised I didn't want to make this a second career. Instead, I enrolled for a writing course. The ideas had been bubbling away beneath the surface, but it was the first time I had written creatively since my school and university days. It poured out of me. I had written poetry and fiction as a teenager, but never thought this could be a career. It wasn't until this stage in my life that I began to write professionally. The years since then have been a revelation, in that I have not only had many poems published, won poetry prizes, had poems read on BBC Scotland, but also I regularly give poetry readings. [Sheila's full schedule and her success were well illustrated. I interviewed her on 30th November 2016. She had in her bag, ready for delivery, her entry for the annual James McCash Scots Poetry Competition — a competition she had already won twice. Then, the following day, one of her poems was published in *The Herald*.]

I enjoyed the first few years of just scribbling like mad without any weight of expectation on me. In 1998, at the age of 57, I finally got something published. It gave my confidence and self-esteem a big boost. However, once you start being noticed and building a reputation, win a few prizes, get invited to give readings and so forth, it's a whole new ball game. Expectations are set up, both in yourself and in others, which has made the writing process harder for me. Now, every time I face a blank page, I think, 'Will this be good enough?' So, that's another challenge for me, something to overcome. As far as I can see, the best way to get over it is to think back to how it was when I wrote something purely because I wanted to write it and focus hard on that. It's difficult to do that, though, when you are given commissions. Steven King talks about 'letting the boys in the boiler-room do the work' — letting the subconscious mind solve the problems and overcome the block. I agree with that. Going for a walk, in nature especially, seems to allow the subconscious mind to get to work and to offer up new thoughts. I find it helps to go out of the house to write — there are too many diversions in my home.

My main area of interest in writing is poetry, in both Scots and English, but I have also had some short stories published. When I was living in Troon in Ayrshire I joined the Ayr Writers' Club. A lot of the emphasis was on writing stories for women's magazines and children's stories and I had a wee shot at that and had a romantic short story published and a children's story in one of the D.C. Thompson publications. I also entered the Scottish Association of Writers competitions. I had a go at just about every category of writing and won a few prizes at the SAW annual event, including first prize in the poetry competition (2002) and first prize in the children's novel competition (2003). But although I enjoy writing fiction, I decided to concentrate on poetry. My head prefers only one hat at a time.

I currently live in Glasgow, but I come from Aberdeenshire, so when I write in Scots, it's usually North-East Scots, the Doric

Scots. I feel most at ease, 'truer' somehow, writing in Scots, though I write in English too. I haven't used Doric to speak for fifty years, not in any uninhibited way. Whether it's a different mind process from writing in English depends on how deeply immersed in it I am. Doric is embedded in my childhood memories and formative experiences. I remember childhood in Doric phrases. I have a CD of my grandmother speaking it and I listen to that from time to time. I'm not hard-wired to write fluently in Scots. Writing poetry in Scots is different, though, because you can take your time over it.

I like to write in Scots the way that people actually speak. My favourite poet writing in Scots today is Sheena Blackhall. I'm a big fan of her work. She uses Doric as she speaks it...and she has a wonderful, wide ranging vocabulary in North-East Scots. Reading Lewis Grassic Gibbon's work when I was young also had a big influence on me. He doesn't actually use Scots words very much, but he uses rhythm and sound to convey the sense that's it in Scots, even though the words are in English. Jessie Kesson's work was also an influence. I wish I had known her, but I didn't find her work until after her death. We did not study either of these writers, either at school or university in Aberdeen in the 60s. Amazing that they could be so ignored! Though I believe Lewis Grassic Gibbon is now on the Higher English syllabus.

When I was a child we spoke our broad Scots all the time, then in school we had to speak 'proper' English. Even my grandmother, a primary teacher at our village school, did exactly the same. An English friend, looking at some of my poems in Scots, said to me with complete sincerity, 'I didn't realise you were bilingual.' There is an argument that North-East Scots is another language, not a dialect, because it is so different from other forms of Scots...the actual vocabulary is different. I'm not sure about that, though certainly a lot of vocabulary is different in Doric.

I've not lived in the North-East now for a long time, so my own vocabulary in Scots is now much diminished from when I was a child. And even then my vocabulary was much less than say, my grandmother's. I remember her going over a passage with me from the 19th-century novel *Johnny Gibb of Gushetneuk*, for a school project...and some of that even then was like a foreign language to me. I mean...*nowt* meaning cattle; *hummel-doddies* meaning mittens! Who could know that? I love rediscovering words I knew well in childhood, becoming reacquainted with them, putting them into poems. There's a richness in Scots which is not as available in English. The words are juicier in Scots!

I am very interested in the themes of parenting, with all the attendant issues and emotions from childbirth to teenage years. Before moving to Glasgow nine years ago, I worked with parents as Poet in Residence at the Harbour Arts Centre, Irvine, in an innovative project enabling parents to write poems about their children. Another theme I write about is the experience of being a woman, and relationships. After moving to Glasgow I was invited to participate in the Living Voices initiative — a national programme developed by the Scottish Poetry Library and the Scottish Storytelling Centre. It offers older people, usually in care homes, activities that use a mix of story, song and poetry to prompt conversation, reminiscence and creative response. From 2012–14 I travelled to Aberdeen once a month to do this. More recently I have collaborated with A.C. Clarke and Maggie Rabatski in translating each other's poems — Maggie's from Gaelic, Anne Clarke's from English and mine from the Doric. I had to think a lot more than usual. It stretched me in new directions and really getting to know another person's work has developed my own writing.

Soon after taking early retirement from teaching I joined a Heartfulness meditation course and then started daily meditation. Through meditation I learned to slow down and listen to what was in my heart. I've been doing it for twenty-three years, both on my own and in groups. I think it is necessary to have a good look at yourself and meditation helped me do this. It gives me a way of facing myself. For me, it's the only way to live, to be able to do that and to realise who you really are, rather than the person you have invented. One of the big shocks in my life was to discover that training as a counsellor and helping people professionally wasn't what I wanted to do. I'd always believed that's who I was, so this was a shock to my system. That's when I began listening to my heart and found my first creative writing class. But it is one of my core beliefs that, if you can get inside a person's feelings, then the door is open to the end of anger and hatred and the beginning of understanding and forgiveness.

I define creativity as facing the fear of going inside yourself and coming out with what you find — facing myself and having the courage to express what I find. As a child I would only sing if I could hide under the table. It's rather the same with poetry — making my inner self public. It's also about going back in memory and discovering things afresh, being surprised by them.

A lot of my creative and personal development has been about overcoming low self-esteem and finding that missing confidence and self-belief. The first time I joined a writers' group, at my first meeting I was shaking all over at the thought of saying out loud my name and that I wanted to be a writer. Up till that moment I had kept my desire to write a secret. It was a huge step forward for me to give witness that I intended to be a writer and then dare to put something of myself on paper. When I've met people I had been at school with, often if they've come to a launch of one of my poetry collections, they said they had been amazed at the imaginative things I had written. And yet, at the time, I never thought of myself as a writer. Parents and grandparents didn't give out much praise in those days in case you got 'too big for your boots.' Low self-esteem was considered an attractive quality in a child. In that sort of mental climate, it never crossed my mind to send off anything I'd written to newspapers or magazines. I had to wait until I got early retirement before I had the time, the money and the belief in myself to think of myself as a writer. It was still a struggle, though. I still harbour fears that people might laugh at my pathetic efforts. The process of working my way through that informs my writing and provides the necessary tension in my poetry. As I get older I care less about what people think of me and that helps counteract the stresses of trying to maintain high standards. Reading at Mirrorball, for example, where really high level poets read, still makes me nervous, but I'm beginning to get on top of this.

On an Arvon course I was sitting next to Liz Lochhead. We were both working away and I had completely dried up. I turned to her and said, 'I don't know what I'm doing here.' She looked at me and said, 'So?' I was shocked. I had been expecting sympathy. It took me quite a long time to understand the importance of what she had said to me — that this was normal, that established writers like herself experienced the same droughts. Her 'So?' was a huge learning experience for me. She had paid me the compliment of responding to me as she might have to any established writer.

After the Arvon course something changed in me. I became more interested in the feedback from what I had written than in my own feelings about having my work criticised. I was able to separate my personal feelings from the objective lessons to be learned. I think everyone who wants to write well has to get to that point where the quality of what they write has to matter more to them than their own hurt feelings.

I have always been an avid reader. When I was a child I took a library book out almost every day. And if we visited somebody's house, I would head for the bookshelves. I read a lot of poetry, of course. At school all the poets we studied were male poets who didn't write about topics close to women. Then I discovered female poets like Liz Lochhead, Mary Oliver, Kathleen Jamie and loads of others. Reading them liberated me from intimidating preconceptions of what poets had to write about. Up till then I didn't believe that anything that interested me could be a legitimate topic for poetry. There has been a male establishment tendency to look down on writing about ordinary domestic stuff. Once I got over that, it was a huge breakthrough for me. I tend to read the poets who write like I write. It's a sort of affirmation that it's OK to write the kind of things I do.

Has the nature of my creativity changed? Well, it's blossomed because I now have the time, a pension and the confidence and self-belief. I'm still developing hugely, I think. Starting late has meant that I have a lot of stuff that's been waiting to be written about, and a lot of life experience to draw on. I'm never short of ideas. It's sitting down and turning them into something more substantial that's difficult for me.

My motives for writing have changed, too, but not through ageing, but through being published and being commissioned to write things. I have moved from writing about whatever was in my head to being more discriminating. Perhaps I need to go back to my former ways and just see what comes. I have always liked writing about nature. Now I try to move from pure description to connecting it to other things.

When my cousin and then my younger sister died in fairly quick succession, I became depressed and quite fearful for myself. Writing about it and processing the whole thing has been very helpful and healing. Now that I am over that, I see myself continuing to be creative for as long as I am alive. Another element in that healing process has been that Larry Butler, a good friend of mine, invited me to join the Die-a-Log group — eight of us talking about anything we felt like that was related to death and dying. This has been enormously helpful to me, as it's a topic we don't talk about easily in our western culture.

I fear becoming helpless and particularly being unable to communicate. I haven't written about this yet. I feel that, if I dwell on it, I might somehow contribute to it happening. On the other hand, the poet Vicki Feaver said that some of the best writing comes when you write about the things you like to keep hidden, the things you are ashamed of, or frightened of. That's something I've taken mental note of. Actually I have written about this in a poem about my grandmother — after she'd had a stroke and was regularly given tea with milk by her carer. She hated milk in her tea, but couldn't communicate this.

I don't like my vocabulary being less than it used to be. These days I sometimes have to fumble for the right word. The other downside of ageing for me, at the moment is having to rest more. I can't take my body for granted like I used to.

The positive aspect is that I'm not so worried about what other people think of me. The big black birds sitting in the branches of the tree of my mind have become smaller and less fierce. And that's a great boon. And just being able to say 'No' for the first time in my life. I used to agree to things and take on things purely so that people would like me — well, not purely, but that was a part of it. Now I don't do things, or spend time with people unless I really want to, which is a great positive factor of ageing for me.

My grandmother was my role model as regards ageing. She was creative and had a very active mind. She read a lot; she loved crossword puzzles and whist. Moreover, she was a woman who'd had a career which wasn't all that common in NE Scotland in those days. Because of her, it never occurred to me that I wouldn't have a career of some sort. She was really active until about 91. I also learned from her the idea of looking out for your neighbours. It was a core belief of hers. Although that is not directly to do with creativity, it is relevant because it is part of what shaped me and made me who I am; and this emerges through my poetry and my creativity.

My advice to people who want to continue being creative in later life would be: work at and maintain the important relationships with the people you love and who love you. World-weary cynicism that can accompany old age is counter-productive to creativity. The opposite of this is a kind of awe and innocence. Never stop being curious. Always retain your sense of wonder.

A sample of writing done since passing 70

I chose the following poem for Robin's book for a lot of reasons. It's in Scots. I find that more and more I am drawn to write in the language of my childhood in Aberdeenshire. Often, a first thought, a first feeling for a poem will come to me in Scots. I don't speak much in my native Scots...a long career in education meant that I always had to communicate in English...and I haven't lived in Aberdeenshire since I was in my early twenties. But a lot of my thinking happens in my gweed Scots tongue! And 'workin men' were such a feature of my childhood. Men who worked with their hands. My maternal grandfather was a joiner, a sapper in WW1, his family were farming folk; one great-grandfather a stone-mason, the other a farm labourer; further back, great-great grandfather a miller. And my own father, first a farm labourer, then a railway line maintenance worker, learning skills on the job, until eventually he became a 'Permanent Way Inspector for East African Railways and Harbours'...and not a paper qualification to his name! So he was able to provide for myself and my siblings to stay in education...a luxury he was denied, having had to leave school at 12, his wages needed to keep the family afloat. So this poem is written in gratitude, homage and love for all these fine working men.

Workin Men

I miss thaim. Miss their quait
haans restin lowssed
oan dusty overalls
deen wi the day's wark,
wachty buits ackwart
in their sklaik o glaur
or pentit spleiter;
the carefu wye they sat
on buses, gaan hame.

My granda's waak
the pleesure o his waak
his hertsome dander up Station Road
lang widden jyner's rule pokin oot

208

the nairra pooch o his dungers
spleet-new saadist furrin his jaicket.

An my faither, tall chiel
swingin alang a hyne-awa railway line
lang sicht taakin swatch o aathing
unner his ontak; fish-plates, bowts,
ivery sleeper in its cinner bed,
on the keevee for onything amissin
— yet his een shairp-set
oan the blae far-awa, the mischancie
o twa bairns, heelster-gowdie
ower steel-glaizie rails,
racin lik a pair o slung-stanes
tae walcome his hame-comin.

Published in *Talking About Lobsters: New Writing Scotland 34*
(ASLS, 2016) and in *Gaitherin* (Red Squirrel Press, 2016).

You may also wish to consult www.sheilatempletonpoetry.com and
www.redsquirrelpress.com

SHEENA BLACKHALL (Age 70)

Sheena Blackhall is a poet, novelist, illustrator, traditional ballad singer and storyteller in North East Scotland. Sheena was born Sheena Booth Middleton in Aberdeen in 1947. She was educated in Aberdeen, attending the College of Education to qualify as a primary school teacher. She took a degree in psychology with the Open University, graduating in 1995, and gained an M.Litt with distinction from Aberdeen University in 2000. From 1998 to 2003 she was Creative Writing Fellow in Scots at Aberdeen University's Elphinstone Institute, and in 2007 she was Creative Writing Tutor at the Institute for Irish and Scottish studies. With Les Wheeler she co-edits *The Elphinstone Kist*, a Doric website with downloadable resources. In 2016 she became an Honorary Fellow of the Word Centre for Creative Writing at Aberdeen University.

Sheena is a prolific writer, having published four Scots novellas, four Scots books for bairns, fifteen short story collections, and well over one hundred poetry pamphlets, and has won many prizes for her work. Alan Spence edited and introduced her poems in *The Space Between: New and Selected Poems* (Aberdeen University Press, 2014). Many of her stories have been broadcast on Radio Scotland, two of her plays have been televised, and three of her short story collections are online.

In 2009 she became Makar (Poet Laureate) for Aberdeen and the North East.

In August 2017 I met Sheena in the magnificent Sir Duncan Rice Library, which is part of the University of Aberdeen. Sheena's 70th birthday had been only a week ago. I had left her to the very end of my interview list so that she met the project's requirement of being over seventy.

'My grandmother stayed with us and she had been brought up in a Doric rural speaking area. The way she spoke was half a century behind how younger, less isolated people were speaking it. The Doric I was learning from her would have been from the latter part of the 19th century. My father, who was manager of a country bus service, spoke nothing but Doric, but slightly different from my grandmother. My mother, because she had trained to be a private secretary, could switch to English. My brother went to a prestigious local school where all the teaching was in English. And I had to speak English in primary school, but the home language was Doric. My son Ross and his Vietnamese wife Nga live with me (he is an electrical engineer). He speaks some Doric and their elder daughter Jessica recites Doric poems she has learned at school.

A lot of people say that the Doric is an emotional, physical language and English is cerebral. I agree with that and this is probably reflected in the poems I write in Doric and in English. Sometimes, if I'm not happy with a poem I've written in English, I try it in the Doric and it's much, much better.

My eldest son died last July of a heroin overdose. A highly intelligent, musical man, he had been an addict for twenty years. One of my daughters is disabled with anxiety and depression and the other edits a business magazine. In total I have four grand-daughters, aged 10 months to 7 years. My grandchildren have been a joy to me. They look at everything through fresh eyes and the childish imagination knows no bounds.

I had originally intended to be an artist, but I failed the art college course in everything except sculpture. So I had to rethink my career and trained to be a primary school teacher. I continued painting, but wasn't very successful, so I turned to poetry which I saw as a kind of word painting. I was at home when the children were small, so I did the Open University degree in Psychology. As part of this degree I put out questions to poets about how they thought. Some thought in smell, some saw things in black and white. Some people in my survey thought only in words and one man thought in pure mathematical symbols. Others, like myself, saw things as an ongoing film — an eidetic image which can be scanned or watched as if it was a real image. As a child, I found watching these images in my mind much richer than outside life.

I started writing short stories when a friend from teacher training college was approached by Frieda Morrison, the BBC producer, to write stories for youngsters. She didn't want to do it and gave my name to the editor. I was sent a list of themes to choose from and had to send in stories, but only got paid if they were selected. I had thirty-six stories published this way.

I had a breakdown at training college, related to failing at art college. One of the tests I was given as part of my treatment (The Thematic Apperception Test) was to look at a series of pictures and say which one I was particularly drawn to. I chose one of a little boy looking sadly at a violin he was holding. I immediately identified with him because he wanted to express himself through music and couldn't, and I could relate to that.

Later on, I came across a book by John O. Stevens (*Awareness*, I think it was called) and he had exercises in guided fantasy. I did some of those and out of that came a story called 'The Honey that came from the Sea' which the BBC broadcast.

Twenty years later, when I was forty, I had a much more serious breakdown, which was terrifying. I had gone into Aberdeen to see the artists' exhibition. I went upstairs and out of nowhere had this strong impulse to throw myself over the balustrade. I got in touch with the psychotherapist who had treated me 20 years before, who was now working in Sheffield. He, Dr J. D. Gomersall, was then based at the Centre for Psychotherapeutic Research. He agreed to treat me by correspondence. He would send me picture postcards and ask me to write stories in response to them. In return, I agreed to let him discuss these with his students. You have to be completely honest for psychotherapy to work. That made a big impact on my poetry. At that time, my husband (now my ex-husband) was an alcoholic. My psychotherapist sent me a quote which said, 'A relationship is like a dance — when you are tired of the dance you are allowed to sit down.' I thought that was wonderful. I had never thought that I was allowed to finish the marriage. I had carried this weight for so long. It was like somebody had cleaned all the windows in the house.

I was sectioned for fourteen days. In a sense that was very good because, such was the attitude to mental illness, nobody wanted the marriage to be repaired. I continued writing and sending my pieces down to my therapist. My handwriting changed completely and became very small. There is no doubt my illness contributed to my eldest son's problems and his drug addiction.

When I found my son in July 2016, he had been dead for over three days. When I had my first breakdown, unable to cope, I had signed him into care. After that he went from one institution to another and then into the army, which is also a kind of institution. He was so used to the institutional life that, when he came out of the army, he couldn't handle it. I have written about it quite a lot. It helps if you externalise it, share it with the page. I put all my poems onto the PoemHunter website. They are available there.

I think I will always write poetry. It's like a dear friend, like somebody you converse with. I was asked, 'Who is your listening ear?' It's not the way I work. It's always just been between me and the page.

Is there an inherited aspect to writing poetry/song? Well, my crofting grandfather wrote cornkisters in Doric...is it in the genes? My family trees have been compiled in depth, several centuries back, by other family members. My father, a Middleton, has DNA shared with the majority of Irish folk, traced back in Scotland to the 1100s. He married his second cousin, related through the Crabb family, who came to Deeside from Flanders in the 16th century with Johann Crabb. The Philip family are thought to have come to the North East from Spain. What makes us who we are? The Scots poet Alistair Mackie, when he first met me, remarked, 'I detect a touch of the tar brush'. Neighbours often thought my mother looked Spanish, and a Dutch colleague at university inquired if I was a Sephardic Jew. According to a maternal DNA test, I'm an Ashkenazi Jew!

I have, in fact, written about the Holocaust in a poetry pamphlet, *A Visit to Planet Auschwitz*. The poems were written in the two weeks after I visited Krakow in July 2009 when I visited Auschwitz with my son Morven.

My family have always sung. My father had a beautiful voice. He mostly sang traditional Scottish songs. As a child I had croup and my mother was told that the way to strengthen my lungs was to have singing lessons. At teacher training college I had the opportunity to learn the guitar. An old traveller, John Stewart, who worked as a lollipop man, saw me go into his school with my guitar and asked me if I wanted to learn to sing — to really sing. He gave me a song to learn and I played it over and over until finally he was satisfied with it. I asked him what I'd done that was different. He said, 'You were in the song before. It's not about the singer, it's the song that's important.'

I worked at the Elphinstone Institute[1] and shared an office with another Traveller, Stanley Robertson[2]. He told stories and gradually I learned them. I listened to his stories during the day and wrote my poems in the evenings and at weekends. When I gave readings and performances, it was usually Stanley's stories they wanted, rather than my poems.

You never know what an audience want until you are face to face with them. Mostly they prefer the funny poems to the serious ones. There is a vast difference between poetry performed and poetry read from the page. Some people write wonderful poems but ruin them when they read them out. Others put on a riveting performance, but when you see their words on the page, they are nothing very much, just thistledown.

Larry Butler trained me to work with Survivors' Poetry Scotland and the first time I was in front of a group, he pointed out that I had never asked their names, or why they were there, or what they expected. I always do that now. I had never really thought about my audience up to that point.

I made a set of CDs in a local sound studio — a mixture of songs for children in Scots, and other songs and poems in Scots. I gave those to the Scots Language Centre[3]. I am often asked at readings if I have CDs for sale, but I'm happier just to have them kept in one place of reference. Music impacts on my poetry. I find it very hard not to rhyme. If you have any musical ability, it's difficult not to. As for reading, it's most often poetry, and often poems in translation from other world cultures. This hasn't changed at all throughout the years.

Buddhism has been a big influence in my life and on my poetry. Meditation has been a great solace to me, calming me and clarifying my thoughts. When I came out of hospital after being sectioned, I went to yoga classes and that was very helpful. The tutor was a yoga teacher called Ian Scorgie, who had trained in India. He was in great demand by people troubled with anxiety and depression.

I went to China ten years ago with my younger daughter Kenna. I'm always interested in going to Buddhist countries. I went to see the Buddhist temples in India, and Thailand and to Vietnam because my son got married there. I have always been interested in how other cultures operate. It feeds creativity and brings new dimensions to what you do and introduces new poetic forms. I'm less keen to travel long distance now because of health factors.

With my diabetes I tend to sleep a lot. The disease makes me lethargic. I've had to struggle against that. I would quite happily sleep all day. I'm much calmer than I was. On my second breakdown I was judged to be bipolar. The medication helped immensely and I have kept on taking it, even though I was told I could now come off it. There was a huge surge of writing during my second breakdown period. It was probably deeper than the sort of things I write now. It was coming from a different place. It needed to come out and it did.

Death doesn't bother me. It's not when I go, but how I go. I've signed one of those 'do not resuscitate' forms. I do not want to be trailing around peeing into my slippers. I have seen it and I don't want it for myself.

I hope to continue as I am for my remaining years. I can't see myself ever stopping writing. Currently I'm translating *Jane Eyre* into Doric, and I'm delighted to say that Sheila Templeton has agreed to be my co-translator. Otherwise, the page and I will continue our lifelong friendship.

My role model, someone who gives me hope of continuing to be productive into later life, is Michelangelo. The critic Cuthbert Graham once said to me that he didn't assess writers by age; he assessed them by whether they were *open doors* or *shut doors*. Some people can be ancient but their door is ever open, so that they are always receiving and giving out. I can receive nature and give it out as poetry. That would be my advice to people who want to go on being creative — be an open door sort of person and never let it close.'

Notes

1. The Elphinstone Institute at the University of Aberdeen is a centre for the study of Ethnology, Folklore, and Ethnomusicology and promotes the culture of the North and North-East of Scotland.

2. Stanley Robertson (1940–2009) was a Scottish storyteller, ballad singer, and piper. He was born in Aberdeen into a Traveller family which had settled there. His family background was rich in tradition, and from his aunt, folk singer Jeannie Robertson, he inherited a huge repertoire of Northeast ballads. He was the key worker for the Heritage Lottery-funded Oral and Cultural Traditions of Scottish Travellers project at the Elphinstone Institute.

3. The Scots Language Centre is based in the A.K. Bell Library, Perth. It aims to promote the Scots language and to give people who speak Scots the chance to learn more about their own language.

A sample of writing done since passing 70

One English poem, one Doric poem

I couldn't wait to share the news of the Scottish earthquake with the
page. In the great scale of things it wasn't the worst of disasters.

The Earthquake

5 August 2017. 12:02am. The largest earthquake to be felt in
the west Highlands of Scotland in more than 30 years was
recorded on Friday. The British Geological Survey (BGS)
recorded the magnitude 3.8 tremor in the Moidart area just
before 3.45pm.

A yowe in Ardnamurchan
Lost two teeth and a fleeceful of fleas
When the earthquake struck

On Ben Ledi two tourists
Feeling the earth move beneath them
Thought that the Highland air
Had boosted their libido

A scone on a plate in Kilmahog
Slid two centimetres to the right
Into a blob of raspberry jam
(A jar from a batch that hardly set at all)

Ochone said the old woman
Gardening in Moidart
The curse of the wind farms
Has surely cast a large spell upon us

A mole in velvet livery
Had his ceiling crumble like curdled cheese
Around his dainty ears
Indicating the end of the world

Though nobody was killed, mislaid, or injured
Although the signs and portents weren't good

Recently I had surgery, and to convalesce, my farming cousin at New Deer kindly invited me to stay a few days with himself and his wife. My bedroom faced a large sycamore tree. At 11.30pm a barn owl appeared like a ghost on a branch. For half an hour, till midnight, we both stared at each other. I had to write about the experience after he left. I wonder what the owl made of it.

The Hoolet

The hoolet sat in the hoolet's tree
He cockit his lugs an he listened
An fit wis his name I canna weel gie
Fur I'm nae richt sure he wis christened

He sat on his branch, I lay in ma bed
We twa watched ane anither
He fleched his oxters, he preened his wings
Wi niver a skreich nur a blether

He furled his heid frae wast tae east
He cast his een up tae the meen
He pykit his clooks an he shoogled aboot
Syne dauchled as still as a steen

The meen wis fite an the hoolet wis fite
He wis winnerin 'Fa's thon vratch
O a fremmit body abed in the hoose
In a neuk o ma huntin patch?'

He luikit lang wi his glimmrin een
His feathers pluffed oot bi the win
Twa carnivores in the mids o nicht
Jist takkin each ither in

You may also wish to consult: http://sheenablackhall.blogspot.com
(blog showing covers of complete set of books, with info.)

http://www.bbc.co.uk/scotland/learning/secondary/nonfiction/
users/leerie.shtml

Conversation between Sheena Blackhall and Sheila Templeton
(as recorded by Sheila Templeton)

Sheena's bus from Aberdeen was early, so she was waiting for me at Buchanan Street Bus Station, a new poem already written on seeing *Wincher's Stance*, the bronze statue by John Clinch, which welcomes the thousands of travellers passing through the busy Glasgow bus station. I was embarrassed to own that I'd never actually looked at its name! I like the statue a lot, and have often admired it, even touched it for some kind of travelling luck. But I'd always assumed it depicted a soldier lad back from a war, his bunnet planted exuberantly on his lass's head as he lifts her off her feet in his embrace.

Winchers' Stance is such a good name...literally translating as 'Courting Stance', a little pun on the dozens of bus stance numbers throughout the station. So this was an excellent beginning to our meeting: a new poem already as a welcome to Glasgow and an intriguing start to our conversation.

> *Wincher's Stance*
>
> He'd a broo like Andy Stewart
> He'd a Rab C Nesbitt sark
> Wi his bovver buits an jeans on
> He was vrocht for navvie work
>
> Wi her Tam o Shanter bunnet
> Wis she jist his Heilin fling?
> Wi her frock half up her bihoochie
> As he clinched her in a swing
>
> She wis aff her feet wi passion
> Glesga style: The Wincher's stance
> Close as a mat tae lino
> Glesga: city o Romance.
>
> —Sheena Blackhall 26/09/17

Sheena had thought about how we might interview each other by going through my interview with Robin and picking out similarities in our lives. I thought this an excellent idea. It's only in the last few years that Sheena and I have got to know each other, meeting at an annual poetry weekend in Callander, though I've been a huge fan of her work for a long time.

The 'cross-overs' in our lives, the similarities, turned out to be much more than any differences: Both of us schooled in Aberdeen at secondary level, but also much experience of country life, Sheena in Deeside, myself in Donside; extra strong relationship with grandparents, indeed living with them, so a strong experience of extended family and also of grandmother being a major care giver; both fathers left school reluctantly at 12; both dads worked in transport, mine on the railway, Sheena's on Deeside buses; both brought up speaking N-east scots (Doric) in an unselfconscious way; both showing an early love of words and writing; both with miserable school experiences; both drawn to spiritual exploration; both with family secrets; both with family colonial experience... not an unusual thing in any Scottish family.

SB: My dad worked on Deeside Buses, based in Ballater. He managed the bus company for his sister. Ivery weekend an aa the simmer, we'd be in Ballater. Dae fit ye like. Doric spikkin.

ST: My dad worked on the railway. First in Dyce where he met my mother, then when I was 3, he took a job on the West Highland Line and we bade in an incredibly remote place on Rannoch Moor, then other places back in the North-East, until finally he took the job out in Tanzania when I was 7. So I'd 2–3 years in East Africa until I was 10 and then I was left at my grandparents in Dyce, after being home on leave. The rest of my family went back to East Africa and I stayed at my grandparents until I was nearly 18. Of course, family would come back regularly, and in 1955 my brother was also left in Dyce, so there were the three of us kids, myself, my brother Allan and cousin Sandy, all living at our grandparents. It was a big extended family. I shared a bedroom wi my Grunnie. Nae jist the room. We shared the bed! I used tae watch her getting dressed in the mornings, though I dinna suppose she knew that.

SB: Aye, I shared a bed wi Grannie tae! She sung aa the time. I learned sae mony sangs fae her. My grannie married a farmer. She was widowed when her daughter, my mither, was 13. She bade wi her brither, my uncle until he wis mairrit, but then twa wimmen in ae kitchen wisnae gaan tae work oot, so when my mother mairrit my dad, Grannie came tae bide wi us in Albert Terrace in Aberdeen. Grannie spoke broad Doric.

ST: An schooling? Fit wis your experience o school? Hiv we got similarities there?

SB: My first experience wis being tested and telt I wis a moron! Faan I wis 5 year auld, I was sent tae the High School for Girls to be assessed. The teacher showed me a selection of farm animals and asked me tae name them. 'Show me a cow'...'Show me a horse!'...in a posh English voice. Of course, I had niver heard English wirds for fairm beasts, so I didnae ken fit she wis on aboot. I kent *nowt*. An *coos*. An *stirks*. An *beasts*. A horse wis a *shelt* or a *cuddie*. But I'd niver heard *cow* or *horse*. So when we were waitin tae hear the outcome, my mother and me, we heard her say, 'not the sort we want here. The child's a moron!' That wis that. I didnae get intae the High School for Girls Primary, though I went there for secondary schooling. Fit aboot you?

ST: My first taste o primary school wis a terrible thing...though for different reasons fae yours. We were livin in a wee place called Tillynaught, inland fae Banff, due to faither's job. And my mother decided I'd be better gaan tae the school in Banff, raither than the local little school. So at 5 year auld, I'm put oan the train wi the rest o the kids. They bullied me, stole my ticket, my faither waiting at the ither end, presumably tae see I wis okay, saw me being sneaked under the ticket barrier and thocht I wis being cheeky, so I got a terrible row, and was spanked, later on, at hame. Then for days I couldnae find the dinner hall and ended up spending dinner hour wi the only cratur seemed friendly — a local prostitute's daughter! I was seen comin oot o her hoose one day by my Auntie Annabel, father's cousin bade in Banff, so a big stooshie ensued and efter that I went tae Annabel's for my dinner. I loved that. My days became better but I dinna remember anything aboot my school experience except colouring in an aipple and playing 'In and out the dusty bluebells'!

So both of us had less than wonderful experiences of early schooling. Sheena didn't get into the High School for Girls and my first year of school was traumatic to say the least. My schooling continued to be erratic, with my father moving us around the country and then to East Africa, where I had first, home schooling, then 18 months at a convent school in Dar-es-Salaam. When I resumed school at Dyce Primary, I was moved down a class so I could catch up and it was only then that I began to blossom at school.

Sheena was already shining at primary school, even if it wasn't the Girls High. She was writing pieces, encouraged by her mother and remembers being slapped by a primary teacher for changing tense in the same piece of writing. So already, high standards were expected. Then in secondary school (by this time, she was attending the Girls High!), Sheena remembered being accused not only of copying another girl's work, but also being told even if she hadn't copied, she couldn't have written the piece because she wasn't capable of it.

SB: When I went tae secondary school, I wis still writing but this wasn't known to my teachers. And I tended not to invite school friends round to my place because we spoke Scots at home and that was private. But one day a school pal asked if I'd done my homework essay and could she see it? Of course I let her come home with me, and see the essay, and unbeknown to me, she copied it word for word. The teacher, a Miss Gordon (whose brother was not only a poet but the Ambassador to Vienna, so high connections), at first accused me of copying. Then she said 'that even if you did write it first, you must have copied it from somewhere. You are not capable of writing that!' I said when I got hame, 'I'm nae gaan back tae that school!' Mother said, 'You must!'

Neither of us had a wonderful experience of education over all, though certainly once I was settled in Dyce under my grandmother's care, my experience of school became much better. And due to a wise primary head teacher, I was allowed to sit the city 11+ exam and get into Aberdeen Academy, rather than the local junior secondary school in Bankhead. Sheena and I were both educated in Aberdeen schools, though as I am a few years older, and we followed different higher education routes, our paths didn't cross then.

Another connection between us is that we've both followed a spiritual path. Sheena to Buddhism, myself to Heartfulness, which comes from the same source as Buddhism does, from the ancient practice of Raja Yoga. I didn't find my meditation practice until I retired from teaching, so creative writing and meditation both started for me aged 52. But for Sheena it was much earlier.

SB: I turned to Buddhism when I was 14. I could not stand my mother's narrow religious views. She'd nae time for pagans or unbelievers, so I searched until I found something which fitted me. And that was Buddhism. 'Better to wear shoes than cover the roads with leather'.

ST: It's only since I stopped teaching and had some space in my life that I was able to 'come out' about both liking to write, and needing a spiritual path. I was reticent about both, had to keep it a secret.

SB: Oh secrets! Did your family have secrets?

ST: They certainly did! I was, as I said, brought up at my grandparents, along with my cousin Sandy, who also lived there. He'd been born to my mother's older unmarried sister and his parentage was always kept a secret from us, even though obviously the older generation knew fine. I remember him and I having a very serious conversation once about...was he my uncle or my cousin? We really didn't know. The truth did not come out until many years later when he needed to see his birth certificate for applying to join the RAF. And Grunnie just passed it to him without a word! It was never discussed. Imagine keeping such a secret!

SB: Oh aye. Same in our family. My father's sister who owned the bus company would go off periodically 'to Perth'. I never knew why, and then discovered many years later that she had regular spells in Kingseat Mental Hospital in Aberdeenshire. It was never spoken of! Sae mony things never spoken. Bodily functions...periods...never explained. I ran aa the wye hame when it happened, thocht the blood meant I wis deein! My mother, so religious, all I got was a lecture about original sin.

ST: Oh me too! Only the lecture came from my father. He happened to be home on leave that summer and my mother had told him I'd started, so he insisted on telling me all his family history, where his grandmother had 4 children, all to different fathers, and never married! The implication being that now I was a woman, I'd better be extremely careful, I suppose! But it's all been grist to a writers' mill. So did you always want tae be a writer?

SB: Well I wrote from an early age. And there wis a lot of encouragement from my mother, who'd always wanted tae be a writer herself. She'd stand at the sink and declaim Sir Walter Scott's 'breathes there the man with soul so dead!' And there wis niver ony doubt about Christmas or birthday presents! My choices were Dickens or Scott! Nae that I minded. I loved Dickens, so visual. My real love was art, though. I started off at Gray's School of Art, but that didnae work oot, so efter the first year, I transferred to a primary school teacher training at Aberdeen Teacher Training College. I nearly didnae finish that, because I was ill a lot o the time, having had typhoid in a serious epidemic. But my mother made sure I finished, and qualified. And I was aye writing. Fit aboot you?

ST: I only began to write my own pieces when I was about 14. I began to keep a journal, which I still have! Maist o the writing is angst aboot boys…lads…and frustration at the family. It's curious reading it, because I've blocked out all that teenage rage at the grown-ups, but there it is, in the journal. And because I'm by then living with the extended family, I have a lot of grown-ups tae rage at! But there are also a lot of 'lyrical' pieces, mostly descriptions of nature, in my journal. Which of course I showed to no-one! I wis aye very private aboot my writing. Though I remember in 6th year taking in pieces to my English teacher, Mr Webster, and he would give me feedback. But it niver occurred to me to send them off anywhere or try to publish. I had no self-confidence, and in the family, and in the village, drawing attention to yourself for ANY reason was a sin! Even though my Grunnie loved poetry and would recite yards of poems like 'The Night Before Waterloo' and 'Charge of the Light Brigade'. She was very fond of Tennyson. But still, in the family and in the village there seemed a sense that writing poetry was something to mock…there would be back-spikken if you did sic a thing. So I didn't write after I went to university. Didn't write until 30 years later, after I got early retirement from teaching.

Our writing careers have followed very different paths. Sheena has been writing, and had poems and other writing accepted for publication practically her whole life, a lot of her work being in North-East Scots. She's built up a reputation as the foremost poet in Scotland writing in Doric and has published many collections of poetry, including a *Collected Poems* which came out last year from Aberdeen University Press. She also referred, fairly casually during our interview, to having had a long correspondence with Flora Garry![1] I've come much later to recognition, finding that writing in Scots gives me great satisfaction, and having that affirmed by being a regular prize-winner in the annual McCash Scots Language Poetry Competition.

So the writing in Doric is a huge connection. And that comes from being brought up in the country, living with Victorian-born grandparents who spoke Scots unselfconsciously. It was literally, our 'first language', though we had both learned English too, as the language for school and doctors' surgeries and interviews, anywhere where 'proper' was expected. But we both find that Scots is a rich language for writing poetry. It has a juiciness, a descriptive range, which is not possible in English. Sheena asked me as a final question, 'why do you write?' And the honest answer that came out of my mouth was, 'I write because I just have to write.' And for a lot of the time that writing for both of us has to be in Doric Scots.

Note

1. Flora Garry came from the farming lands of Buchan; trained as a teacher, she wrote stories and drama for radio from the 1920s, and poetry from the 1940s, though her work was not collected in book form until 1974, when *Bennygoak and Other Poems* was published by Akros. Her poems, in rich Buchan dialect, depict the landscape of that area and the working lives of its people, with the experience of women in particular having a central role in validating the literary use of Scots.

8. AUTUMN LEAVES OF DIFFERENT HUE

Carl MacDougall
Bernard MacLaverty
Lee Gershuny

In this section a writer born and bred in Scotland who left school at 15, a dramatist from New York who did a PhD, and a writer who spent his childhood and early manhood in conflict-ridden Belfast come together. All, in their different ways, now contribute to the Scottish literary scene and Scottish culture.

CARL MACDOUGALL (Age 76)

Carl has written novels, collections of short stories, non-fiction, journalism, plays, radio programmes and television series. However, he is most at home writing fiction. His work includes three prize-winning novels, four pamphlets, four collections of short stories and two works of non-fiction; and he has edited four anthologies, including the best-selling classic collection of Scottish short stories, *The Devil and the Giro*. He has also written and presented two major television series.

Carl was born in Glasgow and spent his childhood between Kingskettle (Fife), Fortingall (Perthshire) and Oban (Argyll) where he still has strong family connections. He left school at 15 and worked in a variety of jobs before leaving Glasgow to spend two or three years mostly in England and Europe.

Back in Glasgow he worked for ten years as a copytaker[1] on the *Scottish Daily Express*. At this time he was also heavily involved with the burgeoning folk song movement, working on the influential *Chapbook* magazine with Arthur Argo and Ian Philip. On leaving the *Express* he published two collections of folk tales, then moved to Fife, where he founded and edited *Words* magazine, in which first appeared extracts of Alasdair Gray's *Lanark* and stories by James Kelman and Agnes Owens.

When I visited Carl in his flat in Nithsdale Road, Glasgow (next to what was once Sammy Dow's pub), he was looking trim and in good shape. He still goes hill walking, he told me. The flat is spacious, comfortably lived in and crammed with books, the remnants from his days as a reviewer. For 14 years he was *The Herald*'s chief fiction reviewer and also worked for other papers.

Carl lives here on his own during the week and enjoys frequent visits from his daughter and new grandson. Fortified by coffee, I turned on the voice-recorder:

It didn't take me long at all to identify the kind of internal censors that whisper to you, the black crows that sit on your shoulder — the things that inhibit free writing; and it didn't take me long to realise that I had to shake them off. As a person, rather than as a writer. I did that while I was still at school, at about fourteen or fifteen.

When I was six my father was killed at work in a railway accident at Burntisland. Within eighteen months my mother lost two brothers and a sister, as well as her husband. Two of these deaths were violent. There was my father and then there was my Uncle Charlie who was killed when a wall collapsed on him when he was building St. Joseph's Chapel in Greenock. Only four days before that, my Aunt Eva died in Canada. I'm not quite sure what caused her death — no one is. I believe it was a heart problem. The family simply went to pieces. I realised, as an adult, it wasn't that I was not loved, but that these people were trying, unsuccessfully, to deal with their own grief. But this was not at all clear to me at the time and, three years later, I had a nervous breakdown.

The Child Guidance counsellor said, 'How would you feel about going on a nice holiday?' Of course, any nine-year-old would say 'yes'. I saw my mother sewing on name tags and I thought this was me about to go on that nice holiday. A man and a woman turned up at the door on a Saturday morning and off we went, my mother in the back with me. It was the first time I'd ever been in a car. As we passed Glasgow Green I had to get out to be sick. When we got to Nerston, I sat in the hall with my suitcase and someone came along and said, 'Follow me.' So I went upstairs and my mother disappeared into the office to see Miss Hassan, the Headmistress. From the dormitory window I saw my mother being driven away and turning and looking out of the back window. I felt confused and the confusion deepened. Some of the children there were very disturbed. It dawned on me that this wasn't the nice holiday I thought I'd agreed to. And I was made to do activities I didn't enjoy, like boxing.

On top of that they found out, while I was there, that I couldn't see properly. It had to do with reading, When I was asked to read aloud I couldn't make out the words on the page. The memorable part of that was having to go to Glasgow to get my eyes tested. I got the bus on my own and my mother met me at Buchanan Street Bus Station. I had my eyes tested at McQuilkin opticians in Sauchiehall Street, just round the corner from Buchanan Street, and the memorable part is that I was away from Nerston. We went back to the house in Keppochhill Road, saw my grandparents whom we lived with — my Granny was blind but always said she was pleased to see me — and it was the return to normality, even for part of an afternoon, that was exciting. My mother and I got back to Nerston about nine o'clock. They weren't too pleased and next day I was asked why it took so long to get my eyes tested. I think they expected me back around three or four o'clock. I told them to ask my mother.

Part of our routine was to attend church in East Kilbride on Sunday mornings. The Minister would lead the congregation in prayer. 'I want you to remember our visitors, these children here,' he said. 'And I want you to pray for the tender mercies that God can offer them in their condition.' I wondered what 'tender mercy' was and thought I wouldn't mind having a bit of it.

I was there for about four or five months. I felt a strong sense of alienation which deepened when I came out, because by that time, everybody had moved on. We had already moved from Fife to Glasgow when my father died. I had just started to make friends when I was sent to Nerston. And, when I came out, I had to go back into school, but not with my former friends. For much of my childhood I was very confused, lonely and very frightened. There are so many instances that it's difficult to pick a typical example, but I suppose bullying of one sort or another was fairly common, though not very persistent — but it only needs to happen once to make you fearful of a repetition. The biggest fear was loss. Having experienced these early losses, for most of my childhood I felt loss was inevitable. It was simply a matter of time.

My childhood never showed me how to bond with other people. I had to learn that as an adult. I used my childhood as a means of separating me from other people. Once I identified it for what it was, came to terms with it and accepted it, I could then move on to do something else; and also begin to see that I wasn't the only one who had experiences similar to mine — perhaps not as acute, but everyone has known fear, loneliness, anxiety and all these things.

I felt angry at the time. I no longer do. I have accepted that people were doing the best they could. I have written about this in a sort of autobiography of my life up until ten. I wrote it about fifteen years ago. I called it *Relative Strangers*. My agent really enjoyed it, but it was at the tail end of that era when there were a lot of autobiographies coming out. I don't think she showed it to any publishers. Also, I knew my aunts would object to things that were in. I have this thing about writing, that when I finish something I'm done with it and don't want to go back, though obviously I have done so and when I do I am often surprised. I've thought of having another look, but my childhood was pretty relentless and the idea of revisiting it is pretty unappealing. Also, I question my motives and maybe the motives of anyone who would read it. I think I wrote it as a way of understanding rather than simply recording, that by laying out the events I could come to terms with them, accept them as mine. But what would potential readers be looking for? Why read a story of loss and misery? This is why I haven't done a subsequent book. The story didn't get any better, not for a long time.

I have no idea if I became an alcoholic or if I already had the virus. It's the nature or nurture argument. I've no idea which it is, whether you are one or you become one, I don't know and neither does anyone else. Eventually, rather than going to a counsellor for help, I went to people who'd had the same experience as me. I don't know whether having a nervous breakdown at nine was behind this or not, but this was when the internal censors you mentioned earlier returned.

I haven't had a drink now for forty-five years. When I stopped, I absolutely knew that I was finished and I wanted to be finished with it. Drinking held neither mystery nor interest and I never even considered thinking I couldn't hack it. I never gave anything up, I actually got rid of something and I think the difference is extremely significant. That's why, as far as I'm concerned, what has happened subsequently is far more interesting. For example, I started writing. I did write a few things when I was drinking, but I never took them seriously or gave them any kind of thought and I certainly didn't see myself as a writer.

I left school at fifteen, at the first available opportunity and travelled, leaving Scotland for several years. When I finally returned, I knew it was time to settle. I was working in Birmingham and an editor at Caters News Agency asked me to write something about Paris. He didn't think much of it, but he showed me how to improve it and asked me to rewrite it. Several months later, he presented me with a cheque for, I think, twenty pounds, but it may have been fifteen. When I came back to Glasgow, the employment exchange offered me an interview as a copytaker at the *Scottish Daily Express*. I was interviewed by the News Editor, Ian Brown, who gave me the job. I did it for ten years and it's the best job I've ever had.

Newspaper offices can be exciting places and they tend to attract interesting people. I'm still in touch with people I met then, which is surprising, not because of time and distance, but because drinking tends to isolate you and I worked there towards the end of my drinking.

I am not really aware of my mind working differently when writing fiction as opposed to non-fiction. It's a different approach. With non-fiction you have to maintain the veracity of what you write. Also in journalism and reviews you have to stick to an allocated number of words and learn to compress your ideas. Write to length and write on time. With novels and short stories I feel more in charge and that there is more of me in them. They're more fun. Playing with ideas and possibilities is so exciting. I am very lucky to be able to do what I do; and I have always seen it as a learning process. I long ago gave up the freelance attitude in which you say yes and then see if you can do it. I now turn down quite a lot.

I agreed to become President of Scottish PEN[2] a few months ago, because it needed to be done. I have been a member for a long time and always believed in what PEN stands for. I admired the people who did the work. I was asked to join the committee and found it far more interesting than I expected. When Drew Campbell retired as President, I was asked if I would take over. I felt I didn't have enough experience, but was assured that that the committee would give me a lot of help. I think PEN is needed more than ever since the rise of UKIP and of Trump. Loss of basic human rights like freedom of expression is happening in this country, not just in far off places. Our 'Many Voices' project works with marginalised people in our own country.

My recent book, *Someone Always Robs the Poor*, [3] explores themes of poverty, migration, alienation, accountability and alcoholism.

Choosing what I write about is an act of sympathy, an attempt to understand. Politically I identify with the Left because of where I was brought up. I am still angered by injustice and abuse of human rights, but I am not so shocked by it. I am more aware of the realities of life. It is not the ideals that have let us down, but the politicians, and that angers me.

My creativity has changed with growing experience. It's not a question of it becoming easier, but that I am more familiar with the process, so that, when I hit problems, they no longer baffle me. I now know that this is to be expected and I trust myself to find a solution. I think I am now much more playful. When you sit down and it works and you are in the flow, there is nothing better than that. By the same standard, when it's tough and when the words don't fit — that business of starting with a blank page and battle through to a finished piece — that, too, is exciting and satisfying. My motives for writing have become clearer, but they haven't changed.

Of course, I feel I made all my mistakes in print, but I know I was finding my voice. Some writers seem to arrive with their voice intact, I had to find mine and then I had to learn to trust it, and to trust the way it adapted to different approaches, themes and so on. I suppose that's what I mean by a learning process and why I feel I am still learning, always will, I hope. There are some things where the voice and tone haven't changed, but changes depend on the subject. I think it's become much freer and I depend on it more than I used to.

I am now writing less about Glasgow and more about Scotland and I am writing about things other than an urban environment. But Glasgow is very familiar to me and it's always nice to return to the familiar.

I have read avidly from early childhood. I always have a book on the go, but I have become less tolerant. When I reviewed books, I had to finish them. These days I abandon books if they aren't working for me. I think I read more non-fiction now. One of my abiding fascinations is Vincent Van Gogh — the vibrancy, the colours. For me, it's the struggle he had, as an individual, to create something. His letters are fascinating. Similarly, Mozart, for the very opposite reason — he arrived so complete. Sometimes I think I care more about painting than I do about writing, because the whole process of creating a painting is a wonder and a mystery to me.

So far, the things that we accept as part of ageing haven't affected my life in any negative way. I have become deaf in the last fifteen years or so, but I can cope with that with the help of a hearing aid. I still walk in the hills. I love being in that landscape and being part of what's there. I have taken up wild swimming. It's now an absolute part of my life. I don't have a wet suit — it's just in you go! But only in summer! I make no concessions to ageing. Most people I know who have not aged well have become old in their heads first — how they think of themselves — and the rest follows.

I am not a church goer. Like everybody else I have looked up at the stars and wondered who or what made us all and what the point is. I am interested in astronomy and in what's out there. A sense of wonder fills me; and that wonder can equally be captured when I look at something like a fish. I have a curiosity about life that naturally leads me towards what I regard as a form of spirituality. It seems to me that the idea of there being a Power greater than yourself is as sensible as there not being anything, that we are nothing and come from nothing and the whole thing is pointless. We just don't know. I do have a spiritual belief that is about finding my place in this universe. The curiosity and mystery of it all attracts me.

A great deal of the ageism one comes up against is so casual. The world of the media is mostly populated by the young. Jimmie MacGregor[4] once said to me, 'You can't get a job in the BBC if your balls have dropped!' And this leads to a lack of a depth of understanding. I think that these days the people who make the decisions about what gets published and what doesn't are not the editors, but very often the publicists. They are looking for things other than writing — youth and good looks being amongst them.

It's difficult to say what piece of writing, done since passing seventy, has given me the most satisfaction. Different things are satisfying in different ways and different things have had different beginnings. Something that has taken years to grow and mature and presented problems to overcome gives me huge satisfaction when I complete it, whether published or not. There is a tendency, too, for whatever I am writing at the moment, the thing I am most involved with at the time, to be the most important to me. I've got two novellas I'm working on at the moment.

The writer who changed my life was John Steinbeck. Reading *Cannery Row* and living in Keppochhill Road, I couldn't help making a connection. Steinbeck interested me because he kept working. He wrote *The Winter of Our Discontent* long after what we think of as his big novels — and it was a good one. He never stopped writing, nor did Muriel Spark. Other creative artists interest me in this respect, too. Monet was painting well into old age, Picasso and Matisse are absolute exemplars; Verdi was composing music in his eighties and lots of actors keep going. If you are able to, why wouldn't you keep on doing it? If you keep trying to get it right, then one of these days you might just land it.

My advice to younger writers is to find out what kind of writer you are and keep doing it. If you want to go on writing into old age, I think, if you are a writer, you will.

Notes

1. A copytaker is a person employed to type reports as journalists dictate them over the phone.

2. Scottish PEN is the Scottish branch of PEN International, a not-for-profit organisation that champions freedom of speech and literature across borders.

3. *Someone Always Robs the Poor* — a new collection of short stories by Carl MacDougall (Freight Books, 2017).

4. Jimmie Macgregor is a Scottish folksinger and broadcaster, best known as half of a singing duo with Robin Hall. Born 1930.

This is the opening of Wild Bells, *chosen because I was working on it when Robin called.*

On Sundays we go up the High Street and sit at the back of the gallery with chains at our legs, tied to the pews for morning service; and we sometimes get to the evening watch at 6, but that's where daft Willie Paterson asks God to tell him the lassies' names.

I have been promised: even though my sins are great and my circumstances strained, Mistress Robertson assures me God's mercy is greater than all our sins.

She pays for this room, a small damp and sullen place with little comfort, a table and a chair, a straw mattress, a blanket and sometimes a fire. I have the Bible, a candle and daylight from a window too high to reach. She brings dip pens, ink and paper, has given me clothes and food. I walk the yard twice a day and have two breaks, morning and evening.

She has told me not to let William Paterson upset me, says he is a poor soul, one for whom God has provided us with special love, but I want rid of him and his snotters. They think they are doing him a favour bringing him to church, but he laughs and slavers behind their backs, puts his hand in his breeks and tells the lassies he'll let them know what Jesus tells him when he comes in the night, riding on a horse: 'Come ben the back with me. Come on. You will, sure you will. I think you might. I've got sweeties.'

Then when we praise God with our singing, he builds in verses about the wee dog, the wee pig and the wee elf, puts them to the hymn tunes and giggles, 'They're back there and I'm up here, so who's the daftie noo, eh, who's the daftie noo? It's no Willie Paterson, no, it's no him. Willie Paterson makes things up and sings them.'

You may also wish to consult www.carlmagdougall.co.uk

BERNARD MACLAVERTY (Age 75)

Although short stories have provided the spine of MacLaverty's career, he has also written five novels including the Booker short-listed *Grace Notes* (1997) as well as *Lamb* (1980) and *Cal* (1983), both of which were turned into acclaimed films. As a screenwriter and director MacLaverty was nominated for a BAFTA for best short film — and won the best first director award from BAFTA Scotland — for *Bye-Child*, his adaptation of a poem by Seamus Heaney, a Northern Ireland contemporary and a fellow member of an early-60s writing group. He has written for radio, films, television and opera, but over the decades has continually returned to the short story form.

Bernard was born in Belfast in 1942, and moved to Scotland in 1975, where he lived in Ratho, near Edinburgh, then on the Isle of Islay, and now in Glasgow. After leaving school he became a Medical Laboratory Technician, later studying at Queen's University, Belfast, and becoming an English teacher. He has been writer in residence at the University of Aberdeen, and Guest Writer at the University of Augsburg and at Iowa State University. For three years, at different times he was visiting writer at John Moores University, Liverpool, and visiting Professor at the University of Strathclyde. He is a member of Aosdana[1].Bernard is married with four children, all successful in various branches of the arts, and eight grandchildren.

Bernard's house, in the West end of Glasgow, is not far from where Alasdair Gray lives, or where Carl MacDougall used to live. And, of course, they all know each other. Hanging in Bernard's hall are large framed film posters of *Cal* and *Lamb*. There are bookshelves in every room — one full of poetry, another of short stories, shelves of art and photography books, and one with hundreds of CDs of classical music.

'If you want to know what someone's real interests are, look at the books in the loo,' he tells me. I last saw Bernard nearly twenty years ago, but he hasn't changed and that smile still hovers around his mouth.

Tea, biscuits, comfy chairs, recorder on:

After Ratho, we moved to Islay. I was there for eight years, three of them teaching Higher English. It's the only time I have lived rurally. It was exciting to be within sight of the sea. I was an Irishman in Scotland, teaching English. Things were beginning to come right for me at this stage — my first novel, *Lamb*, was accepted for publication; one of my short stories grew into a TV play, another turned into a radio drama. To keep all this work going and teach in school was becoming too much. I asked for a year's sabbatical to write the next novel, but was refused, so I left. The novel was *Cal* and there was an irony there because it ended up being studied in schools and here was me losing my job because of it. That was 1981. From that point onwards I have made a living through writing and all the things that go with it — readings, school visits and so forth. I have been married to Madeline for coming up to fifty years. She is my first port of call as a writer, the first to read and comment on new work.

There has been a sixteen-year gap between *Midwinter Break*, the novel which is coming out later this year, and my previous one. It is simply that I have been very busy with other things. First of all, each of my eight grandchildren deserves a share of care and attention. They are all living in Glasgow and all have much the same postcode as here.

At another level, in those sixteen years, I have written a book of short stories, *Matters of Life & Death*. Then it was proposed that I had a book of collected short stories — *Collected Stories* (Vintage, 2014) — and that meant reading all the earlier stories and going over them. What I really wanted from this collected edition was a retrospective in the same way that you have a retrospective exhibition of a painter. It's all under the same roof. And I love the idea of things coming out of the attic that were made in the 1960s being presented alongside newer work.

In this same sixteen-year period I also wrote and directed a film — a short 15-minute film, based on Seamus Heaney's poem *Bye-Child*. That took me nearly two years to do. It was nominated for a BAFTA for the best short film of that year and I won a BAFTA Scotland for best first director. In addition to all this, I was approached by Scottish Opera to write a 15-minute libretto. I was introduced to another Irishman, a composer, named Gareth Williams. We hit it off and worked well together. I had heard a story about King James IV, who was curious to know what language a child would speak if not subject to the normal process of language development. So he sent orphaned twins to the Bass Rock with a dumb wet-nurse. I called the opera *The King's Conjecture*. The conjecture was that the children would speak Hebrew, the language of the Bible and of God. To crush that into fifteen minutes was hard in a way but Gareth's music was great.

I then wrote another short opera based on just one chapter from a big, fat Russian novel, *Life and Fate* by Vasily Grossman [2]. A number of years later, Gareth Williams and I had another idea, starting with a true story about an elephant in Belfast Zoo and the first woman keeper in Great Britain. This was during the war and she was worried about the baby elephant if Belfast was bombed. She started taking it home every night on a lead. When the blitz did come to Belfast, the baby elephant was safe outside the city. In the opera it was an opportunity to bring in the children playing around the elephant, their singing, the Easter Mass, the sound of the bombs. We put it on in about twelve places in Scotland. In each place we linked it to a primary school and drew upon the children to be in the performance. The elephant was like a pantomime horse, done by a comedian who was very good, very funny [3].

For five years I wrote a screenplay of Robin Jenkins' novel, *The Cone Gatherers*. It didn't work out and disappeared without trace, but it's another reason why there has been a big gap between one novel and the next.

My stock answer for when I'm asked where my creativity comes from is to say that it is a kind of play activity left over from childhood. I used to have a pretend miniature farm and would act out the dialogue between the farmer and his wife. Games like this are not far away for a story like *Cal* where he's out in the country and goes to a farm. Play is a very important basis for later creativity.

I'm always on the lookout for things that start a story going — things that chime, new ways of putting things together. A jag — that's how it happens. I see or read something; and then it begins to put on flesh. Sometimes you get a jag, but you don't get the craft with it and it doesn't work. The jag that started 'My Dear Palestrina' was when I was on my way out for a shovel of coal. The radio was on and somebody was being interviewed — a woman with a foreign voice, a piano teacher, was saying, 'and there I was, standing at the piano and I was crying.' I thought, why was she crying? Why was she talking to this interviewer? And I found myself constructing a fictional woman who had fled Europe and ended up in a Northern Irish village, teaching this boy piano, a boy with problems of his own. The whole story flowers in front of you. You work on it; you craft it and then you do further work on it.

By 'crafting it' I mean…well, for example, my novel *Grace Notes*[3] is about a woman who is a composer. Therefore there is a dominance of sound pictures in it — doors squeaking on their hinges, shoes squidging across the boards and so on. Then there is a different level where the father makes a joke about homophones — those things that sound the same. He's a pub owner and he talks about 'bar talk' which for her is the same as 'Bartok'. And then I write about divisions of sound. When I was living by the sea in Islay, I talked with the children about the idea of breaking down the time intervals of the sea. The biggest interval is the tides; then within the tides there are waves that come on the shore. All of those things about sound and time intervals are important in music. And there were things in my own life that I plucked out to put in the story. In terms of research, there was a composer who came to Glasgow and gave a public workshop. I went along to that. He invited ten students onto the platform. He told them to think of something, then make a sound that represented it, then make the sound again, then give it a head and a tail. He told the people to just make a sound breathing. A huge range of different sounds came out of us. The world seemed different because of what I was hearing. Aspects of this went into the novel, too. That's what I mean about crafting. It is absolutely necessary that each line you write contributes to the story you are telling. It's about the construction of the story. People might not notice it, but it's there and a vital element of what makes the story work.

There were no such things as writing classes when I started. You learnt on the job, so it's not surprising that I find a few of my earlier stories a little embarrassing when I read them now — not candidates for the all-embracing collection. Over the years I hope the craft of my writing has improved. I have not left out quite so many of the later stories as have of the earlier ones.

There are a number of things that have turned up in my stories right from the start: love, religion, Northern Ireland, and anti-violence, although to have a stance about anti-violence, you have to write about violence to discredit it in some way. I said in an interview, a while back, that anger is one of the things that makes me write.

For the last thirty years, Belfast has been in a war situation — bombs, terror, death. It just made me so angry. What right have they to blow people to pieces? Out of that rage came my first novel, *Lamb*. It was my way of writing about the Troubles in Northern Ireland. The second novel *Cal* was about someone on the fringes of violence. The third, *Grace Notes*, was about being on the verge of peace. It is in two parts. One part has a happy ending, and the other part ends not so happily. It was reflecting what was happening in Northern Ireland at that time. And then I wrote *The Anatomy School* and at the end of that novel the boy knows he is going to do something good and it's a positive ending. So, there is a progression from pessimism to optimism, reflecting the Troubles situation.

That's the kind of wee universe that I have and, throughout the years, this hasn't changed. The biggest change for me, articulated in *Grace Notes*, has been that religion has fallen away and art has taken its place — seeing what mankind is doing and recreating that in some way, whether it be through music, painting or words or other forms of artistic expression. It's mankind reflecting on itself.

Midwinter Break, which is coming out later this year, [4] is about an elderly couple from Northern Ireland on a break to Amsterdam. The answer to 'is the old couple in the novel you and Madeline?' is 'yes, and no.' It's not us, it's a creation, but the creation is looking over its shoulder at the kind of thing I have been talking to you about. There's an interweaving of fiction and real life. The old man, Gerry, is not me. I feed Gerry with things I have done, but he is not me. That's what creation is. You take a raw material and you manufacture it and you take a bit of this and a bit of that and you make it up and it comes alive.

The aspect of ageing I fear most is losing my memory. It's happening already. That's why I carry a small notebook now — so that ideas and phrases don't get lost. I often think my brain is like Gruyere cheese — it's full of holes. And then I think, 'is it Gruyere, or some other kind of cheese?' Yesterday, I said tulips instead of daffodils. The words just got interchanged somehow. Because I'm so taken up with words, I'm doubly dumfounded when I can't find the right ones. I forget people's names and even their faces. That's the worry. I console myself that I have produced a novel in my 75th year, so I can't be all that bad.

One of my stories, 'The Assessment', is about the struggle of a son putting his mother into a care home. She is not eating and is beginning to dote. This is a story crafted out of that dilemma. I then turned this into a radio play. One interesting result of this was that a woman, Professor June Andrews, who was the head of the Dementia Unit at Stirling University, contacted me. She said she had heard it on the radio while driving and had pulled over onto the hard shoulder and listened to the whole play. Later, she asked an assembled cast of Belfast actors to give a reading of the play at her unit's annual conference. I was delighted because this was nothing to do with literature; this was to do with dementia. She said, 'I want to use it as an education tool for nurses and others in the caring professions, because the note that you strike is absolutely right.' From her scientific point of view it was right; and from my literary son-and-mother viewpoint I had also done something right. This was performed for three years in succession. Then they offered to print it and I changed the name from *The Assessment* to *The Woman from the North*, because the woman in the play is as geographically misplaced as she is mentally misplaced.

The first time I visited my mother in the care home, she asked about her sister, Betty. She had forgotten that Betty was dead. When I told her, it was a terrible shock, with oceans of tears. 'Why did nobody tell me?' Every time I visited her, she would ask after Betty. I found ways of changing the subject and not answering. Wee details of that kind are in the story.

I am aware of time running out. Because I am self-employed, I have to keep the big red book with the accounts in it. They are very expensive books. When I was buying a new one, there were two — one for fifteen years, and one for seven years. I took the one for seven years. I remember hearing a ninety-three year-old man on the radio, who was asked the same question. He said, 'well, I'll put it this way — I don't buy green bananas!'

No longer believing in an after-life causes me no worry. I see death as a completion. Once you're dead, it's over. Roman Catholic ideas of infinity and eternity and pain, burning and suffering — they must have driven people mad.

For many years, my drinking habits and reading habits clashed. Madeline would go to bed an hour earlier than me and I would sit up, listen to music and have a couple of whiskies. So, when I got to bed, I went straight off to sleep. But I stopped doing that about five years ago and now I read at night. It's not the best way to read a book. The best way is to read from start to finish at one sitting. There's a guilt involved — if I am up and in work mode, then I should be working. If the work doesn't come, I'll do emails and that sort of thing. It would be a total luxury to take a book, sit down and read for six hours. I've just finished Julian Barnes' novel about Shostakovich, *The Noise of Time*. Nowadays I read more poetry. Poetry was not such a factor in my early life. I so love it now.

I don't consciously think about or analyse my own ageing process. I recognize, though, that grandchildren have been a huge bonus, a huge joy in my later life. I know that death is tapping me on the shoulder, so to speak, but I don't have any terminal condition.

As regards my plans for the future — my immediate plans: I read a story in the newspaper a few weeks ago. I want to take it from the public domain and make it a private story. I haven't had a jag for a short story for about three or four years and suddenly I want to write one. But I haven't time at the moment because I'm involved in the possibility of my novel, *Midwinter Break*, becoming a screen play, so I'm concentrating on that.

I draw and paint a bit. I've done that throughout my life. Five or six years ago I got an iPad and I use that now for making images.

I enjoy it tremendously — heads, characters, cartoons, illustrating a holiday we had with the grandchildren, that sort of thing. When my own children were wee I would tell them stories, then I started illustrating them. It recharges the batteries for the writing. I would love to do another children's book. I've done two and a whole series of short radio stories about a boy called Andrew MacAndrew.

I think what I would suffer from, as a form of ageism, would be not being taken seriously because I was old. Robin Jenkins, whom I knew, was quietly angry that nobody paid enough attention to him in later life.

There's a part of writing that says 'me, me, pay attention to me!' Everybody who takes up a pen must have experienced this. You would like to be the best you possibly can be and if no one pays attention, it's disappointing. As an English teacher, I delighted in making pupils readers, of recruiting people into that world where books and writers were exciting.

One of the questions you sent me in advance asked how the tendency to be calmer in old age sits with the need for some kind of nervous tension to spark creativity — the grit in the oyster that produces the pearl. I can answer that in one word — Trump! I've left behind the conflicts in Ireland, but there are other social things that make me angry and therefore make me want to write. Somebody like Ken Loach — all he has to do is look around him. He's 82 and making work that's brilliant.

I'm a story teller, not an academic. If you begin with a jag and develop it, you suddenly get a blaze. You don't ask where it's coming from. Flannery O'Connor talks about writing being a series of pictures — I think that's great!

Your mind can take you anywhere. I don't enjoy writing, but I love having written, particularly when it comes out right.

Notes

1. Aosdána is a unique Irish artistic institution with the objective of supporting artists and their creativity. It is funded by the State through the Arts Council.

2. Vasily Grossman (1905–1964): Russian journalist and novelist. His report on Treblinka was one of the first to tell the world of the Nazi death camps. His novel, *Life and Fate*, sharply criticized Stalinism. It was suppressed and never published in his lifetime. Copies were smuggled out of the Soviet Union and it was eventually published in the West in 1988.

3. Based on the end of his novel, *Grace Notes*, Bernard wrote the libretto for another short opera for Scottish Opera. Performed in March/April 2018. Composer: Samuel Bordoli; director: Kally Lloyd-Jones.

4. Since the time of the interview, *Midwinter Break* has been published to great acclaim and has won the Novel of the Year Award for the 2017 Irish Book Awards.

The Fountain Pen

Recently I lost my fountain pen but discovered it again in the pocket of a rarely used jacket and my first action, naturally, was to try to write with it only to find that it functioned poorly — the flow of ink to the page was stultified and intermittent and no matter how often I changed the cartridge there was no improvement — as a result I ceased to use the pen for some time but I missed handling it — the heft of its heavy metal barrel — so much so, that I took it into a pen shop to have it repaired at whatever the cost — enquiring of the pleasant woman behind the counter if the pen could be fixed and she puckered her mouth, looked at the nib through a magnifying glass and asked if it had been damaged at any point and on hearing that it hadn't she recommended that I take it home and immerse the top half of the pen (the engine room, she called it) in cold water and leave it overnight demonstrating as she talked the inside of a new pen by unscrewing it and revealing its gills where the ink gathered before making its way, via the nib, onto the page with the advice, 'These can become clogged but the overnight steep should clean it out,' she said as she screwed up and capped the demonstration pen, 'But you must make sure, when the pen and its ink has been freed, to write with it every day — a long sentence,' to which I said, 'Writing is a life sentence,' and, like the good boy I am, I did as she bade me, plopping the pen's engine room into a full Waterford crystal glass, changing the inky black water many times over the evening and the next day rinsing and drying and reassembling the pen, complete with a new black ink cartridge and as it was singing sweetly across the page I realised that the tense had changed and it is what I am doing at this moment with this very fountain pen — completing a long sentence.

*

I chose this piece because it is the right length and complete. It is also appropriate because it deals with writing, time, creativity and decrepitude. This piece appears in *Funny Bone: Flashing for Comic Relief*, an anthology of flash fiction published by Flash: The International Short-Story Press in 2017.

You may also wish to consult: http://www.bernardmaclaverty.
com/

Bernard MacLaverty, Contemporary Irish Writers — a Bucknell
series by Richard Rankin Russell.

LEE GERSHUNY (Age 78)

I met poet and playwright Lee Gershuny at the Scottish Storytelling Centre in Edinburgh, a place she knows well, having had some of her plays performed there. I had forgotten how petite she was, but the helmet of white hair, the radiant smile I remembered. She was born in New York City, but from the age of 10 lived in small towns in northern New York State.

'I left the University of Rochester, New York in the middle of my third year even though I was an honours student with full scholarships. I didn't know why I was studying and couldn't connect to what I regarded as superficial materialistic values of my classmates. I went to Israel because I felt there was a community of like souls there — courageous people, some who survived the concentration camps, people who had walked thousands of miles to create a new life and who gave up religion to discover who they really were. That inspired me. I lived in Jerusalem for about a year where I discovered the poet/visual artist William Blake and, inspired by his work, dedicated my writing to touch people as deeply as Blake touched me.'

Lee has been described as 'spiritual'. Yes, that came across. 'My parents were spiritual socialists in following various esoteric paths that focused on service to humanity. I was brought up to live consciously and creatively in harmony with myself and the rest of humanity.'

When she returned to the Big Apple, her birthplace, she not only completed her undergraduate studies in Literature and Linguistics, but also her graduate studies with a PhD in Applied Linguistics. There she totally immersed herself in the city's cultural and social life of concerts, theatre, opera, poetry readings, exhibitions, parties, etc.

In New York, she enjoyed a successful career teaching in colleges and universities while continuing both academic and creative writing. Although she loved research and publishing scholarly articles, she realised that what she really wanted was to focus entirely on creative writing. With the support of a university faculty award in creative writing, she was finally able to do this when she came to Edinburgh in 1988.

Just about the first thing Lee said to me was, 'I got married recently!' Her new spouse is Rodney Stares, her life partner of thirty years, an Englishman she met in New York. It was Rodney who brought Lee to Scotland. He felt that Edinburgh was the best place in the UK for both of them to do the work they loved and follow their other interests. But if she preferred to stay in the US, then he was okay with that as long as he was able to have a garden! The way Rodney described Edinburgh struck a deep chord in Lee. Without hesitation, she said, 'Let's go to Edinburgh. I've never been to Scotland.'

'After all, I'm a wanderer,' she says and explains that *Gershon*, in Hebrew, means 'the exiled one' or 'wanderer.' Adding 'uny' onto the end makes a complete Hebrew sentence that means 'they threw me out.' Part of being a wanderer is that she doesn't identify with labels even though she acknowledges that she's 'a woman, American, a New Yorker, Scottish, Jewish, a teacher, an artist and "everyone who crosses my path."'

Thirty was the right number of years on which to finally marry, Lee informs me, because three is a special number — the Trinity of Body, Mind and Spirit. Rodney and Lee had a simple ceremony with just two guests as witnesses in the Leith Registrar's wedding room in what was once the Leith Theatre. 'How appropriate,' she says.

On the back of the card announcing their marriage in Edinburgh on US Thanksgiving Day (24th November 2016) is a poem written by Lee:

Map to Eternity

We found a map to Eternity
with no lines connecting the dots,
no signs pointing the way,
no reason to go and
no reason to stay.

We dress for the trip
with no change of clothes,
nothing to find and
nothing to hold,

Only the map and
the light on the road.

Lee has been busy arranging for her company, The Elements World Theatre, to go on tour later in the year with *Reflections of a Constant Monk*. Lee set up the company, which grew out of the community theatre work she had been doing, in 1992.

'I am its sole writer, but I work with amazing artists, dancers and musicians who are on the same wavelength as I. *Reflections of a Constant Monk* premiered at the 2016 Luminate Festival of Creative Ageing. The musicians and I were all over fifty, you see. When I was writing in Mexico on holiday, there was one voice that was mine, but not mine — the voice of the monk, the wanderer, anyone. It just poured out of me. I was in the flow.'

A few samples from the flyers and press release show us the sort of performance it is:

'Incorporating storytelling, poetry and original music. Join a modern monk as he, or sometimes she, makes a poetical and musical journey through a world of challenging encounters with familiar experiences — gaining weight, meeting a bully, falling in love, etc. Often gentle and funny, frequently poignant and always intelligently observed...rich with a sense of pilgrimage and possibility.'

Lee adds that it's a fusion of poetry, parable, storytelling and music. It is like a surreal riddle or a Zen koan [1]. Basic questions emerge through a series of small adventures, questions like, who am I? Why am I here?

The poem on the reverse side of their marriage announcement is the opening poem from this production. Lee, who also teaches meditation, tells me that, for her, there is no separation between life as it is and the meditative state. 'I'm in a meditative state right now by simply being alert now and speaking from inner peace. I don't need to have my eyes closed.' Lee teaches a form of meditation known as the Bright Path Ascension. In its simplest form you learn four initial techniques based on Praise, Gratitude, Love and Compassion. 'And we ask what do you most want to bring into your life? What is your deepest longing?' Lee's name as a meditation teacher is Srivani, which is another name for the goddess Saraswati, Mother of the Arts. The Bright Path Ascension meditation has been taught to prisoners, the warden and guards who volunteered to try it in the most violent maximum security prison in Mexico. 'A documentary film, *A Mindful Choice*, was made about how individuals and communities have benefited from meditation practise. To see the bliss and the peace on the prisoners' faces was inspiring. They finally felt they were somebody and they had a life to lead in peace. The reduction in the level of violence in the prison was extraordinary.' The film has been inspiring many people all over the world to make that 'mindful choice' to find an approach to meditation that works for them.

Next week Lee will be attending a conference in Edinburgh on Spirituality in Prisons. 'I'm very interested in teaching meditation in prisons and also in schools. I was delighted to learn that Conflict Resolution, mediation and meditation are taught in some Scottish schools.'

Lee sees a strong connection between creativity and meditation. 'Everyone is naturally creative and meditation allows us to go more deeply into the inner sources of creativity. The chattering mind settles down stress-free without trying or forcing the mind to stop thinking. A greatly simplified way of saying this is that, in meditative states of being, the rational left side of the brain rests in harmony with the non-rational, creative right side of the brain. You don't know what might emerge, but you let it take you wherever it takes you and amazing, magical things happen. You become like a child, innocent, playful, but far more aware and attentive to what's happening both inside and outside of your physical "reality." Jesus said it beautifully: "Until you become as little children, you cannot enter into the Kingdom of Heaven". So, here we are, becoming younger all the time!'

Lee goes on to qualify this by saying that, although we never lose the awe, wonder, curiosity and innocence of children, we also cultivate the wisdom that experience may bring. This life journey reminds her of Blake's *Songs of Innocence and Experience*.

When they moved to Edinburgh, Rodney set up the Foundation for Community Leadership Development to help community leaders in council estates — places where people often felt trapped in negative situations — to have more confidence and develop natural creativity skills as community activists. Lee's input to this was to develop a course called 'From Coping to Creating.' The course asked: what do you most want to create in your life — both for your community and for yourself? It was based on a course Lee had been teaching in the United States called 'Technologies for Creating.' Rodney and Lee were joint directors of the Foundation. They had a team of facilitators, many of them trained as gestalt therapists[2].

'Our leadership style was one of collaboration, rather than the top-down hierarchical model, often seen in community development programmes. When the funding dried up, I focused most of my attention on writing and developing a theatre that was both cross-cultural and, when appropriate, interdisciplinary, including text, dance, music, poetry, film, etc.

I had studied and taught Conflict Resolution skills which I believe helped me become a better playwright — all drama deals with conflict. A theme that runs through all my plays is the potential we all have to stop in the midst of conflict and change course. It was a conscious decision on my part to allow the characters I developed to find a new way of looking at their conflict. In other words, become more conscious of what really mattered to them, their values and priorities. Themes of redemption and transformation characterised my work in merging the healing and creative arts. My style tended to be absurd and surreal with what one reviewer called an "idiosyncratic sense of humour."'

Lee says that she sees herself as 'something of a mythologist.' She has written a series of poems called *Love Fables* in which there are different animals in love relationships and her plays deconstruct and transform well-known myths.

'The first major myth we explored was *Return to Eden* in 1992. It was a community theatre event preceded by a week of workshops in an Edinburgh park. The collaborative workshops generated a structure for devising the performance with the "audience." The audience and actors played together to build the set and resolve the dramatic conflict. I remember that we had planted a tree in the park during the workshop period, which became 'The Tree of

Life.' Two workshop participants — one a Ukrainian professional dancer who didn't know English and the other a Scottish wood sculptor — played the roles of lumbermen looking for a tree to chop down. One chose our newly planted 'Tree of Life' over the others' protests and commitment to protect it. The whole audience and workshop participants built a big wall around the wee Tree to prevent its destruction by anyone else. Our job was to find a way to 'return to Eden' and open safe passage through the walls without using force or abuse and without harming ourselves and the 'Tree of Life.' Could we be trusted? I was the 'inner director' and called myself 'The Absent-Minded Storyteller' because I didn't 'remember' the story since it only existed in the moment and was gradually emerging as we went along. I chose the Garden of Eden myth because I was interested in the genesis of evil. Would it emerge in an open, unstructured drama? It actually did — magically and playfully. The 'audience' and the actors processed the conflict like children at play — only the game we played created a win/win resolution with no punishment involved. We could only return in peaceful, 'innocent' play, dancing and laughing together.

We created another version of *Return to Eden* when Penumbra International commissioned me to create a week of events for the Federation of Mental Health International Conference (1998), held at Heriot Watt University. The various events invited conference delegates to play with The Elements team of Edinburgh and Glasgow — professional actors and community folk in different states of 'mental health.' Larry Butler, with members of Survivors' Poetry Scotland, joined us in making non-rational interventions in the seemingly rational conference programme. It was a magical merging of the light from the east with that of the west and the harmonising of rational and non-rational actions. I re-structured *Return to Eden* as part of this for a plenary session, with the audience shouting out answers posed to a classical Indian dancer standing and moving as the Tree of Life. We were a huge hit because we were 'wacky' by making the non-rational as essential as the rational. A Polish psychologist said the highlight of the whole conference had been The Elements World Theatre because we had shown that what we all needed more than anything was unconditional love. I nearly jumped out of my seat with joy that at last someone understood what our work was about. I chose my life's work in art over therapy because I could be free to be 'wacky' and unconventional and it could more easily be accepted via theatre than the more 'rational' theoretical frameworks of the therapeutic arts.

Then there was *Theseus and the Minotaur: A Love Story*, and *The Old Woman Who Lived in A...* They were dramatic storytelling through poetry, music and dance. All of my deconstructed myths illustrate how consciousness and meditation connect with creativity. I feel that theatre is not only an intervention in the collective dream and the collective culture, but also simultaneously makes the individual's dream part of a collective experience. In the theatre a world is created where you are collectively and individually experiencing something which is the same, yet different, for everyone. When you read a novel, you read it alone and it's not the same.

Creativity is as natural as child's play. Creativity is play; and it's breaking the rules and being free. When people ask what I do, I say, "I play." We are all creative. There are so many aspects to it. Defining it is a left brain activity, but creativity itself is a right brain action. Creativity is integral with meditation because you are accessing deep inner sources when you don't know what will emerge. A friend once asked me why I write. My automatic response was, 'to surprise myself.' The unknown, the unknowing is at the centre of creativity. The rational mind knows things and has lots of information and 'good ideas'. Meditation challenges the rational mind to find balance and harmony with the non-rational mind. Meditation allows habits of mind to gradually dissolve while enabling one to access that culturally unconditioned voice that has no rules attached to it. It just is what it is. On a feedback form for one of our productions, someone wrote: "I was deeply moved and I don't know why." That was music to my ears! It's the not knowing 'why', maybe even not understanding, that often opens the doors of perception beyond the conditioned, pre-conceptual closed mind.

I am more relaxed about my creativity than I used to be. Even though I was a "committed" academic, I still wanted to break free from the part of academe I regarded as a "mental institution". I tried to write a play that would be a big Broadway hit and make enough money to support me. I fell into the trap of writing for a particular goal instead of trying to free my voice from all institutions. As soon as I stopped striving for that kind of success, my plays began winning prizes and awards and I returned to my original inspiration to write with the profound simplicity of William Blake.

Something that has changed as I get older is that I don't do a show on the fringe anymore; it's too exhausting. And fairly recently I let go of producing a new play every year.'

I asked Lee what aspects of ageing she feared most.

'I express things more in terms of what I'm going towards instead of what I'm fearful of or avoiding. So what motivates me — and this is partly through meditation and Qigong [3] — is to move my attention away from fear to constant gratitude for what is, and unconditional love. The first time I fell in love I realised I didn't know how to love anyone. I dedicated myself to learning how to love. The second time I fell in love I realised I didn't know how to love myself. I almost lost my life in an automobile accident because I didn't know how to love myself. And I realised that I had to wake up to who I really am or I might accidentally kill myself. Consciousness without drugs was what I dedicated my life to. I used to be a very harsh, demanding critic of myself. Teaching meditation has been a tremendous gentle, humbling opening of my heart. I think that's why Rodney and I decided to get married. We were both on this journey of loving each other and the world unconditionally. It's not always easy! I think Donald Trump is an awkward blessing to the American people. They are waking up to their own greatness; they are fighting back, they are actively standing up for each other and what we collectively value: the Planet, freedom and peace. It's inspiring.'

The conversation turned to reading.

'I don't read as much as I used to. I rarely read novels. The last novel I read was James Robertson's amazing book, *The Professor of Truth*. Beautiful language is not enough for me. I'm interested in something that inspires. Or, as one of my students and closest friends said years ago, "Move towards what opens you." I read a lot of stuff on the web in following a thread of interest, sometimes about the various activists and political figures both here and in the U.S. whom I support — financially when I can, and through meditation, and through various pressure groups and activities.

I'm dedicated to promoting a culture of peace in my writing, political and personal life.'

Several near-death experiences have awakened Lee's sense of what life is about.

'So death is my ally. It enables me to be better at life. Each time I came close to death — a car accident, being threatened with a knife, illness — I just accepted it. Letting go, not holding on, is something I practise regularly in meditation. Whatever emerges is what I deal with. Through Ascension meditation I feel I am able to rest in Nothingness and Silence without fear.'

In reply to my question about the gifts that accompany ageing, Lee says:

'I am learning to see slowing down as a gift. I used to have very little patience. I was a New Yorker, trying to pack it all in. I am learning patience and to give myself space. Other gifts that have come in later life are deeper self-knowledge and feeling connected, both to my true self and the Grand Design. Recently I asked an ageing artist friend what was most important to him. And he said, "Gratitude. I'm so grateful I'm alive. So many people I know have died just in the last year." I feel the same way. I'm so grateful that I can love unconditionally, that I can have pain without popping pills or suffering, that I am more present. I don't know what lies ahead, but I'm grateful for what is now and just to go with the flow.'

Since passing seventy, which of her plays have given her the most pride and satisfaction?

'I am proud of my whole body of work and the way it has evolved from community theatre to professional productions. I feel I have produced some great work. It's difficult to pick out just one. I am proud of everything the Elements World Theatre has produced since I founded it in 1992.

I have to mention *Theseus and the Minotaur: A Love Story* (2012) and *Lockerbie Lost Voices* (2013), which I did for the 25th anniversary of the Lockerbie air disaster. Although I didn't realise it until recently, my whole life expresses a longing to connect with the Divine, but religion never quite hit the spot. In my play,

Messages From a Mental Institution (2014) I felt I had connected with the Divine. The mental institution of the title is the chattering monkey mind we accept as life and as our true selves. In the play, a woman's husband has disappeared and in her search for him she believes he's sending her messages from a mental institution. She wants to help him, but she doesn't know where he is or why he's there. She looks everywhere and consults various authorities, all played by the same actor who plays her husband. Where is this mental institution? Who is really sending the messages and why? An absurd, surreal production with plenty of laughs invites the audience to leave their preconceptions behind and be totally unprepared for whatever happens. And, of course, there is my newest work, *Reflections of a Constant Monk* (2016–17) with its parables and surprises — totally different from anything I've ever written or produced before and the first time in almost 20 years that I'm actually presenting my own work on stage.

Lee's advice to those approaching later life is, 'be present and stay committed to your heart's deepest desire regardless of whether you 'think' it's possible. Just see what happens and trust yourself. I feel that, in later life, we have an opportunity to "return," not to childhood but to our essence, forgetting what we've learned and remembering who we truly are as human beings.'

Notes

1. A koan is a riddle or puzzle that Zen Buddhists use during meditation to help them unravel greater truths about the world and about themselves.

2. Gestalt therapy is an existential/experiential form of psychotherapy that emphasizes personal responsibility, and focuses upon the individual's experience in the present moment, the therapist—client relationship, the environmental and social contexts of a person's life, and the self-regulating adjustments people make as a result of their overall situation.

3. Qigong is a holistic system of co-ordinated body posture and movement, breathing and meditation used for health, spirituality, and martial arts training.

From *Theseus and the Minotaur: A Love Story.* Dialogue between Theseus and the Minotaur. The theme is Love.

MINOT:	I'm everything you'd want to be.
THESEUS:	Man or Beast? A false dichotomy.
MINOT:	Now you can see the beauty of me.
	Now you can see I'm all humanity.
THESEUS:	Man, Beast, God...
MINOT:	Theseus, you're decidedly odd.
	Don't forget you're here to cut off my
	Bullish head,
	Not fall in love with me.
THESEUS:	Forget? Not me. Who am I killing?
MINOT:	Is it the Beast you want dead?
	Something you imagined or
	Something I said?
THESEUS:	...or the blindly frightened Monster
	swirling around in my head?
MINOT:	What took you so long to see your fear?
	Now see in me all that you care for.
	Face me, embrace me. Embrace all that I
	am.
THESEUS:	I know you, you arrogant Monster.
MINOT:	What a laugh. You're confused.
	You're here to be consumed
	by your own arrogance.
THESEUS:	I'm here to end your gluttony.
MINOT:	I'm immortal, the Sun God of the Cretans.
	King Minos and I are one:
	The Bull is Sun, Fertile, Rich,
	Life giving, eternal in Nature.
	I am the Creator / the Destroyer in One.
	I will always live in the minds of men and
	women.
	They long for me eternally
	as they wander through the Labyrinth of
	memories and mundane fears.

THESEUS:	I come in peace, Great Minotaur.
MINOT:	Really? Which piece? The rump, the tongue or the brains?
	I eat it all!
THESEUS:	I admire you, great Minotaur.
MINOT:	Of course you do. How nice. I've heard that one before.
	Pass the salt.
THESEUS:	No thanks.
MINOT:	The mustard too.
THESEUS:	I'm not hungry.
MINOT:	I have a treat in store for you.
THESEUS:	No, thanks.
MINOT:	I have longevity, beauty, youth, power and lots more.
THESEUS:	But no friends.

You may also wish to consult http://www.the-elements.org.uk

9. TWO ISLAND VOICES

John Purser
Pauline Prior-Pitt

John Purser lives on Skye and Pauline Prior-Pitt lives on North Uist. Both have come under the spell of island life and are influenced by the wild environment of the Western Isles. In addition to writing, both also express themselves through another art-form — John through music, Pauline through painting.

Photograph by Terry Williams

JOHN PURSER (Age 75)

John Purser has been described as one of Scotland's most important cultural ambassadors. He was born in Glasgow of Irish parents in 1942. In his early twenties he took diplomas in Composition, Singing and Violoncello at the Royal Scottish Academy of Music and Drama. With the aid of a Caird scholarship, he continued to study composition with Sir Michael Tippett and Dr Hans Gál. As a mature student he took a First in English Literature at Glasgow University (1980), followed by a PhD (1989). In 2009 he was awarded the degree of *Doctor Honoris Causa* by the University of Aberdeen.

He has been a freelance composer, cellist, musicologist, critic, poet, playwright and broadcaster, as well as lecturing on classical music for many years for the Glasgow University Extra-Mural Department (as it was then called), and has lectured and broadcast on Scottish music world-wide. He was the first Manager of the Scottish Music Information Centre, 1985–1987 and was joint editor with James MacMillan of *Stretto* magazine.

More recently, John studied Gaelic at Sabhal Mòr Ostaig (the Gaelic College on the Isle of Skye) where he has assisted in course development. In 2006 he was appointed as a Researcher, and was Gaelic Music Course Director there from 2006–2008. He was one of the team of researchers for the project, 'Window to the West — towards a redefinition of the visual within Gaelic Scotland', funded by the Arts & Humanities Research Council [1]. In 2007, already established as the greatest living authority on the history of Scottish music, he completed an expanded and up-dated edition of his book, *Scotland's Music*, and a series of 50 radio programmes on the same subject for BBC Radio Scotland. In 2009 he published a critical biography of Erik Chisholm [2]. His collection of new and selected poems, *There is No Night*, was published in 2014 by Kennedy & Boyd.

John lives on the Island of Skye where he and his American wife, Barbara, are crofters. He was Chairman of the local Common Grazings Committee from 2003–2010 and Vice-Chairman of the Strathaird Community Association from 2004. He was Secretary of the Elgol and Torrin Historical Society, 1996–2002, and Secretary of the Strathaird Management Committee, 1995–2001. He was a Trustee of The John Muir Trust from 2001–2004. An article in the *Sunday Herald* described him 'as infectiously passionate about mackerel fishing and cattle herding as he is about the ancient history of Scotland's music.' [3]

John very kindly invited me to coffee and to lunch at his home near Elgol in the South West of Skye. Unfortunately, I had to cancel this trip because of ill-health in the family, so John offered to send me written answers to his questions.

Your poetry collection, There is No Night, *has been described as 'steeped in the natural world'. Could you please expand on this. Do you feel that, as you get older, your connection to the natural world becomes stronger?*

My connection with the natural world has been with me since I was a little boy. We walked, we climbed, we swam in rivers and mountain pools and the sea, and we did so at all seasons and wherever a bus or train would take us. Later I rock-climbed (never very proficient but had the privilege of my very first rock-climbing lessons from none other than Bill Murray). We climbed for pleasure and for a love of nature; not competitively. My parents taught us the names of all the plants and trees, birds and animals. In the summers we stayed on our grandmother's farm in County Wicklow and helped with everything from calves to hens, stooking oats and barley, to weeding turnips. The connection was and is so fundamental that as soon as I was able, I moved to Skye and started crofting, keeping cattle and a boat.

Could you please say something about the different creative processes involved in composing music and writing poetry.

Composing music is ten times more labour intensive simply because of the physical business of setting it down on paper. It is also much more demanding because the techniques involved are not only linear (essentially all poetry is linear) but vertical and contrapuntal. On top of that, the exigencies related to the respective musical instruments (the human voice included) and, frequently, specific performers, requires a much higher degree of artistic flexibility. It also requires a higher degree of (for want of a better word) 'visualisation' because, while it is easy to read a poem off the page, it is far more difficult to read, say, a string quartet or a symphony off the page — though one or two lines can be read fluently by those who are good sight-readers — and I mean here, without recourse to any instrument, keyboards included.

I know you have studied Gaelic. Do you do any form of creative writing in Gaelic?

Scarcely any and that not for publication. I am not a native speaker, nor am I fluent enough in the language.

Why did you stop writing radio plays?

Because of a change of commissioning policy in the BBC which centralised control in London. I submitted a scenario to BBC Scotland which was accepted for production but turned down in London. I am an award-winning radio playwright and of my six radio plays, my three full-length ones were Sunday plays and very well received. I have not got time or energy to put up with that kind of imperialism.

How much of having been to Fettes [4] still remains with you?

Quite a bit. I acted in many plays, sang many solos as well as in the choir, played in the orchestra, debated in the Paramecium (we looked down on the debating society as a vulgar body!), painted in the art room, listened to many LPs in the music department, and was well taught by intelligent and thoroughly engaged teachers. The school also kept us very fit and fed us very well. The CCF tolerated my latent Irish Republicanism and taught me how to blow things up. Best of all was going on camp with the RAF Mountain Rescue. We got to climb mountains, go on long treks, the food was better than the army's and we managed to sneak in some alcohol now and again.

What was the subject of your PhD?

The Literary Works of Jack B. Yeats. Jack was known to both sides of my family and two of his oils were in my parents' house, as well as some of his novels, largely regarded as wayward and incomprehensible — which intrigued me. I loved them and, while they may seem wayward, they are not so; nor are they incomprehensible. My thesis was published as a book in the Princess Grace of Monaco Memorial Irish Library series.

How do you react to the description of yourself as 'an iconoclastic rogue'?

Timothy Neat states that this is how I have been described — but by whom, I know not. I am rather proud of it though it is wildly and sadly inaccurate. 'Iconoclastic' I am not, because I love visual representations of anything and God (the grey-minded old sod) can be included in that: but if by 'iconoclastic' is meant breaker of norms and fashions, then it will do fine. As for 'rogue' — I am more mischievous than roguish.

Does religion or any form of belief system play a part in your life? If so, has this changed over the years, and does it influence your creative work?

Other people's belief systems have had a profound effect upon my creative and academic work, and Christianity is central to that: but I am not a believer and if I have any religion, then it is music. In the process of researching and writing up *Scotland's Music* I had to come to terms with the Christian religion from its earliest days in Western Europe, and into the later mediaeval period, through the High Renaissance into the Reformation, and on into our own days where both secular and Christian spiritual motivations remain strong. In my role as an historian and broadcaster I did my best to inhabit the worlds which inspired the different musics and to empathise with them so that I could convey to others something of their inner depth and meaning. I am also interested in philosophy and theology.

Have your motives for writing changed at all as you grow older? And have your motives for composing music changed?

Not really. I have worked throughout my life almost exclusively to commission — whether financially guaranteed or performance guaranteed — and have composed very little purely for its own sake. I am essentially a communicator and a social creature and much of my poetry is for others rather than purely self-reflective. For the same reason I was not going to work up elaborate scenarios for radio plays on spec and I turned down Scottish Opera when they asked for an opera proposal from a number of composers of whose work only a proportion would be chosen.

In general, has the nature of your creativity changed with the age-ing process? Have these changes affected you as a writer and you as a musician in different ways?

As a writer I have become more assured and fluent. As a composer, much less productive and more overtly influenced by traditional music than hitherto.

To what extent does reading inform or stimulate your creativity? Are your reading habits changing?

I read very widely, but in the last years the focus has been increas-ingly on academic work, both Gaelic related, music related and philosophically related. When I read for relaxation, I prefer a relatively mindless detective novel, so long as the writing is good enough.

Have you experienced a 'late life crisis'? What form did it take and what sort of things triggered it? Has it affected your creativity?

I had a mid-life crisis, if you like — divorce and re-marriage and all that that entails. New love is always inspiring.

What, from your own personal experience, have been the most neg-ative aspects of ageing? How have these impacted on your creativity both as a writer and as a musician?

Loss of energy and physical capacity. My brain is functioning as well as ever, if a little differently, but my body is no longer a match for my requirements despite the splendid efforts of our NHS.

What gifts has old age brought you?

I *hope* I am more patient and more interested in others. Self-know-ledge? Well I believe I know myself and can live happily with who I am, but that has always been the case, and anyway, who are we kid-ding? The giftie hasnae been given us. Humour is fundamental.

How do you envisage the remaining years of your life? Do you see yourself continuing to be actively creative into even later life?

Yes, I expect to be creative to the last, if more sporadically.

Have you experienced ageism as a writer or as a musician? What actions are needed to counteract this?

Not really. By my age I have taken up a good deal of the world's time and attention and it would be greedy to seek for more.

Of all the things you have produced as a writer since passing 70 (not necessarily published), what gives you the most satisfaction and pride?

Some dedicatory poems — one for Dame Beryl Gray, then *in memoriam* Leslie Henderson, and one for the Irish poet Paddy Bush and his wife Fiona. In each case these poems came to me prompted by events or memory, and they came to me as fully-formed and spontaneously as though I were speaking and almost as rapidly. They required very little revision and each one of them reaches beyond its immediate subject matter because the people for whom they were written are or were themselves amongst those who reach out.

Did you, when younger, have any role models as regards continuing to be creative and productive in later life?

Hans Gál[5]. He was very old, still very productive, he was a patient teacher, devoted to truth and disdaining of fashion, with a passionate love and respect for, and a truly profound knowledge of the work of the great composers of the past, such that he could also point out to me their mistakes and how they themselves had learnt from them. I always left his company feeling a little taller. He made me feel a part of that great tradition and to understand the responsibilities that one was therefore taking on.

One theory of creativity is that creative energy comes from 'the quarrel with ourselves' (to quote Yeats), the inner tension, the grit in the oyster that produces the pearl. How have you found that this sits with the tendency in old age to be calmer, more tranquil and generally more at peace with the world?

Too many assumptions in this question and to hell with sanctimonious W.B. I would prefer Swift's *saeva indignatio*[6] and I think that more than anything, love and gratitude have increasingly motivated my work.

What advice would you give to younger writers and musicians who aspire to continue being productive into old age?

Stay young. Stay young any way possible — and by young I mean very young, when laughter and tears are equally close to the surface and concealment unmanageable. But since we do grow old one thing we gain is the depth of memory and experience and a higher degree, one hopes, of awareness of beauty and the possibility of creating it as well as appreciating it. That is why, if I had a religion, it would be music. But eventually voices falter and fingers stiffen, ears deafen and eyes dim. Then the world of imagination and memory can not only occupy those spaces but fill them with a different kind of richness. I summon Plotinus[7] here to my aid — describing The Beautiful:

This is the spirit that Beauty must ever induce, wonderment and a delicious trouble, longing and love and a trembling that is all delight. For the unseen all this may be felt as for the seen; and this the Souls feel for it, every Soul in some degree, but those the more deeply that are the more truly apt to this higher love — just as all take delight in the beauty of the body but all are not stung as sharply, and those only that feel the keener wound are known as lovers. ('Ennead I.6', trans. MacKenna.)

Notes

1. Window to the West — *Uinneag dhan Aird an Iar*: the development of the University of the Highlands and Islands has resulted in a significant growth in research into Gaelic culture. However the place of the visual arts within this culture has largely been neglected and is only defined as a footnote to the broader history of the visual arts in Scotland or to the music and poetry of the Gael. This project addresses this imbalance. The fundamental premise is that by placing the study and practice of visual art at the heart of

a multidisciplinary research project, it creates a new focus for the understanding of Highland culture (*Gaidhealtachd*).

2. Erik William Chisholm (1904–1965) was a Scottish composer, pianist, organist and conductor often known as 'Scotland's forgotten composer.'

3. This introductory section is slightly adapted from John Purser's website.

4. Fettes College is a leading independent school in Edinburgh. Originally a boarding school for boys, it became co-educational in 1983 (after John Purser's time there).

5. Hans Gál OBE (1890–1987) was an Austrian-British composer, teacher and author.

6. *Saeva indignatio*: 'Savage indignation,' a feeling of contemptuous rage.

7. Plotinus was a major Greek-speaking philosopher of the ancient world. In his philosophy there are three principles: the One, the Intellect, and the Soul. His teacher was Ammonius Saccas and he is of the Platonic tradition.

A sample of writing done since passing 70

This poem is relevant to the whole issue of age and death and also to my views on religion, written this year (2017).

For Sheila, In Memoriam Leslie Henderson

When your widow asked for roses to be
bedded into soil, I asked in turn
that one such plant might be
the little white rose of Scotland:
for there was much of Scotland in you —
a hard metamorphosed spirit, multi-
coloured, often contorted, but utterly itself.
No compromises here; a geological
certainty, and a beauty determined
by realities — none harsher than those you faced
fighting a long slow retreat.
No comfort from Boethius there. If God
existed he would be, as my father once maintained,
a grey dispiriting creature. But it was you
who freed me from religion; probed with your scalpel mind
into the rotten sentiments, the shifty morals of the primrose
        path.
And so that little rose, clean-scented in critical mountain air,
recalls you to me now on the last lap of my race
and I am free to salute you in astonished retrospect
when what I am will yield all its alignments and disperse —
but not before I've penned
this single tribute to my first best friend.

You may also wish to consult www.johnpurser.net

PAULINE PRIOR-PITT (Age 77)

I was born in Hull, enjoy being a Yorkshire woman and am grateful to have had one Irish grandfather. I trained as an actress and drama teacher, and later took and later studied for an advanced degree in Special Needs and Dyslexia at Birmingham University. I then became the Teacher Adviser for thirty primary schools in Coventry, organising Special Needs in-service training courses for serving teachers. I was also a part-time lecturer at the University of Warwick.

Although not born with a pencil in my fist, I have been a verse speaker for most of my life, so that when I began to write in my late thirties, the knowledge about verse forms, structure, sounds, what makes a poem, was deeply ingrained. Scotland has always pulled me northwards and in 1997 I moved to live permanently on the Isle of North Uist.

I write poetry, mainly about women, although men tell me I'm writing about them. The poems are written to perform and with a slight introduction are accessible at a first hearing. I enjoy trying to make the ordinary, extraordinary; taking the domestic scene, family life, relationships between men and women, and heightening them. Some of the poems are humorous; usually with a sting; and always with serious intent. Lately I've been writing obsessively about ageing and dying.

The other strand of my poetry concerns North Uist. I collect images from the landscape; write about this land of water, wind, and stone, and the awesome sea. My collection *North Uist Sea Poems* won the 2006 Callum Macdonald Award for pamphlet poetry.

Your poetry collection Be an Angel *is described as being about the preoccupations of women. What preoccupations do you have now that you didn't have when younger?*

Well, I'm much freer now than when I was younger. I can please myself more, although I still have too many commitments involving other people; organising poetry events on the island, running a writing group etc. I would like to be even more selfish. Other people's illnesses take up my time as well. I'm more philosophical about life in general. And I have time to walk beside the sea. My main preoccupations are writing, painting (in my own painting shed), spending time with my husband, children, grandchildren, and meeting friends. Time is the main thing. I'm not in quite such a hurry as I used to be.

The blurb about Meeting the Stone *refers to 'coming to terms with the difficult issues that face us all, especially as we get old.' And your collection* Three Score Years & Some *is largely about the experience of ageing. Could you please say something about what, for you, these issues and experiences have been.*

Well, I began writing about ageing when I was in my early 60s, when I wasn't old at all. My poems were humorous, about being forgetful, lines on my face etc. Now I write about dementia, other people's illnesses (not my own because I'm fortunate to be in good health), but you are not prepared for how the ill health of relatives and friends will affect you, and their deaths; their funerals. An old friend told me that 'old age is like living in a foreign country.' I haven't begun to experience that yet; most of the time I don't think about my age. I'm preoccupied with death though and wrote a complete pamphlet called *Disappearing Out*, to try and rid myself of the threat of it. I'm in a group of four friends who meet to talk about death. And I have written an Advance Directive because I don't want to be kept alive artificially.

Then there are the unexpected joys of grandchildren. I have two teenage grandsons who live in England, and now, living across the road, two grandsons aged 3 and 6 and they help to keep me fit. I also have a very loving relationship with my husband and my children and my sister and very good friends.

I know that you are a successful after-dinner speaker. What topics do you speak about?

Mostly women's issues, a sort of cradle to grave look at women's lives through my poetry. Most of my after-dinner speaking was to Ladies who Lunch, who always bought masses of my poetry books afterwards, which was encouraging.

Your website says that, amongst other things, you write about love and death. Please can you say more about your thoughts on these topics.

Well, I think these are the two most written about topics in poetry, don't you? But when you have been married for a long time, it can be hard to capture that initial rapture in a poem. I write copiously about the sea and recently have been working on a series of poems imagining that the sea is in love with a woman who walks along the edge of the tide. Death, as I have already said has been a pre-occupation for many years. I just don't want life going on without me, which is such an egotistical remark to make, but you do want to know what will happen to your children and grandchildren. I still miss my mother who died when I was twenty, before we really knew each other.

Could you expand on the extent to which North Uist has fed your creativity and influenced your writing.

Yes, when we moved here 19 years ago, I didn't think I would write about the landscape at all. Up until then I had always written about women's lives, but gradually island images crept into my writing and I wrote a book of poems called *Storm Biscuits*. Then, being obsessed by the sea, each time I walked on the shore, I wrote about how the state of the sea was on that particular day...a sort of journal, which eventually grew into a pamphlet called *North Uist Sea Poems*, which won the Calum MacDonald Award. Now images from the landscape and the sea just get mingled in with any of my poems. My sequence of poems about Alzheimer's called 'Slipping' uses sea and beach imagery.

How do you define creativity and has your definition of it changed over the years?

Oh my goodness yes. I used to think that creativity was just to do with the arts, but now I think it is life itself. How you live your life is to do with creativity, planting a garden, relationships, bringing up a family, preparing a meal, thinking, dressing, problem solving, being. They all require a creative mind.

Does religion or any form of belief system play a part in your life?

If so, has this changed over the years, and does it influence your creative work?

I was brought up as a Christian, sang in the church choir twice every Sunday. I still believe that the philosophy is fine, as is Buddhism, but I don't believe in God or life after death. Organised religion, with its hierarchies, its rules, its power, seems wrong. The established church is very wealthy, but it doesn't appear to be helping the poor. We shouldn't be arguing about who has the true god. All those divisions in religion are ridiculous. My belief is that everyone should be looking after the earth. It's all we have and we should treasure it, not plunder it or pollute it or sacrifice it for greed. We should realise that the planet might be better off without us, and that we are privileged to be here.

Have your motives for writing changed at all as you grow older?

Well, I don't think my motives for writing have changed that much. My poems are written to be performed and I feel that I am my true self when I am sharing them with an audience.

To what extent does reading inform or stimulate your creativity? Are your reading habits changing?

Reading does inform my writing. It makes me more daring sometimes. I'm an avid reader of fiction and of other people's poetry. I read a lot on my iPad. More recently philosophy and books about mindfulness and meditation have been very helpful. I used to read *The Guardian* every day, but just read the Saturday *Guardian* now because that's the only day it comes to the island, although I read some articles on the iPad. I certainly read more now than I did when I was younger, because I have more time. And I don't have a television.

In general, has the nature of your creativity changed as you get older?

It depends now on what we are calling creativity. About 15 years ago I enrolled on a drawing and painting course with the idea of learning a new language, and a new way of looking in order to stimulate my writing about the landscape. I learned to paint, seriously paint, and now exhibit my paintings during the island's open studio event in the summer, and at my very modest painting shed, which overlooks the sea at the bottom of the garden. Painting and poetry feed each other very well. And it adds to the Ps; Pauline Prior-Pitt, Poet, Painter.

Have you experienced a 'late life crisis'? What form did it take and what sort of things triggered it? Has it affected your creativity?

Not a late life crisis, no. Moving to North Uist when I was 58, was a complete change of lifestyle, but an exciting one, not a crisis.

What, from your own personal experience, have been the most negative aspects of ageing? How have these impacted on your creativity?

Less energy and not yet learning to say NO. Turning down opportunities to do readings because I can't fit them in. This is because living on a remote island means I can't go and come back in less than three or four days.

What new gifts and joys have come to you with old age? How do these impact on your writing?

There have been many. For example: gaining wisdom and a more relaxed attitude to problems. Acceptance that some things just are as they are. Learning to follow my intuition (very important, the gut reaction). Not sure what impact they have on my writing though. Writing has always been a learning process and it still is, Maybe my writing isn't quite so strongly feminist as it used to be.

How do you envisage the remaining years of your life? Do you see yourself continuing to be actively creative into even later life?

That's the good thing about writing and painting. As long as I can hold a pen/brush or tap a key, I'll just keep going.

Have you experienced ageism as a writer? What actions are needed to support writers in later life?

I don't think so, more sexism than ageism. The poetry editors are still mostly male.

Of all the things you have produced as a writer since passing 70 (not necessarily published), what gives you the most satisfaction and pride?

Since passing 70, I have published three books, two pamphlets, and a CD. The book that has given me the greatest satisfaction is *Be an Angel*. It is a selected work of poems about the preoccupations of being a woman taken from my seven previous collections. It was suggested to me by the prize winning author Marion Molteno, who helped with the selection. We met last year at the Wenlock Poetry Festival and I really enjoyed the collaborative process of working with another writer.

The CD was a another collaboration, working with the composer Catherine Eunson on a suite of music based on my pamphlet *North Uist Sea Poems*. The piece was composed for flute, cello, fiddle, harp, and my speaking voice, and the performance was funded by Atlas Arts.

Do you have any role models as regards continuing to be creative and productive in later life?

Tessa Ransford was a great role model for me. I'm never sure how old people are, but there are lots of us around still writing and painting; lots and that's encouraging.

One theory of creativity is that creative energy comes from 'the quarrel with ourselves' (to quote Yeats), the inner tension, the grit in the oyster that produces the pearl. How have you found that this sits with the tendency in old age to be calmer, more tranquil and generally more at peace with the world?

Yes, I understand that quote and as a younger woman I was more feisty in my work, but there are plenty of issues to be faced, and even though I think I'm calmer now, I can still get very involved with the political. Dignity in Dying is occupying my thoughts and some poems.

What advice would you give to younger writers who aspire to continue being productive into old age?

Just keep going, meet other writers, keep learning, follow your intuition, don't follow money, have fun.

A sample of writing done since passing 70

The Dead

They walk with you
the dead.

Some skip along in front
some walk beside

some, like naughty children,

drag behind.

Others walk on top of you
crush you into nothing
or demand to be carried
like shopping.

A few slip like loose change
into pockets.

And one or two
lie curled together,
stitched into the lining of your heart.

I was in a shopping mall, waiting for a friend, people watching as we do, and I know this isn't an original thought, but as the crowds were walking towards and past me I just saw that they were carrying their dead with them. At the time it seemed like an important poem to write and in time it has taken on a life of its own. It's been used as the frontispiece in a couple of academic writings on death, and it has been used at several funerals, because mostly, to the people who are mourning, the person who has died is stitched into the lining of their hearts.

The poem is taken from my pamphlet on death, called *Disappearing Out*.

You may also wish to consult www.pauline-prior-pitt.com

www.scottishbooktrust.org.uk

DISCUSSION

After reading each other's interviews, John Purser and Pauline Prior-Pitt corresponded by email and asked each other questions arising from what each had said.

JOHN'S QUESTIONS TO PAULINE AND HER RESPONSES

I am going to probe not too seriously and perhaps sententiously — but we are being presented as wonderful old creative creatures whose ideas are assumed to be of interest to others and yet there is no hint of criticism or judgement, no justification for our having been chosen: just something approaching a 'puff'. I am uncomfortable with that. It's all too cosy. So here goes:

You write a lot about women and their preoccupations. Why?

Women and their preoccupations were uppermost in my mind when I began writing poetry in my late 30s. It was rather a dark period in my life. To summarize André Gide, the things I was making my happiness out of were not the things I had dreamed of making my happiness out of. Poetry was my way out. I had been a prize-winning verse speaker since the age of five, studied drama at college, knew about verse forms etc., but most of my examples were male poets, mostly dead. For seven years I wrote in secret about women, their juggling lives; coping with men, children, the domestic scene, gynaecology, and of course, loving and dying. I was trying to get to the truth of my experience of being a full time worker and a wife and mother, and just what that meant in the 60s and 70s. A lot of the poems were humorous. I was not confident that these subjects were the stuff of poetry, but attending a Women's Studies evening course at Warwick University persuaded me that they were, and with the encouragement of my lecturers I published my first collection, *Waiting Women*.

Should I have been writing about men and theirs? Am I already guilty?

I'm sure you were doing that naturally. Most poetry was about male preoccupations at a time when the domestic scene was not considered a suitable subject. However I am not implying that in the past women poets were only preoccupied by domesticity, far from it.

What do these questions imply to you?

To me these questions imply that you may not have realised how difficult it was for women poets to be taken seriously by male editors and publishers. Some of their writing was thought to be too personal. I remember being so thankful when I heard the wonderful Irish poet, Eavan Boland read her poem 'Night Feed', on *Woman's Hour.* It gave me courage.

You moved to North Uist and have been there for many years, its nature impinging upon your creative work. What about the language? Have you considered learning it, at least enough to converse or read in it? If not, why not? Has age made it seem too late?

I wish I had learned Gaelic when we first moved here. It all seemed too complicated and I was immersing myself in the life at Taigh Chearsabhagh Arts Centre and Museum, acting as their voluntary literature person, organising poetry evenings and writing workshops. And everyone spoke English. I do regret it now. I would like to be able to re-write some of my poems about the island in Gaelic. My two grandsons are taught in Gaelic at the nursery and at school. I did use a Gaelic phrase in a recent poem. I am tempted to learn it even at this late stage, but when I try, and my six year old grandson corrects my pronunciation, I realise just how hard it is.

You appear to have a troubled relationship with death, notwithstanding your own self-declared reasonable health at 77 and your acceptance that there is nothing hereafter — so what is the problem?

The problem is that death is forever and we won't get another turn. It's King Lear's 'never, never, never, never, never.' Sometimes I envy those who have a belief in an afterlife. I think it was Julian Barnes who said 'I don't mind the dying, it's the being dead afterwards.' That sums it up for me too.

I wrote this poem just recently on the subject. What say you?

For Dame Beryl Grey

Twice you have danced the role of Death,
and now, approaching ninety,
you speak of Death's authority,
your eyes smiling with absolute assurance.

On parting, as I reach
to kiss your proffered cheek
I have to steady myself, my hand
upon your firm slender waist.
You accept its presence there
as you have done
hundreds of hands in gestures
of strength, of beauty, and of tenderness.

Oh Death, I am smitten.
But when you stand at my bed-head
I will not ask that it be turned
to cheat you of your rights.
Instead, I will look up
and smile into your eyes
awaiting that last forever lift
high into weightless space.

This is so real John, what a lovely way to celebrate your meeting with Beryl Grey. You have brought so much more into the poem; it's beautiful, and the double meaning of 'smitten'. That is such a striking line. I love the idea of being lifted into weightless space, the dancer and the spirit.

See below my poem about death. In this case, death is a woman, of course.

Death

She clings to my lips, my breath,
covers my breasts when I dress,
strings pearls round my neck
fashions her words in my mouth.
"Forever," she says, and again,
"Forever," and "Never, ever, again."

And in bed, her head on the pillow
with mine, nightmare screams,
dreams caught in her cloak,
falling into the depths below.

And day after day at the sea, she
beckons me in to the slow dancing waves,
splashes my face, licks my cold skin,
swims below me, above me, beside me,
twists her legs round me,
pulls me close in to kiss,

whispers the bit about less
than a grain of sand in the surf,
and never again, and forever.
She knows about this.

*When you describe your reading you only mention one newspaper
(and no books or authors), and that an English one. Why not read
a Scottish newspaper?* The Herald *is reasonable,* The National, *remarkable,* The Scotsman *as poor as it has ever been but at least
related to the nation's culture.*

Yes, I wonder if I had become tired by this time. I do read *The
Herald* on Saturday, and sometimes *The Stornoway Gazette* and
Am Paipear. I'm interested in your saying, 'remarkable' about *The
National,* I'll have to give it a try. On the whole though I don't read
too much news; so much of it is opinion rather than news; so much
is just sensation and I don't give a damn about celebrities. People
all over the world are suffering because of greed. I don't understand
why some people need so much money. I hate tax avoidance. So
much of the news makes me feel angry and impotent.

Books/authors: Salley Vickers novelist and psychoanalist. Her
book *The Other Side of You* is a firm favourite, as is Ann Michael's
Fugitive Pieces. Too many others to mention, but Maggie O'Farrell,
Kathleen Jamie's poetry and prose, Nan Shepherd, Bernard
McClaverty's *Grace Notes* and his latest *Midwinter Break.* Julian
Barnes, John Williams.

I would like to know what philosophical works you are reading. I too am interested in philosophy. Are we conditioned not to venture forth with philosophical thoughts?

I'm not a philosopher like you. I read Sarah Bakewell's book, *How to Live: a life of Montaigne*, which I found enhancing, and her book *Existentialists Café* about Sartre and de Beauvoir, Heidegger, etc. I found them to be indulgent and hedonistic, and unrealistic. But then they weren't committed to a family life.

I really enjoyed *Philosophy for Life and other dangerous situations* by Jules Evans, and embraced Epictetus' art of maintaining control; how we are only in control of our own beliefs. I think I may be a stoic, but each of those Greek philosophers has a lot to offer the world.

My question is always 'if so much about life was understood 2000 years ago, why haven't we learned from it? After 9/11 why didn't Bush call in the philosophers instead of the warriors?

Other writers more to do with lifestyle are Thich Nhat Hanh, Eckhart Tole, Jon Kabat-Zinn. Most mornings I try to meditate, practice Tai Chi, and write morning pages in my journal.

I am much in agreement with your views on humanity's responsibilities to the earth. Do you feel a sense of responsibility to society and, if so, how far does it reach out beyond the society of the household and with what cultural parameters?

I'm a volunteering kind of person. Before I moved here, I was the secretary of a Cancer Support Group. I also organised all the poetry events for the annual Warwick Music Festival. Since living on the island, I have been involved in a Complementary Therapy Group promoting events and conferences. As an offshoot of this, four of us now host an annual fun day for elderly women, called Celebrating the Cailleach. I was on the Board of Directors at Taigh Chearsabhagh, and have been the chair, secretary and now just a committee member of the Uist Art Association for 19 years. For eighteen years I have been the Voluntary Literature Officer at Taigh Chearsabhagh, organising monthly poetry events, running a monthly poetry workshop, and curating poetry cards on the café tables.

What are your political views with respect to the current situation in the UK and specifically in Scotland?

I am appalled/made afraid by the state of politics in England. Big business has always been in the background of politics, but now it appears to have the upper hand and we are scuppered. The austerity measures were a smoke screen, causing untold harm to the poor and weaker members of society, and did nothing to decrease the debt. There appears to be a mafia of rich unscrupulous people who want to take over the world. We need more philosophers.

Although I would not wish to create more borders, it would appear that Scotland could benefit from independence. But HOW DO WE REALLY KNOW? How can we know the truth?

Is a double-barrelled name an advantage or a curse?

Both. It's not a combination of our previous names, it's my husband's surname and when we married it didn't occur to me not to change my name. The disadvantage is that people assume I'm rich and maybe a snob. Neither is true. The advantage is being PPP poet. It's easy to remember. I can easily be found as there are so few of us, which is both an advantage and a curse.

PAULINE'S QUESTIONS TO JOHN AND HIS RESPONSES

You say that you have worked mostly to commission, whether financially or performance-guaranteed and yet you appear to be someone who knows his own mind, slightly intolerant, wanting to do things your own way.

The art forms I have worked in most are primarily co-operative. You cannot compose successfully for musicians or write successfully for actors, or talk successfully on radio to a varied and unquantifiable public, without working at the most profound as well as the most practical levels of co-operation. Of course one must know one's mind and it helps performers if they know you know what you want. Nowadays, many performers have taken over from composers and writers — often, I suspect, because they can easily do as well themselves. I am intolerant of incompetence and wilful ignorance and loathe the self-indulgent navel-gazing stuff, peppered liberally with the most superficial existential angst, that passes for deep feeling and sensitivity and is very largely meretricious. No names, no pack drill...

Didn't working to commission inhibit you somewhat?

No, it stimulated me. I am a communicator and a social being. I have been amazingly fortunate in having the chance not just to indulge personal feelings in the privacy of an ivory tower, but share them with others — and when commissions in one area of creative life have dried up, I have started up in another — hence the variety of art forms and genres to which I have contributed. Jack of all trades...flibbertigibbet?

Has this restricted your creativity at all?

Not in the slightest. I was never asked to write a symphony, but I doubt if I had one in me. In any case, I don't miss it.

Has it made you less free to be spontaneous?

I have enjoyed a life of unremitting spontaneity and nobody and nothing is capable of inhibiting it. Why? Because I was born that way — born happy and loving life, and when things have gone wrong, spontaneity often takes over — for good or ill. Spontaneity is not necessarily a good thing — but I enjoy it.

Maybe you would like to say more about the commissioning process that you experienced.

The variety has been amazing. In music from opera to *a cappella*, pieces for orchestra, pieces for prehistoric instruments, solos for lute, for violin, quartets, songs and so on. In literature, from radio plays (6) to poetry, innumerable radio scripts, music history (*Scotland's Music, Erik Chisholm, Scottish Modernist*), literary criticism (Yeats studies, notably *The Literary Works of Jack B. Yeats*), journalism (music criticism for various publications), CD liner notes (very many). The process has been mostly positive and efficient — especially on the part of the performers and producers — wonderful producers (Stewart Conn, Martin Dalby, David McGuinness, Susan MacKay). Administration of said commissions has mostly been very good but occasionally alarmingly haphazard, as when I was informed of a commission for an orchestral overture two weeks before the premiere — only they had never verified the commission. I did it and it went well — *Overture Clydefair*. I still like it, but it was composed in one hell of a hurry.

Are you attached to any particular school of philosophy?

I do not believe in 'schools' of anything and am therefore blissfully unattached.

Or any particular philosopher for any particular reason?

Plotinus in the translation by Stephen MacKenna — the most beautiful philosophical prose in the English language.

I'm slightly jealous of your statement 'new love is always inspiring'. Would you like to elaborate? Maybe not!

Maybe not.

You say that if you had a religion, it would be music. Can you say why?

It's international, appeals to all ages from the child in the womb to an old person on a death-bed; it can celebrate love and death and war and peace; it is the world's best passport; it is the rhythm and pitch of the universe as we know it; it combines the highest mechanical achievements of the human body with our most sophisticated tools (because not only are they virtuosic in their design and competent performance, but they can also convey emotion, which is not given to many tools apart from the brush and palette knife); it does not become trapped by the specificity of words. If the gods aren't interested in it, I am not interested in them.

Do you have any rituals that you follow most days?

I always make a hole in the shell of my finished boiled egg so that the witches cannot use it as a boat and drown sailors. I have saved many lives by this simple precaution, taught me by my mother who also initiated me into music. She, and her ways, are therefore deeply embedded in my soul as is my father's poetry and philosophy.

In one of my poems called 'In the End', the last line is "you will be grateful for what is left of love and beauty". Is this something you would agree with?

Wholeheartedly, my dear. Wholeheartedly.

Echoing one of your questions to me: What are your political views with respect to the current situation in the UK and specifically in Scotland?

I have always wished and voted for an independent Scotland and am profoundly grateful to this beautiful country and its people for my education and my living, for which I can never fully repay the debt, though I have made a good effort. What is happening in England is a tragic disaster, brought on by an appallingly unbalanced society, incredible incompetence and mendacious politics — and it is having the worst of influences upon Scotland. One should be sorry for the English. They have lost their way — but then they deliberately chose the road of isolation and separation. It is they who are the separatists.

10. THREE EDINBURGH VOICES

Richard Holloway
Jenni Calder
Stewart Conn

Although none of these three writers originate from Edinburgh, all of them now reside there and have contributed to Edinburgh life and to Scotland as whole in significant ways: Richard as the former Bishop of Edinburgh and Primus of the Scottish Episcopal Church; Jenni as a senior figure at the National Museum of Scotland and a central figure in the Edinburgh cultural scene; and Stewart as the first Edinburgh Makar and Head of Radio Drama at BBC Scotland. 'Though happily "of this parish"', he says, 'I remain in part an instance of being able to take the boy out of the west but not the west out of the boy.'

Photograph by David Eustace

RICHARD HOLLOWAY (Age 84)

Richard Holloway, FRSE, is a Scottish writer, broadcaster and cleric. He was Bishop of Edinburgh from 1986 to 2000 and Primus of the Scottish Episcopal Church from 1992 to 2000.

Born in Possilpark, Glasgow, and brought up in Alexandria in the Vale of Leven, Dunbartonshire, Richard was educated at Kelham Theological College in Nottinghamshire, where he went as a boarder at the age of fourteen. Later, there was further study at Edinburgh Theological College and the Union Theological Seminary, New York City. Between 1959 and 1986 he was a curate, vicar and rector at various parishes in England, Scotland and the United States.

He resigned from these positions in 2000. It was only several years after he had become Bishop of Edinburgh that the tensions between being expected to uphold the orthodoxies of faith and his growing disbelief in the certainties of the system became too great. The last straw came over the refusal of the Lambeth Conference of 1998 to accept any softening of its harsh attitude to gay relationships. His departure from the Episcopate was hastened by the publication in 1999 of his book *Godless Morality*, which provoked a hostile reaction from certain quarters of the Church.

Richard Holloway is now regarded as one of the most outspoken and controversial figures in the Church, having taken an agnostic worldview and commenting widely on issues concerning religious belief in the modern world. His own theological position has become increasingly radical and he has described himself as a Christian agnostic.

Richard is well known for his support of progressive causes, including campaigning on behalf of gay and lesbian rights in both Church and State. He was carrying out gay marriages well before the Church officially sanctioned them. He is a patron of LGBT Youth Scotland, an organisation dedicated to the inclusion of young LGBT people in the life of Scotland. He has questioned and addressed complex ethical issues in the areas of sexuality, drugs and bioethics. He has written extensively on these topics, being the author of more than 20 books exploring their relationship with modern religion.

Richard was elected as a Fellow of the Royal Society of Edinburgh (1995) and was awarded their Royal (gold) Medal in 2008. He holds honorary degrees from the Universities of Strathclyde, Aberdeen, Edinburgh Napier, Glasgow, Dundee, Open University, St Andrews and the Royal Conservatoire of Scotland. He was Professor of Divinity at Gresham College in the City of London. From 1990 to 1997, he was a member of the Human Fertilisation and Embryology Authority and held the position of chair of the BMA Steering Group on Ethics and Genetics. He was also a member of the Broadcasting Standards Commission and is a former chair of the Scottish Arts Council and is the current chair of Sistema Scotland.

Richard has been a reviewer and writer for the broadsheet press for several years. He is also a frequent presenter on radio and television. His best-selling book, *Leaving Alexandria: A Memoir of Faith and Doubt*, talks about his life from childhood. In a review of this book Mary Warnock said: 'What he loves about the [Christian] narrative is its central figure, who possesses endless pity for human beings and is endlessly subversive, in preferring compassion to rules. What he came to hate about the church is its insistence on rules, which turns it to cruelty, not pity. The attitude of the church towards women and homosexuals, which Holloway in the end could stand no more, illustrates the way the supposed rules drive out love.' (*Observer*, 19th Feb, 2012.)

Richard lives in Edinburgh with his American-born wife Jean. They have three adult children (two daughters and a son) and two grandchildren.

In a lovely terraced house in the Merchiston area of Edinburgh, Richard was looking out of his sitting-room window, awaiting my arrival. He greeted me on the doorstep, tall, erect, very fit for his age. 'Don't send me any questions in advance,' he had said. 'I prefer to wing it.' And wing it he did, with an amazing fluency and clarity of thought:

I'm still a pretty driven human being. How much of that is my DNA I don't know, but I suspect that some of it is related to the sense of divine mission that Kelham had, that you were on Earth for a purpose, that you had to sacrifice your life. The way I put in it *Leaving Alexandria* was 'the given away life.' The ultimate ambition was to be a completely self-given saint. I never achieved that and in my own thinking about personalities I realised I am not that kind of person. I have known some 'given away' people who were unaware of themselves in the sense that they were unselfconsciously for other people, didn't get in their own way and were almost instinctively unself-regarding, whereas I've always had a self-awareness. I have known the kind of person I would have liked to have been, but increasingly over the years have realised that I wasn't. We tend to long to be what we are not and I sometimes try to act the kind of person I wish I had been. I think quite a lot of that is still in there.

I have just finished my latest book. It's on death; it's called *Waiting for the Last Bus: Reflections on Life and Death*. It's about my own relationship with death, because I've buried people and sat beside the dying. As well as thinking about my own death, it's an extended meditation on death as such. My editor at Canongate prompted me to do a bit more self-examination, with the result that quite a lot of my recent writing has had that element in it. I conclude at the end of the book that I do have a driven personality and that it has made problems for me. I keep working, I keep writing, I keep walking. How much of that was inherited and how much instilled at Kelham I can't now say, except that I remain a religious person in that I am still asking these ultimate and unanswerable questions. I don't now think that there is a personal god, personally prompting me towards a life of sacrifice, but I guess that some of this is rooted in me, because I continue to work hard and to write and to be as good a person as I can be with my complicated nature.

The after-life is one of the many things I'm agnostic about. When I'm being flippant I say, 'None of the prospectuses attracted me.' But if you've counselled and tried to comfort dying children it's hard to be certain about it. There's a lot in my forthcoming book about the way death haunts us and the way we defy it. I think that, in some ways, god was invented to give us immortality, to guarantee us something beyond death. Personally, I neither desire it, nor expect it. But, life is so uncertain that I might be surprised. I'm not afraid of death, nor am I in any hurry for it to arrive at my door.

Julian Barnes wrote a book about it: *Nothing to Be Frightened Of* (Cape, 2008) and Larkin wrote his famous poem, 'Aubade', because he dreaded the thought of being dead, which is kind of absurd because he wouldn't be there to experience it. When I was a young priest, I would preach sermons defying death, I would read the great Resurrection passages, 1 Corinthians.15 in particular. The transition in my thinking happened quite suddenly. Walking down a hill in the Pentlands I realised I didn't want life after death and that I didn't believe in it any longer. But I still quite like the Christian defiance of death because death is a horror and it robs us of people and love. I see Christianity's response to death now almost as an artistic protest and I like that about it, because it's a monster, death. I've been to really tragic funerals, of children in particular. Loss stuns us. As in most things, I'm mixed up! You know MacDiarmid's Caledonian Antisyzygy — competing and opposing polarities within the same entity, a kind of Jekyll and Hyde binary self — I'm conscious of quite a lot of that in me.

As a young man I used to write poetry that was very imitative of Gerard Manley Hopkins. I wrote poems probably until my early thirties, but not since. Although, more recently, a group of nuns took a chunk from a speech I gave at a religious conference and metered it. I sometimes wonder if I will go back into it as a very old man. I regard my non-fiction writing as creative. All writing is creative, if only in the sense that you are editing memories, you are being selective. For example, in *Leaving Alexandria* I recall my father getting up very quietly in the morning so as not to disturb anyone as he went to work. I describe him lighting his pipe and standing at the window and me wondering what he is thinking about, and I say I remember, with a pang, what a considerate man he was. A woman at a writers' workshop I was running asked me if that was an actual memory of me as a boy, or an adult memory. I said, probably both, but the language would be of me now. It's the old man looking back at the boy watching his father. So, in that sense, all writers, especially autobiographical writers, are editing their lives, editing it into form and remembering selectively. Occasionally writers adjust facts to fit the truth, because the truth is not just factual accuracy, but they contain deep truths. It's a larger thing. I am more aware of doing that and more comfortable with it. In the book I'm working on at the moment, I talk about the various kinds of people I have seen into death and there's a little bit of editing and tweaking and conflating going on in that. It's not deception, but an artistic or poetic bringing out of a deeper truth. A lot of people are confused about whether religious narratives are fact or fiction. They are myth, which is truth through story. They may be factually inaccurate, but that's a very difficult distinction to get people to grasp.

In writing about my own life and thoughts, one of the things I'm after is to know who I am before I die. I'm a determinist in the sense that we come into this world programmed to go in a certain direction and the only freedom we acquire in life is knowledge of that determining background.

Much of the time when I go for walks it's all happening in my mind. I don't notice what's going on around me. I'm not good at mindfulness. I'm easily distracted. What I derive from Buddhism is awareness of the compulsion of desire, of the need to break free from that cycle of wanting and getting and then wanting more. I think that was Buddhism's single greatest insight. I achieve peacefulness of mind in different ways — from reading poetry or from walking in the Pentlands.

In the past I have written as though my opinions were set in concrete, what they call apologetics, arguing for a particular Christian position. The further on I went, the less certainty I had and the more I began to prize uncertainty, without falling into absolute scepticism, which I think is paralysing. We have to hold all our beliefs with a kind of provisionality, because history teaches that we may have to drop them. We believed in slavery; we believed in the subordination of women; we believed that gays should be beyond decent society. I call it existential jazz — living in a way that enables you to listen to new things and develop a new ethic. I believe in a radical kind of provisionality, except that, in order to function, we need a certain level of institutional firmness — but not so firm that you can't abandon it when you realise it is wrong, or is no longer appropriate. It's quite a taxing way to live and it's not popular. People have entrenched political or cultural positions because it gives them a sense of being in harbour, or being safe. In evangelical terms it is what sells.

One reason I have upset a lot of people is that I can be very per-suasive. I make converts and then, a couple of years later, I have taken a different position. I have given them enough grounds to stay in a particular place along this journey, then I am no longer there myself. I say to people, 'Listen to me, but don't fundamen-talise me.' There's an anarchic streak in me — not in the wrecking sense, but in the sense that I tend not to prioritise law as being more significant than it is. We need law, but if you absolutise it, it's absurd. It makes you a bit of an ass. Jesus gave us the text: 'The Sabbath was made for man, not man for the Sabbath.' I realise now that I don't have the gene for powerful institutional loyalty. You do need institutions and laws, but you also need people like me who stick more lightly to them, because they do become absurd if they become marble rather than something more plastic. It was always in me to shift to a more radical challenge on the gay issue, but I hadn't thought my way through to a strong position to chal-lenge these orthodoxies until I was in my thirties. I married my first gay couple in 1972.

I admire the conservative temperament and share its sense of loss at the way we constantly discard good things — books, buildings, religions and tradition. But the anarchic side of me understands how the conservative mind can conserve the bad as well as the good; and that it can maintain cruel traditions as well as useful ones. Of all the vices, cruelty is the one I hate most.

One of the things I've noticed is the drift to the right in people as they get older and I daresay that is probably happening to me. However, if you're a writer, your attitudes tend not to harden quite so firmly, because you are constantly examining and questioning things. I am more accepting now about living with uncertainty. I just don't want to be too certain of my uncertainty.

I don't pray anymore in the way I did as a priest, but I do a kind of praying. I read poetry for spiritual nurture and I read it with in-tensity. For this purpose, I read (amongst others) Gerard Manley Hopkins, Don Paterson, Michael Donaghy, Yehuda Amichai, the Israeli poet, and Larkin, too, the great poet of regret and elegy. Increasingly, the poetry I like is melancholy and elegiac. Larkin said that a lot of poetry is an attempt to pin down the past before it disappears. And I find that when I'm out on the hills, I do address something. I take concerns with me and I pray, not as Hopkins puts it, 'dead letters sent to him who lives alas away,' but just addressing the universe and ultimate reality, being intentional towards people I love, and I think of that as prayer because what is prayer but a kind of beseeching, a kind of longing. So, I don't pray in the sense of trying to change the mind of the Almighty Cosmic Organiser.

Good preaching is when it's a soul wrestling with itself. The little preaching that I do these days is me preaching to myself, wrestling with myself. Next month I'm doing a sermon at the graduation ceremony at St. Andrews University — they are giving me an Honorary Degree — and the topic I have chosen is that life is not a pool, it's a river and that surprises keep us living. I will be trying to fortify this conclusion, arrived at through my own experience, by talking about it.

One of the pieces of writing done since passing seventy that I'm most pleased with is *Leaving Alexandria* — both with the reception of it and with the writing of it and the fact that my editor helped make it a better book and helped me appreciate the value of learning from a good editor. He challenged me. In terms of broadcasting, I did a long series of Radio 4 programmes: *Honest Doubt*, which was examining a lot of these preoccupations of mine. When I first started presenting radio programmes, I was self-conscious and worried about being tight and unrelaxed. I have got better at it as I learned to relax and wing it and to listen. One of the things I have most enjoyed about my latter life is becoming a good radio broadcaster. I write less journalism now and do fewer book reviews. I am much happier with the long form. Being commissioned to research and write a book — *A Little History of Religion* (2017) — was a new departure for me. It is very satisfying, at my age, to be still learning and still acquiring new skills.

I haven't had any role models as regards positive ageing, but I've encountered the opposite — models of what to avoid becoming. I've met a lot of boring males with endless stories of their glorious past — anecdotage, as it's called.

My advice to people who want an active old age would be: work hard at keeping fit and well and take exercise. The easiest form of exercise is walking. Push yourself a bit, but don't overdo it. Above all, keep active mentally — keep reading, keep an interest in politics, do stuff and go to things. And write, because everyone can write, even if you don't write for anyone else. Try to leave something of yourself behind, even if it's just a memory bank for your children. Keep alive, keep vivid, keep curious. And don't moan.

My twelve years at Old St. Paul's were a happy time for me [as rector from 1968–1980]. They were particularly intense, our children were young, it was a very vivid, packed time; we were very engaged with the neighbourhood and the city and with needy people, the music was wonderful, the congregation were very interesting people; and Old St. Paul's is a wonderful building. It was a very charged time. It was a big stage on my journey towards living without certainty.

Despite that, I would say that now is the happiest time of my life. I am having a good old age. I am on record as saying that no longer having to defend things I don't believe in is one of the great joys of my later life. But I'm encountering other joys, too. I've been lucky with my health. I walk at least one hour every day and try to get on the Pentlands at the weekend for a longer walk. I am rediscovering the joy of a life together with my wife, the routine together, the evenings we have. I am financially better off now than I was when younger and, increasingly, we enjoy going out to dinner. I'm enjoying a new and closer relationship with my children. I'm adoring being a grandparent — I have two grandchildren, one of thirteen and one of fifteen. No-one could have prepared me for the joy of that. That's probably been the biggest gift of old age. I have time to cherish the people who are important to me. There's a poem by Clive James about enjoying the cosmic blaze before it's taken away. When I'm on the hills I notice that kind of beauty more than I used to. Gratitude, I feel gratitude. I continue to enjoy the movies. I have been addicted to them since childhood. I still get a huge kick out of reading, but not fiction so much these days. I enjoy journals, biographies and autobiographies.

And I'm enjoying my charity work. I started a charity called Sistema Scotland which uses the orchestra as an instrument of social transformation in areas of deprivation. We have youth orchestras in Raploch in Stirling, Govanhill in Glasgow and Torry in Aberdeen and Douglas in Dundee. We are working with about three thousand kids in Scotland now. We employ wonderful charismatic young musicians to work with them. To change these communities, you need to do it slowly, organically, strategically and patiently. I tell politicians, 'Think in half centuries, not in electoral cycles. Quick fixes don't work.' Being in touch with young people has been colossally rewarding and energising. Along with my love for my wife, my children and grandchildren and the hills, this has been one of the great gifts of my old age. I'm having a great old age and I'm writing better than I ever did. My writing is more considered now. I always rushed things before. I never used to call myself a writer, but I do now and I get a tremendous kick out of it. And I will go on doing it until I pop. It's a privilege to have something you don't ever have to retire from. Writing is a good way to grow old.

A sample of writing done since passing 70

I've pasted a short passage from my next book, Waiting for the Last Bus: A Memoir of Death — *to be published by Canongate next year — because it seemed appropriate to the theme of* Autumn Voices. *In autumn leaves begin to change their colour and start falling from the trees. In this short passage I try to show how our bodies have their autumn, too.*

I remember when I noticed that coloured patches like stains on old stone had started to appear on my face and body. When you get old the garbage disposal mechanisms designed to clear out waste in your skin cells start to break down. Instead of clearing the rubbish away, like lazy bin men they leave it lying around in the street, your skin. And it clots into those yellow brown patches called *lipofuscin,* better known as age spots. A few years ago at the Edinburgh International Book Festival the press team photographed the writers with a special camera that subjected their skin to a ruthless high definition exposure of every flaw and wrinkle. When my picture went up in Charlotte Square a few days later it revealed a face blotched and stained with patches of lipofuscin even I hadn't noticed before. The bin-men of my epidermis had obviously gone on permanent strike. That was when I realised that the wind-down of my body was well advanced and there would be more to come. Mind you, for me the process had started in my twenties, when I started going bald.

Baldness is not a terminal disease, of course, but it is a permanent condition. And I hated it when it started. I fought it in all the usual hopeless ways. I even bought pills advertised in a church magazine. The manufacturers probably thought the readers of *Church Illustrated* would have a stronger gift of faith than other baldies. Their pitch worked on me. I sent off for the pills. Nowadays the law would require an accurate description of the chemistry of the product that came through my letter box a few days later, but none of that was required in 1958.

They looked like little brown Smarties. And like Smarties they were probably made of sugar. I started swallowing one a day. My hair continued to recede. Hopelessly, I flushed the remaining pills down the toilet and started combing what was left on top to the front, trying to look like Marlon Brando as Mark Antony in the movie *Julius Caesar* that was out at the time. It was a vain response to a disagreeable reality. It may delude the owner for a moment, but the comb-over is an embarrassment that takes no one in. Depressed yet defiant, one day I cropped the whole thing off and that's what I've done ever since. It was an early lesson in accepting things about myself I did not like but could not change. I see now that losing my hair was a good preparation for ageing and death, the skeleton being the ultimate baldy. Maybe I've been lucky to have had an early rehearsal.

You may also wish to consult: https://en.wikipedia.org/wiki/Richard_Holloway

Photograph by Rachel Calder

JENNI CALDER (Age 75)

I was born in Chicago, but was brought up mainly in Upper New York State and that is what I remember most. My father, David Daiches, the literary critic and historian, had a position at Cornell University. I was nearly ten when we moved to Cambridge, England. I went to school there and then to the University. At university I met Angus Calder, like me, reading English and much involved in left wing politics. We married in 1963, separated twenty years later. After we graduated, Angus and I lived in London, but when a job for Angus came up at the University of Nairobi we went to Kenya for three years. When the contract came to an end in 1971, we decided that, since we both had roots in Scotland, we would live and work there.

The National Museum of Scotland was my first permanent job. I worked there for twenty-three years in various capacities, including Head of Publications and script co-ordinator for the Museum of Scotland exhibitions. During my last three years at the Museum I ran a section concerned with Scottish emigration, which has remained an interest. Most of my freelance work has been in areas of literary and social history, with a focus on Scottish literature, particularly R. L. Stevenson, women writers, and questions of identity. Of all the Museum publications I worked on, I think the two which gave me the most satisfaction were the book about the Orcadian Arctic explorer, John Ray, and *The Wealth of the Nations*, about the Museum's very diverse collections. Both publications involved extensive collaboration with others, which can be quite challenging. Working at the Museum and having colleagues who were experts in different fields taught me a huge amount, both intellectually and practically. I particularly enjoyed working with designers, who contributed greatly to my visual education, and also being part of the Museum of Scotland team. It was always interesting, always challenging, although often with the frustrations of working within an institution. When I retired from the Museum, I reverted to my previous life of freelance writing and teaching, except this time I didn't have the distraction of children, which was wonderfully liberating. I write on literary and historical subjects as Jenni Calder, and fiction and poetry as Jenni Daiches.

As a child my urge to tell stories emerged in the form of drawings.

My first ambition was to be an artist until I realised I wasn't that good. As a student at Cambridge University I wrote poetry and the occasional short story, and was published in student magazines. I have continued to write poetry, on and off, all my life. After university, in my mid-twenties, I wrote a couple of novels that were never published and then other things took over. The two early novels probably differed from my more recent fiction in that I now write with more experience, both of life and of writing. Maybe I'm still exploring similar themes but the perspective is inevitably different. I think I've always tended to write about the fragility of human relations and the haphazard nature of experience. As my early efforts have vanished somewhere into a loft, and as I don't anyway have much interest in looking at them again, I can't comment on how my approach may have changed.

At the age of eighteen I spent several months in Israel, which was a formative experience for me. The second novel drew on this. Going to Israel was an aspiration that evolved during my last year at school, when I became aware of some of the background to the founding of Israel and had a growing interest in exploring my Jewish heritage. The experience was important not just for what I learnt about Israel, but for the fact that I was travelling alone for the first time and met a range of memorable individuals, from Holocaust survivors to sabras who had fought in the Sinai campaign to kibbutzniks dedicated to communal living and working.

My grandfather was a Rabbi and my father was brought up as an Orthodox Jew. But my mother was a Scottish Presbyterian, although she converted to please her parents-in-law. So, theoretically I am Jewish, but only theoretically although I retain a strong sense of connection with my Jewish heritage. My belief systems are not so much religious as secular and humanist. Both my parents were committed socialists. And my father-in-law was very active in the CND. As regards beliefs, I don't like being labelled, and I find organised religion (and other kinds of organised belief which makes me a bit of a political maverick) totally unappealing although I do appreciate the social and community value of shared celebration. (Celebration was an important part of my upbringing.) My commitment to social justice and a necessary faith in humanity has never varied. Koestler's description of himself as a short-term pessimist but long-term optimist has always stuck in my mind. The prospect of death does not tempt me towards a need for a god or a belief in an afterlife.

I find it difficult to say what writers have influenced me as there are so many ways influence can materialise. Although I have written a biography of Robert Louis Stevenson and read his work with great attention, I would say he has influenced me indirectly, rather than directly, in the sense that his work is a resource and a catalyst. There are places I would never have visited but for him, such as Samoa, and he has brought me together with people I would not have met otherwise. I haven't consciously modelled my writing on anybody. I devour all kinds of fiction and poetry all the time and I suspect that writers I admire do influence me, but I couldn't put my finger on exactly how. It's probably easier for somebody else to detect these influences.

I am always encouraged by writers, particularly women, who are still active in their later years — Doris Lessing, for example. I had the privilege of writing a biography of Naomi Mitchison and getting to know her when she was in her nineties. She was 94 when her last novel was published. Another important example for me was a woman I knew when I was in my forties who in her seventies lived alone in rural Pennsylvania. Her independence and community involvement made a lasting impression.

I wrote my novel *Forgive* because I wanted to create a narrative that explored the whole idea of forgiveness and the way individuals try to deal with it. I admire those who can forgive. It's not an intellectual thing, it's emotional and perhaps implies a kind of superiority. True forgiveness, where you can genuinely say, 'It really doesn't matter anymore,' is very difficult — there are so many levels on which impact and meaning linger. And if I can forgive on my own behalf, taking it upon myself to forgive what has been done to others is altogether another matter. I don't hate anybody. Hatred is negative and often dangerous. It's not in my emotional vocabulary.

I aspire to continue writing and to continue being read. There are still things I want to write about and new ideas bubbling up almost every day. I write mainly fiction now, less poetry, although the reading and writing of poetry remains very important to me. For me, writing is a compulsion and if I go for a long period without writing, I have withdrawal symptoms. I get quite depressed. I need to write, even if it's something I know will never be published.

My love of the landscape comes from two directions. My maternal grandfather was a Highlander and his family all worked on the land — crofters, a gamekeeper, a water-bailiff. My maternal grandmother also came from a farming family. My mother's uncle had a farm in Banffshire which we often visited. We also had family holidays on the Moray coast and other parts of the Highlands. Then, when my children were growing up, we went to Skye, Orkney, Galloway — many rural Scottish holidays. My partner, Arthur, is a keen explorer of the landscape and also introduced me to going out in small boats, so I have now added some of Scotland's west coastline to my appreciation of the Scottish landscape. He has a house in Ardrishaig. My most recent novel very much draws on my time spent in Ardrishaig and Lochgilphead and that part of Argyll. I love to walk, in towns as well as in the countryside. I do find that ideas run through my head while I'm walking; but it's also a good way to take a break from staring at a screen. My usual writing routine is to spend a couple of hours at the computer, then take the dog for a walk, then another couple of hours of writing.

I don't think my motives for writing have changed as I get older. My work habits haven't changed much either, although I don't have quite the same stamina. When I was freelancing and had young children I had to take advantage of every child-free minute and became extremely good at that. (Interestingly, I've just read an interview with Emma Donaghue who describes exactly the same thing.) It taught me discipline and to write even if I didn't feel like it — and I try to maintain that sort of discipline. The children are grown-up now, of course. Rachel, my eldest, is a film-maker and photographer and also works on events and festivals; my second daughter, Gowan, is an actor, director and writer; and the youngest, my son Gideon, teaches Ethics at the University of Swansea and writes widely on related topics.

I am in the happy position of having a modest but perfectly adequate pension. I don't have to worry about whether or not my books make money. I don't have to write anything I don't want to because I need the cash. When I was freelancing I was under that kind of pressure. I was often over-committed because I didn't dare say no to anything, and just as often anxious at the lack of work. Feast or famine. I don't think the nature of my creativity has changed over the years. It's the conditions and context in which I write that have changed. I am very conscious of being in a privileged position, living comfortably with the time and opportunity to pursue an activity I love, with a supportive partner and extended family, and being in reasonably good health. Life in the past was often a great deal more difficult!

Yes, I am of an age when some of my friends and colleagues are dying. I accept that as a natural part of life, but you do feel increasingly exposed as members of your own generation disappear. Hardest to deal with has been the loss of both my siblings, both in accidents. I know people who haven't been able to cope with retirement. I think the whole idea of working full time one moment and then not working at all the next is crazy. I think people should withdraw gradually from their professional lives. Writers are lucky in that there is no compulsory retirement age. I shall go on for as long as I can.

For me, the most negative aspect of ageing is not being as physically capable as I was. I have arthritis and I get tired more easily. I have to accept that I can't do as much in a day as I used to. I enjoy spending time with my grandchildren, and although it can be exhausting, their expectation that I can match their levels of energy is a great boost. Reading to them and just watching them are both great and less demanding pleasures. (My younger grandson, aged seven, when he discovered publishing books could actually earn money, immediately sat down to write a story.) Something I have learned as I've got older is to accept the things that are beyond my control and that there is no point in getting upset about this.

Fiction is the form of writing I love most and, since passing seventy, I have finally got into my stride and had three novels published (though the first was written before I retired). That is a great source of satisfaction. The novel that has given me the most satisfaction is always the most recent, as I feel each one has taken me a bit further forward in terms of my development as a writer and, I suppose, in terms of personal development as well. By the time a book is published I'm usually caught up in the next project and keen to move on, but I know of course that at some point the moving on will come to a stop. My most recent novel, *Borrowed Time*, is partly about the accumulation of years and the consequent imbalance between past and future, and about loss which inevitably increases as the years increase; it of course draws on my own experience.

Do I feel less pressure to conform than when I was younger? As far as my work is concerned, I have never felt a huge pressure to conform, except when I have been writing something that might distress others. But sensitivity to other people's feelings is not quite the same as pressure to conform. There are certain things I would not write about, or which I've had to wait to write about, because of not wanting to hurt people. There are those who are deliberately shocking and hurtful in order to draw attention to themselves. I've never felt I wanted to do that. You can always find indirect ways, alternative ways, to say what you want without hurting others.

I am not sure that creativity is sparked by 'the quarrel with ourselves'. It's more an investigation of the self, an exploration and testing things out. I think the business of giving meaning and shape to one's life is there all the time. It's not something that only arrives with old age. As I've said, it's a constant interrogation of the self. As you get older you have more and more experience to draw on so that this process is deeper and richer. I am more accepting of the person that I am. When I was younger I criticised myself more and resisted things about myself that I now accept. I set standards and goals for myself that were not compatible with the person I really was or with a realistic acceptance of my abilities. When I was young, I felt there were things I should be good at; I wanted to emulate the examples of both my mother and my father. I was going to be a supportive partner, raise children, be an efficient housewife, a brilliant cook, and a successful writer and academic. Almost by accident I was diverted from an academic career which made me realise that it probably wasn't my forte anyway. Gradually I learnt to admit that I was asking too much of myself, that sometimes I had to accept failure or at least settle for second best.

My advice to other writers is to keep writing, keep trying. There are plenty of examples of writers who don't get published until well into later life. If you haven't been published or had success by forty, fifty, sixty, or even beyond that, it's not the end of the road. I think the important thing is to encourage, not young writers, but first-time writers, whatever their age. The early stages of a writer's career are just as likely to be in their sixties as in their twenties. There are lots of awards for writers under thirty. There should me more encouragement for people starting out, whatever their age. I'm fairly sure that there are more readers over sixty than in any other age group and a lot of them prefer books written by authors who are themselves mature.

The publishing world sometimes seems to be dominated by the very young. One of my recent novels was read by two publishing interns who were, at the most, in their early twenties. They weren't enthusiastic and made unhelpful comments. But twenty-year-olds were not who I had in mind when I wrote the novel. Having said that, it is really important to read the work of the young, to be aware of as wide a spectrum as possible of what is being written and published. In my own case, the three most important contributing factors to my activity as a writer of fiction and poetry, aside from the physical business of setting words down on page or screen, have been watching, listening and reading. A story teller has to be, before anything else, an observer and a listener. Reading enables you to do both through the eyes of others. My final advice would be that it's never too late to start and there's no age at which you should stop. And it's never too late to learn, from the young, the old, from the living and the dead.

This passage reflects an ambivalent response to time and place, and the imbalance between past and future. The novel explores notions of belonging and connection, which have always been currents in my writing.

From *Borrowed Time* (Vagabond Voices, 2016)

In a fold of the hills behind me, among the pines and birches, the bracken and thick clumps of nettles, are the few stones that remain of a group of cottages. The landowner, rich on sugar and slavery, decided to improve his estate which meant getting rid of many of his tenants... I walk up there often with the dogs and loiter among the tumbled stones. I can see where the hearth once was. There are times when the forlorn emptiness of such abandonment suits me. I have become acquainted with emptiness. Life fills and fills as the years accumulate. At least, it does if you're lucky, if you have a purposeful occupation and people to love. But there comes a point when for most — for all? — substance begins to drain away. People disappear, and the feeling grows that you live in a territory whispering with shades and spectres.

Beyond the settlement there are standing stones and rocks with cup and ring marks. To be there in a smirr of rain, the sky low and occluded, is to feel a phantom presence. I lose myself sometimes, if I stand long enough with the dogs snuffling in the undergrowth, drawn into an ancient past which diminishes my own few decades of life. There were places in England where I felt stalked by history, but never so intensely and yet so imprecisely as here, making my way up the hillside past a blackened hearth telling of daily labour and the etched rock that speaks of the need for so much more than daily labour... But this is not my country, and these more ancient hauntings have never been flesh and blood presences, though strangely easier to understand.

You may also wish to consult Who's Who in Scotland *and* www.scottishbooktrust.com/live-literature

Photograph by Angela Catlin

STEWART CONN (Age 80)

Stewart Conn's boyhood was mainly spent in Kilmarnock, where his father was minister of St Marnock's, with school holidays in the Ayrshire countryside where his paternal relations were farmers. He was educated at Kilmarnock Academy and then at the University of Glasgow. He did his National Service in the Royal Air Force. In 1963 he married Judy Clarke; they have two sons. He worked at the BBC from 1958, in Glasgow until 1976 and then in Edinburgh (moving there to live in 1977), mainly as a radio drama producer and latterly as Head of Radio Drama, until he resigned in 1992. From 1973 to 1975 he was Literary Adviser to the Royal Lyceum Theatre, Edinburgh. He was appointed Edinburgh's first Makar, or Poet Laureate, in 2002, a post he held until 2005, doing much to raise the profile of poetry in the city, and of the city in poetry, with competitions, readings, projects (poems on buses and in art galleries, for example).

In addition to poet and producer, Stewart has also been a playwright, enjoying success, particularly in the 1960s and 1970s, with varied and powerful plays, including *Play Donkey* (about a Scottish mercenary, gaoled in an emergent African state), *I Didn't Always Live Here* (1930s and 1940s Glasgow tenement life relived through two women's eyes), and *The Burning* (on James VI and the North Berwick witch trials).

RLJ: Tell me a bit about yourself as a young poet.

SC: The first poems I really wanted preserved, written in my early twenties, were the Ayrshire farm poems depicting my father's biblically rooted aunts and uncles. The poems not only showed them set against the rural landscape to which they belonged, and which, temporarily, belonged to them, in the hope of preserving a whole way of life that was slipping away, but were, I suppose, also an attempt to pin down my own identity and genealogy.

After National Service with the RAF (an uneventful desk job in Lincolnshire), I ended up in radio drama. I was very lucky in finding a harmony between working in radio — which although communicating aurally, is essentially a visual medium in that it uses words and sounds to conjure up images — and writing poetry. Rather than there being a clash between the two.

RLJ: The blurb about you in the anthology *Whatever the Sea* says, 'His more recent work explores themes of mortality and celebrates love and maturity.' I'd like to explore this further with you, if I may.

SC: I suppose an interweaving of love and mortality have been pretty well a constant from the outset. The later work revealing an understandably greater awareness of our vulnerability, an inevitable consequence of ageing.

RLJ: Your poem 'Tide' in the collection *Estuary* contains the lines, '...hard to know / Where the river ends and the sea begins.' Could you expand on this?

SC: One night I heard a radio presenter describe the opening two movements of a symphony he was about to play as not having a gap between them, as is customary, but flowing into one another, 'like a loch into a river'. This struck me as capturing perfectly the unobtrusiveness of time passing, and of ageing. In the poem, this is related to the undertow and potential danger you can have to watch out for, when fishing.

RLJ: Another poem in this collection is 'On the Slope'. Tell me more about that one.

SC: The slope round the corner from us, some years ago, was so snow-covered then icy you had to hang on to the railings for fear of falling. At one point folk were actually tobogganing down it. So again there's a question of precariousness. The poem's last line, Bette Davis's 'Growing old sure ain't for cissies', was pre-planned. Usually I let a poem take me where it's going. Not that I abrogate responsibility for it, but there's that exciting moment when a poem takes its own direction — rather like when, in drama, the characters start speaking for themselves. There's one strand in which this is in a sense built in: those poems which draw on paintings, where the speaker becomes either the artist or the subject of the painting. I do that a lot.

RLJ: A review of *The Touch of Time: New & Selected Poems* refers to your 'delight in daily serendipity.'

SC: Yes, the serendipity of looking for a solution, and finding it in unexpected places. One has to be constantly on the *qui vive*. Norman MacCaig wrote prolifically and must have thrown away a good proportion of what he wrote. He called it 'keeping the tubes clear,' so that he was ready for the poem when it came along. My analogy would be fishing: if your attention wanders, you suddenly realise you've had a bite and you've lost the fish. It's a matter of constant alertness. The day our grandson was born, for instance, from my study window I saw momentarily, for the first time in our garden, a bullfinch, who fitted perfectly into a poem of welcome — one occurrence coinciding with another, little signposts that trigger things off. I don't find poems so effusive or so eager to come towards me that I can afford to ignore such signposts.

RLJ: The critic Alasdair Macrae comments on your later work as being 'more reticent emotionally.'

SC: I suppose there's a parallel between how a schoolboy bounces all over the road on his way home and spills ice-cream down his front — you don't behave like that when you're older and in different company. I'm now probably more guarded with emotions. I think at the very start I was expressing feelings I didn't really understand to a sort of anonymous Muse, but latterly it would be a very specific figure and a lot of my poems are directed to, or relate specifically to Judy, my wife. So I suppose there's a reticence in that she's been drawn into the orbit of the poem. Maybe through an obligation towards propriety. Like music that starts off in a major key and then goes into a minor key. And perhaps also through growing less confident about eternal truths. Everything seems to have its own variant and qualification, with the poem likely to be increasingly hard won, through the ramifications and external pressures on it.

One of the tiniest and simplest yet most intimate statements I have made in a poem lay in a drawer for years. I suppose it was reticence that prevented it from appearing in public. It accepted the inevitability that one of my wife or myself was likely to die first. But I went on to say that should either of our boys predecease us, something not in the natural order of things, 'I'll hack out the god of stone / and confront him with it till one / of us lies broken bone from bone'. This was written after close friends had lost their son.

But when it did finally appear in print, it was as a tiny section in a much longer sequence, 'Roull of Corstorphin' — who was elegised by William Dunbar in his 'Lament for the Makaris.' Putting the words into Roull's mouth, as it were, meant I could express my own fears, through him — or if you like, his through me. As if I was wearing his mask. To give another example: in my poem sequence 'The Luncheon of the Boating Party' things are seen through the eyes of characters in Renoir's famous painting — and his own. I suppose in the hope of illuminating the relationship between life and art. But there, too, projecting on to Renoir, or attributing to him, my own feelings about ageing and death.

RLJ: Has the nature of your poems changed in later life?

SC: I'm more aware that my attitude to those poems I engage with has changed. I came to Burns on the farm where they treated him as if he'd just gone out of the room before I arrived. 'To a Mouse' has always been one of my favourites. But now there has been a shift. For instance, to a poem which haunts me: 'O Wert Thou in the Cauld Blast.' I can't but relate to the irony of Burns addressing this poem to the seventeen-year-old girl who was tending him in his last illness. And talking of *him* protecting *her* — when he's in no position to. It's so much a *volte face* of the actual situation. I find more and more that the sentiment in that poem, 'My plaidie to the angry airt, I'd shelter thee, I'd shelter thee', and the circumstances under which it was said, chime with a growing realisation that, in life, there are things you can't protect people from, no matter how much you want to, with that at its most intense when it's loved ones you want to protect. Resulting in a shift in the tone of many of the poems I now write.

RLJ: And has your style as a poet changed over the years?

SC: I find that a difficult question to answer because these changes are not necessarily consciously made. Other people see it more clearly than I do. The farm poems have occasional Scots words and there's a richness in texture. Later, when I thought I had pared things down and had a cleaner line in a collection called 'Under the Ice', one reviewer saw this as a negative thing, whereas I saw it as a positive process towards being more austere and clear. I can't duplicate the rhythms and texture of my early farm poems unless I'm writing on the same subject. So I'm aware of a change in myself. Then again, I started off being accused of *not* rhyming and latterly have been berated *for* rhyming, which I suppose reflects a shift in fashion. But always, even if they don't have end rhymes, consistently there are internal rhymes and assonances and sound patterns, many of which seem fortuitous...a word appearing out of thin air, rather than it being premeditated. That's the area I find most exciting. Also, I have become, or aimed to become more conversational — having a naturalness of speech and syntax. It still has to be crafted and have an element of artifice to make it seem natural — it's the *illusion* of naturalness.

RLJ: Has the nature of your creativity changed as you get older?

SC: The writing process is more tiring than it used to be. Maybe through an increased sense of urgency. And with lengthening fallow periods in between. While instead of, as in the early poems, catching experience on the wing as it were, I now trawl through memories more. Nothing significant to that, just a fact of life. I still re-read certain other poets, as a springboard to ways of seeing. And I like to have something formal, and generally classical — mainly Mozart, or Haydn — as a background to the often lengthy revision process. In an odd way, they seem to keep me on track.

RLJ: Could you please say something about yourself as a playwright and the difference between this and yourself as a poet.

SC: I had never really been confident in myself as a poet. It was nice to be called one but I felt that, if I applied the term to myself, I might be struck by lightning. It feels presumptuous given how elevated the poets I admire are. And in a way, I don't feel entitled to take credit for the poems I've written...so many of them seeming to have been, as it were, written through me. The plays are different. If I put six hours work into a play, at the end of that time I would be six hours further forward, whereas, if I'd spent six hours writing poems, I might end up by throwing them all away. Plays and poetry seem to depend on different factors. I started off writing poetry at school. Some in the form of monologues. One of the triggers being Robert Browning's dramatic poem 'My Last Duchess' and having learned it by heart before I realised that it actually rhymed. The monologues led to duologues, then by extension to dialogue...and the plays. As I say, I've always regarded play-writing as a technical task, whereas writing poetry remained something of a game of chance.

I thought of myself as a playwright until the late 1990s when I had a play called *Clay Bull* in the Lyceum. Riskily, it was set in South Africa. The reviews in the main tended to misinterpret what it was trying to say. At that moment, I totally lost confidence as a playwright, not in fury at the reviewers…but because I lost trust in my own theatrical voice. I thought if what I want to say is not comprehensible to the audience, I have lost my voice. This coincided with the commissions running out and I thought that all I had left was poetry. But, as I say, I didn't regard myself as a poet. I had friends who were so much better poets than I was. I tried for a while to write like Iain Crichton Smith, a dear friend, and draw on the influence of others I admired, but found it beyond me. For a spell I had no sense of direction.

Then, out of the blue, I got a phone call from Paul Scott (of the Saltire Society) saying that Edinburgh were creating a Laureate or Makar post. I grabbed a piece of paper and started jotting down the names of people I thought might suit, not taking in that he was asking me to do it. I thought, 'I'm from Glasgow, not Edinburgh, and I don't write in Scots,' but instantly that was superseded by the realisation that I couldn't even begin to say, 'no.' So I said, 'yes.' I'm still amazed nobody raised the Scots issue. At one time, anyone appointed to the post who didn't write in Scots would've been assassinated. Or at least banned from the Abbotsford. Anyway, I remember the effort I had to make, coming from Glasgow, to adapt to Fergusson's work, and the rhythms and intonation of someone like Robert Garioch, because I had the music of Burns in my head. Discovering Fergusson belatedly was a glorious experience. In the wake of my appointment, suddenly there was this reason for having to write poems. A problem was that I still felt I didn't belong. And then I discovered that my mother's father's licensed grocer's hadn't been in the outskirts as I'd always assumed, but in the High Street, in the Royal Mile. Making me feel, as one poem puts it, 'less an interloper, than one who has been long away'. As well as writing to my own themes, I was given commissions, which served as an oiling of the cogs. And from that, and rubbing shoulders with other poets and speaking their language again, came a self-respect as a poet that enabled me to grit my teeth and get on with it. Out of that came for instance the 'Roull of Corstorphin' sequence I mentioned earlier. It wouldn't have come into existence if I hadn't sensed an obligation to offer some return other than just poems set in the city. I used to find commissions quite scary, but some proved challenging and immensely helpful in driving me back to the coal-face.

RLJ: I note that your father was a Minister of the Church. Has this been an influence on your life? Does any form of religion or belief system impact on your creative work?

SC: My father never tried to persuade me to join the Church. He was one of the best preachers I ever heard. I've never had religious belief, because other things aside I can't accept the concept of a personal God, or the notion of any one particular belief or set of deities being more valid than any other. For all that, one of the things most deeply embedded in me — I suppose along with the Border Ballads — is the King James Bible.

RLJ: Have your motives for writing changed as you grow older?

SC: It's always been to leave a footprint. Or if that sounds grandiose, maybe a thumbprint. Some of my latest poems are about my small grandson, Ellis, and he is now part of that thinking. I also wish my poetry could give comfort, because I find a lot of poetry can be healing. Some of the most touching consequences of writing poetry I've had have been when people have asked to have one my poems read either at a wedding or a funeral.

RLJ: Would you continue to write if you knew that nobody was ever going see or hear what you wrote?

SC: Obviously, you write a play to be performed in front of an audience. The poems are different, except for the commissioned work, of course, which is written for public consumption. But with most of my poetry I'm not anticipating or assuming an audience. That's not what drives me to write my next poem — except I suppose that, in Judy, I have an audience and my poems are increasingly directed towards her. Reaching a wider one's a nice bonus.

RLJ: We have all heard of a mid-life crisis, but have you experienced a late-life crisis?

SC: After passing seventy my circle of friends and the extended family began to diminish. This and realising you're no longer the focal point of your children's — or other folks' — lives. It's partly an ego thing — not being at the hub of things any more. I dread having to be in the care of people I don't know; and of being removed from this familial environment. Luckily, I'm in reasonably good health. It must be quite frightening if you are on your own, but I have my wife to counter any feelings of despair. As for the poetry... I'm often shaken by how suddenly this or that poet's work, once they die, can drop out of sight. More and more these days one has to be around to take part in the media hype. Also, there seems an increasing trend for performance as against written poetry.

RLJ: So what do you see as the most positive and most negative aspects of ageing?

SC: One of the biggest positives has been my grandson's birth three years ago, which puts things in a fresh perspective. By contributing to the optimism-pessimism graph. As time passes and the ageing process affects health, there are vulnerabilities that one becomes increasingly conscious of. He also awakens memories of my own sons at that age and recreates the aspirations, hopes, guilts and fears for them that accompanied that. Another positive, I suppose, is that one is gaining in experience all the time, and this is put at the disposal of one's writing. Negatives would be limited movement and activity. I miss driving at night. And most of all, my regular hill-walking days being over. That led to exercise, comradeship, varieties of climate and unforgettable views...and quite a few poems. Fortunately, I can still cast a line.

RLJ: Do you see yourself being creative into even later life?

SC: I am naturally concerned about 'the dying of the light.' The fear that, as W. B. Yeats put it, the animals might flee the circus ring of the imagination, or are already scarpering. In the face of which all I can do is write what I can while I can. I've just been reading extracts from an American literary editor Robert Gottlieb's autobiography, *Avid Reader*, where he talks about 'starting to recede from whatever limelight [he] had once been in.' Quoting Robert Frost's 'No memory of having starred / Atones for later disregard, / Or keeps the end from being hard,' he responds disarmingly: 'I never felt I was a star. I don't now feel disregarded.

And, yes, the end may very well be hard, but perhaps fate will be kind and at least keep me on reading for a while.' If you substitute *writing* for *reading*, this would sum up my own attitude.

RLJ: Have you encountered ageism in your professional life?

SC: It's difficult to tell if it's ageism or if one has simply reached one's sell by date. But, yes, I think it does exist. Simply in the natural way of things. One instance, you could say, a recent anthology of poems about Edinburgh to which it seems no-one over seventy was invited to contribute. But you could argue that it's time for today's young to have their say. And, as I say, I wouldn't know if I'm too old or if what I write may simply be out of fashion. Maybe it's not ageism, but only natural, that there is a tendency for any inner circle to keep the perks to themselves, as it were. Also, the arbiters of taste in the arts, in the publishing and literary-cum-editorial world, are these days themselves younger people. But latterly, if rather to my surprise, I've been asked to act as a judge, twice for the Edwin Morgan Award and, latterly, by the Scottish Book Trust, when they might've gone for someone younger.

RLJ: Of all the things you have written since passing seventy, what has given you the most satisfaction?

SC: Out of a very serious fall Judy had, for which she spent a spell in hospital, came a group of poems called 'Against the Light,' not a diatribe against the light, but imagining, in a sense, her figure, and strength of spirit clearly defined against it. Satisfying in that, out of that painful experience for her, I managed to fulfil what I think of as my duty as a poet, and to her, by focusing on what she'd gone through and turning it into a sequence. In the same pamphlet are what might be styled a suite of Edinburgh winter poems which stemmed from a commission to write a programme for Radio Four called 'Edinburgh at the Year's Midnight.' The title drawing on John Donne. They gave me a different satisfaction, being more public, as it were, and as a belated thank-you for the accolade Edinburgh gave to me all those years ago.

RLJ: Do you have any role models as regards staying creative into late life?

SC: Iain Crichton Smith springs to mind. The fact that he was able to write poetry right till the end, despite periods of what he called madness, was a triumph, not just of the intellect and the imagination, but of the will in the face of negative and disruptive forces. But he never put poetry on a plinth. He was a human being before he was a poet. A remarkable instance of not just longevity but poetic rejuvenation in old age was George Bruce, for whom I worked briefly in my BBC days — from his collection *Pursuit*, published when he was 90, to the striking sea-related poems he wrote in his final years, in response to images by John Bellany. And the intelligence and velvety lyricism of Douglas Dunn's poetry — younger than me, I know, but of my generation, and he has been through the mill in various ways — have made him something of a constant poetic role model for me.

RLJ: Do you feel less pressure to conform than you did at a younger age?

SC: Yes. As a playwright in Glasgow I was aware of a very real antagonism towards anyone not writing socially committed material with dyed-in-the-wool working-class characters and accents. Whereas the title of my play *The Aquarium* (1973) represents both the stage area it was performed in and the imprisoning middle-class flat off Byres Road where the action takes place. Its claim to fame may be that it was the one play in that new wave in which someone said 'fuck' on stage and the other characters reacted with shocked horror. This didn't apply to my poetry, it was totally accepted as being set in and reflecting what was then W2, where I lived and worked, with its middle-class terraces, and the Botanics with the Kibble Palace not just in the background but, as it were, protagonists. It was only when I came to Edinburgh that I found myself in places disapproved of because my poetry wasn't in Scots. I felt rather elbowed. I am grateful that this Scots vs. English issue has ceased to be so important. There's less pressure for a writer now, regarding this issue, than there was when I was starting. I felt an attempt to put an onus on me to make a choice about things when I didn't see why I should have to. I've always written in the tongue instinctive to me. It also suggested a fatuously rigid dividing line between Scots — or the many varieties of Scots — and English. Negating the sheer range at a Scottish writer's disposal.

RLJ: Do you still experience inner conflict or has later life brought calmness with it?

SC: Recent events — Brexit and Trump, for instance — have so appalled me that my focus is on that, rather than any inner quarrel. These events make my little personal anguishes seem rather trivial. But I'm not a political person and the paradox is that I'm still committed to writing about the inner things. I was asked recently for, as well as a book of the year, something I'd gone back to and I chose Yeats's 'The Second Coming,' from *Michael Robartes and the Dancer*, which ends: 'And what rough beast, its hour come round at last, / Slouches towards Bethlehem to be born?' Yeats was writing about Fascism, but you can apply it to a whole lot of situations, whether it's Syria or Trump. I think my role is to somehow advocate the importance of the human spirit. That is all I can do in the face of the threat Yeats was writing about. I believe poetry, especially lyric poetry, is not rendered less relevant by brutality and political manoeuvrings and cruelties, but all the more so, as a haven that can give succour and hope. We need poetry, to feed the imagination, and to move forward. As soon as you stop believing that, you might as well stop writing or composing or painting or whatever it is you do. I admire those, many beyond not only my experience but my comprehension, who can still do that under the threat of physical cruelty and death.

RLJ: What advice would you give to younger writers who aspire to continue being creative into later life?

SC: 'To thine own self be true,' I suppose. Seek the truth, and be yourself. And to those menaced by what Chesterton saw as the skies growing darker yet, and the seas rising higher, the trust that as at the foot of Pandora's box, they may find — and have it in them to sustain — a glimmer of hope.

A sample of writing done since passing 70

Its title drawn from Horace, this poem's appearance in The Loving-Cup *(2007) coincided with my wife's 70th birthday, five months after my own. I hope it instils a sense of wonder at what is. At the same time I confess the succinctness with which it handles its floral theme owes much to what the poem's observed subject describes as her role 'in doing the bloody pruning.'*

Carpe Diem

From my study window
       I see you
below in the garden, a hand
       here pruning
or leaning across to snip
       a wayward shoot,

a daub of powder-blue in a
       profusion of green,
then next moment, you are
       no longer there —
only to reappear, this time
       perfectly framed

in dappling sunlight, with
       an armful of ivy
you've trimmed, topped by
       hyacinth blooms,
fragrant survivors of last
       night's frost.

And my heart misses a beat
       at love for you,
knowing a time will come
       when you are
no longer there, nor I here
       to watch you

on a day of such simplicity.
       Meantime let us
make sure we clasp each
       shared moment
in cupped hands, like water
       we dare not spill.

You may also wish to consult: www.stewartconn.com/home

http://www.scottishpoetrylibrary.org.uk/poetry/poets/stewart-conn

11. SOME CLOSING COMMENTS

As the title of this section suggests, these are comments rather than conclusions. The sample of writers over seventy is too small for any sweeping statements and much of *Autumn Voices* is about individual stories and circumstances, all of them different. All, however, show that productivity and creativity can be extended well into later life and provide role models for future generations.

The writers interviewed represent a total of over 150 years of life experience since passing the age of seventy. The interviews in *Autumn Voices* are only the tip of the iceberg. To properly appreciate what old age has brought to these writers we need to read their recent work or see it performed. This is where the true expression of their thoughts and feelings is to be found. The online information referenced at the end of each chapter amply demonstrates that, since passing the age of 70, the authors in this book have produced an impressive list of publications and productions and won a heap of awards and prizes; and they continue to be active as speakers, workshop leaders and office-bearers in a range of associations and societies. These Scottish writers in their later lives are proof of Emerson's dictum that you don't grow old, you become old when you stop growing [1]. The responses to ageing and the changes that have occurred may vary, but in every case growth has continued. In *Aging: The Fulfillment of Life* (Doubleday, 1990) the authors, Henri Nouwen and Walter Gaffney say: 'Aging does not need to be hidden or denied, but can be understood, affirmed and experienced as a process of growth by which the mystery of life is slowly revealed to us.' We hear something of this in the autumn voices that speak to us through these pages.

The Introduction commented that it is before, not during later life, that many of the qualities and attitudes that serve so well in old age are developed and these were clearly apparent: qualities and attitudes such as flexibility of mind, forgiveness and the willingness to let go, to move on and step into the unknown, self-confidence, acceptance of change; learning the wisdom of uncertainty, and the mindset summed up in the Serenity Prayer:

'God grant me the serenity to accept the things I cannot change,
The courage to change the things I can,
And the wisdom to know the difference.'

Despite the fact that more than twenty years separates the oldest
and the youngest contributors to this book, and that the twenty-
one writers have different backgrounds and different experiences,
both personal and professional, the advice they give is remarkably
similar. One of the questions was, 'What advice would you give to
younger writers who hope to continue being productive in later
life?' In essence, what nearly all of them say in reply is: keep going,
keep learning, keep trying. Do what is true to your heart and write
what you really want to write. Never stop being curious and open
to new experiences; and never lose your sense of wonder.

This advice comes from men and women who, rather than deny-
ing or resisting old age, have chosen to embrace it, to regard it as
a new and interesting phase of life, full of possibilities. While acknowledging that their later lives are related to their earlier years,
they appreciate that they go beyond them. Their present lives are
not just repeat performances of earlier life. The challenges are
different. There is a realization that as one door closes another
opens; and that the doors which close behind have positive messages about the direction of their lives every bit as much as the
ones that open up in front.

Also there is recognition of the need to let go. Much of our younger lives is about acquiring — acquiring partners, children, a good
job, a house, material things. There comes a period in our lives
when the scales tip and much of life becomes about letting go
— downsizing, coming to terms with loss, letting go of what you
can't change and of unrealistic hopes and plans; and letting go of
grudges and hatreds because it's now or never. In letting go we
help those old doors to close and the new ones to open.

The poet William Carlos Williams wrote about 'an old age that
adds as it takes away.' He showed that ageing need not be defined
as a steady accumulation of losses. Instead, as we struggle with the
losses and changes that accompany old age, we encounter both
problems and potential. The problems become a catalyst for devel-

oping the potential. This can be seen in *Autumn Voices*. The kind of losses spoken of here include loss of friends and life partners, loss of freedom through being unable to drive or because of impaired mobility, a diminishing in faculties such as sight, hearing and memory; and a general slowing down. We see in *Autumn Voices* how these and other problems and sorrows have produced some beautiful, heartfelt, insightful poetry, short stories and other writings — writing filled with a renewed wonder, with a wry humour about increasing infirmity, with unflinching courage and honesty. And we see how the act of writing about these things is central to coming to terms with them.

Autumn Voices, then, turns out to be a book not only about creative ageing, but about successful ageing in general. The two are closely connected of course. Creativity contributes to successful ageing by fostering a sense of confidence, purpose and growth. For many it helps develop self-acceptance through writing about one's true thoughts and feelings. Writing about loss and other traumas can assist in coming to terms with them and coping with them. Loneliness is one of the biggest problems of old age in the UK. Although the act of writing itself is usually a lone activity[2] there is a strong sense of community amongst writers in Scotland. Writers meet each other at literary events, they belong to writers' clubs and associations, attend courses and workshops together, they read each others' work and chat online about matters related to writing.

The *Autumn Voices* project overlapped with the New Frontier project I carried out between 2012–2014. This was a series of interviews with the recipients of the Times-Sternberg Awards which are for men and women over the age of seventy who are still making a positive contribution to society[3]. The remarkable people I interviewed for this project were noticeably mentally and physically fitter than the norm for their ages. The main reason for this in every case was that they were deeply involved in causes that took them outside of themselves. They had no time to dwell upon their own ailments and problems, they were too busy working and caring for people in greater need than themselves.

Something very similar was noticeable about the participants in the *Autumn Voices* project. The mind is a powerful tool in keeping the negative aspects of ageing at bay, and creativity is like a tonic. Being completely immersed in what you are writing, having the mind fully engaged, having a purpose in life, waking up with something to look forward to, and knowing that, through your writing, you are still doing something useful to and valued by society — these things contribute massively to a happy and fulfilled old age.

I think it is significant that, when the writers were paired up and let loose to 'talk amongst themselves,' age-related topics hardly came up at all. Other things interested them more, which is possibly one reason why they are ageing so successfully.

Has the nature of their creativity changed in later life for the twenty-one writers in this book? Although there was general agreement that things were slowing down, that the output was maybe not as prolific as before and that ideas did not always knock on the door quite so often, the actual process was much the same. Much the same, that is, except with the craft of writing honed and refined by long experience and practice. These writers felt that the quality of what they were writing now was better than ever before and more enriched; that they had reached, or were near the optimum combination of knowledge, experience and emotional readiness. The majority of them thought they had greater maturity and emotional intelligence than when younger; they had acquired deeper self-knowledge; they had a wider perspective on life and were more reflective.

As mentioned in the Introduction, the voices in this book are far from being the only Scottish voices to speak of old age. There is, for example, the fine anthology, *Whatever the Sea: Scottish Poems for Growing Older* (Scottish Poetry Library/Polygon, 2015). The blurb at the front of *Whatever the Sea* says:

'Age comes to us all. It is not a unique phenomenon, but it is personal and it can be perplexing. Poetry gives us a fresh way to think about growing older, and these poems celebrate maturity, widen perspectives and confront the inevitable.

The poets acknowledge the advent of age, in rueful or upbeat mode, celebrate the bonuses of friendship and late love, survey the weaknesses of body and mind with black humour, and face the final destination with indomitable spirit.'

As the contributors to *Autumn Voices* (and most other people, too) approach a time when they will probably be counting the remaining years of their lives in single figures, thoughts about death, its manner and its meaning, naturally visit them more often. Almost nobody I interviewed feared death itself, but worries about the manner of it and the lead up to it were commonly expressed, with dementia and complete dependence on other people being to the fore. These fears and worries have been faced with an honesty that produced some very fine writing. Death was accepted as an important part of the journey. Nancy Bost Millner, in her book *Creative Aging* (Davies-Black, 1997), reports an eighty-four-year-old retired school teacher as saying: 'Life is like a good book. You hate to see it come to an end, but you couldn't enjoy it if it didn't have an end.' I sensed that kind of recognition that death is part of a full life in the people I was privileged to meet while writing this book.

Over the years old people have reported that some of the gifts and unexpected joys that accompany ageing are: deeper self-knowledge; feeling more connected to your true self; feeling connected to something greater than yourself; increased acceptance of self, of your limitations and of life as it really is; greater interest in other people; a strong sense of gratitude and a desire to give back some of the things you took from life; more patience; becoming more reflective. These 'gifts' are demonstrated in the lives and in the writings of the contributors to this book. There was a very positive response to my question about what gifts later life had brought. To the 'gifts' listed above they added: a feeling of liberation and of being less afraid of doing and saying what you wanted; time to cherish the people and relationships important to you; a sense of serenity, a growing spirituality and a sense that ageing is the last great adventure.

Gratitude was a word frequently mentioned. Both wisdom literature and well-being literature tell us that cultivating gratitude makes us happier and healthier. Gratitude helps us become more optimistic, more positive, more relaxed and more resilient and it results in deeper relationships and increased creativity and productivity. On the other hand, being ungrateful is related to anxiety, depression, envy, aggression, materialism and loneliness. The writers I interviewed for *Autumn Voices* expressed gratitude, in particular, for grandchildren — the delight they gave and, through them, a rediscovery of playfulness. Gratitude was expressed for the gifts of old age that have been mentioned, including the gift of gratitude itself. Gratitude is there also in expressions of grief. Sometimes, when we express grief for our loved ones, the pain we feel is a form of gratitude for what we once had. Pain and happiness are tied together. The pain of the present moment is made possible only by past happiness.

Having read quite a lot of the work that these writers have produced since passing seventy, it is clear that these 'unexpected gifts' have influenced their writing — the subject matter, the perspective, the mood and tone, the reflective nature of it, a rediscovered playfulness and a new freedom that self-acceptance and the dismissal of the internal censors brings. Guy Claxton in his book *Hare Brain, Tortoise Mind* (Fourth Estate, 1998) points out another way that creativity changes in later life. As ability for quick thinking declines, slower and more explorative thinking takes over. Alexander Pope put it this way: 'Some people will never learn anything because they understand everything too soon.' This type of exploratory thinking is evident in the later works of those who find themselves between the covers of this book.

In *The Creative Age: Awakening Human Potential in the Second Half of Life* (Avon Books, 2000), Gene D. Cohen refers to a Summing-Up phase in later life, shaped by the desire to find larger meaning in the story of our lives and to give, in a larger way, of the wisdom we have accrued. In this phase the lessons and fortunes of a lifetime are shared through autobiography and personal storytelling. Cohen's findings seem to hold true for the *Autumn Voices* authors in that recent publications include quite a number of collected works of poetry, short stories or essays and several autobiographical pieces. There is also the rather obvious point that the longer you live, the more autobiographical material you accumulate and the more writing you have done to put into collections. Later life is a time for harvesting the past. Nearly all of these authors, when they saw their earlier work in the same collection as their later work, thought that the latter was better — better crafted, deeper, more understanding of human nature, more aware of beauty to be found.

Quite a high proportion of the contributors to this book practised meditation in one form or another. They reported some of the benefits of meditation as being that it sharpens the senses, refreshes and clarifies the mind, makes one more receptive to creative ideas, opens the gates to gratitude, forgiveness and serenity and increases the chances of getting into 'the flow.'

Many of the contributors not only wrote in several different categories or genres — adult, children, prose, poetry, fiction, nonfiction, drama etc. — but also expressed themselves through other forms of creativity besides writing, such as painting, drawing, music, dance and acting. Clearly, some kind of internal dialogue goes on between one form and another, each illuminating the other in some way, assisting in the discovery of new sensitivities and awareness. At the very least, having more than one mode of being creative keeps the juices flowing when one of the springs temporarily dries up.

We live in a culture that is still learning how to age. 'To know how to grow old is the master-work of wisdom, and one of the most difficult chapters in the great art of living,' wrote Henri Amiel in 1874 [4]. The autumn voices in this book are moving towards this wisdom and, through their writing and their example, helping others in its discovery.

Notes

1. Very similar sayings have been attributed to Somerset Maugham, Gabriel Garcia Marquez and many others.

2. There are, however, various forms of collaborative writing, such as small groups working together, sequential writing and parallel writing. Comedy scripts are often written by two or more people; and drama of any sort is a team effort.

3. My book resulting from this research, *The New Frontier: Making a Difference in Later Life* will published by ThunderPoint Press, Edinburgh, in September 2018.

4. Henri Amiel (1821–1881) was a Swiss moral philosopher, poet and critic.

12. A SHORT BIBLIOGRAPHY

Anderson, Morag (Ed.). *bundles of bog cotton* (PlaySpace Publications, 2015)

Barnes, Julian. *Nothing to be Frightened of* (Cape, 2008)

Blair, Pamela D. *Getting Older Better* (Hampton Roads, 2014)

Cameron, Julia. *The Vein of Gold: A Journey to Your Creative Heart* (Pan Books, 1996)

Cohen, Gene D. *The Creative Age: Awakening Human Potential in the Second Half of Life* (Avon Books, 2000)

Csikszentmihalyi, M. *Creativity* (HarperCollins, 1996)

Csikszentmihalyi, M. *Flow: The Psychology of Optimal Experience* (Harper Row, 1990)

Cutler, David. *Ageing Artfully: Older People and Professional Participatory Arts in the UK* (Baring Foundation Report, 2011)

Friedan, Betty. *The Fountain of Age* (Simon & Schuster, 1993)

Hennezel, Maria de. *The warmth of your heart prevents your body from rusting* (Pan MacMillan, 2012)

Hillman, James. *The Force of Character and the Lasting Life* (Random House, 1999)

Jones, Ken. *Ageing: the Great Adventure — A Buddhist Guide* (can be downloaded from www.kenjoneszen.com/buddhism-and-social-engagement/ageing_the_great_adventure)

Lively, Penelope. *Ammonites & Leaping Fish: a Life in Time* (Penguin, 2013)

Lloyd-Jones, Robin (Ed). *The New Frontier: Making a Difference in Later Life* (Thunderpoint Publishing, 2018)

MacGregor, Lizzie (Ed.). *Whatever the Sea* (Scottish Poetry Library/Polygon, 2016)

McCrum, Robert. *Every Third Thought: On Life Death and the End Game* (Picador, 2017)

Millner, Nancy Bost. *Creative Aging* (Davies-Black, 1998)

Nouwen, H. and Gaffney,W. *Aging: The Fulfilment of Life* (Doubleday, 1990)

Sacks, Oliver. *The River of Consciousness* (Alfred Knopf, 2017)

Saltire Society. *Second Wind* (Saltire Society, 2015)

Thomas, W. *A. Life Worth Living* (Vanderwyk & Burnham, 1996)

Vaillant, George E. *Aging Well* (Little, Brown & Company, 2002)

Wilson, Angus. *Late Call* (Faber & Faber, 2008)